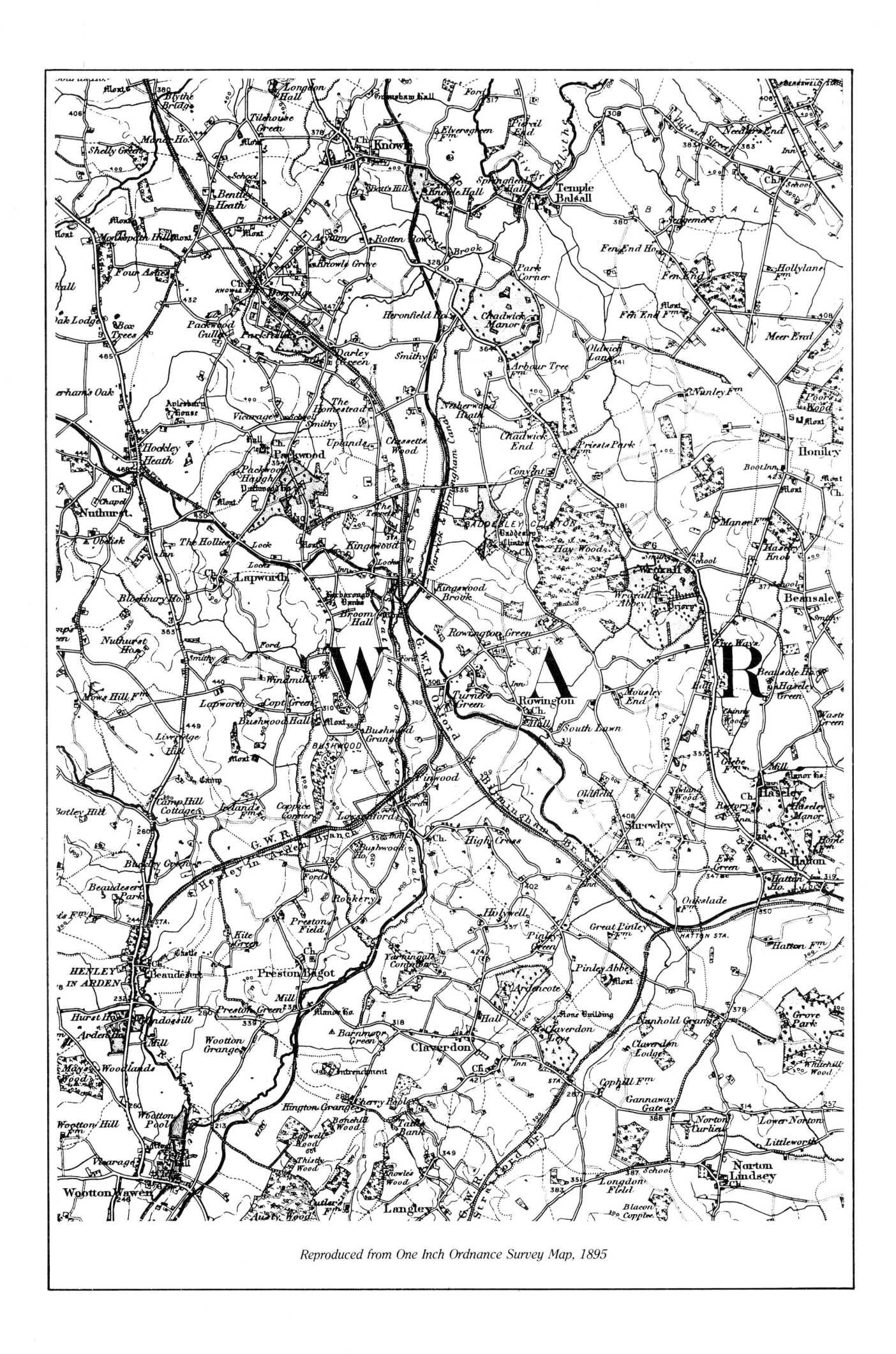

Reproduced from One Inch Ordnance Survey Map, 1895

Portrait of LAPWORTH
in the 18th. & 19th. Centuries

by
JOY WOODALL

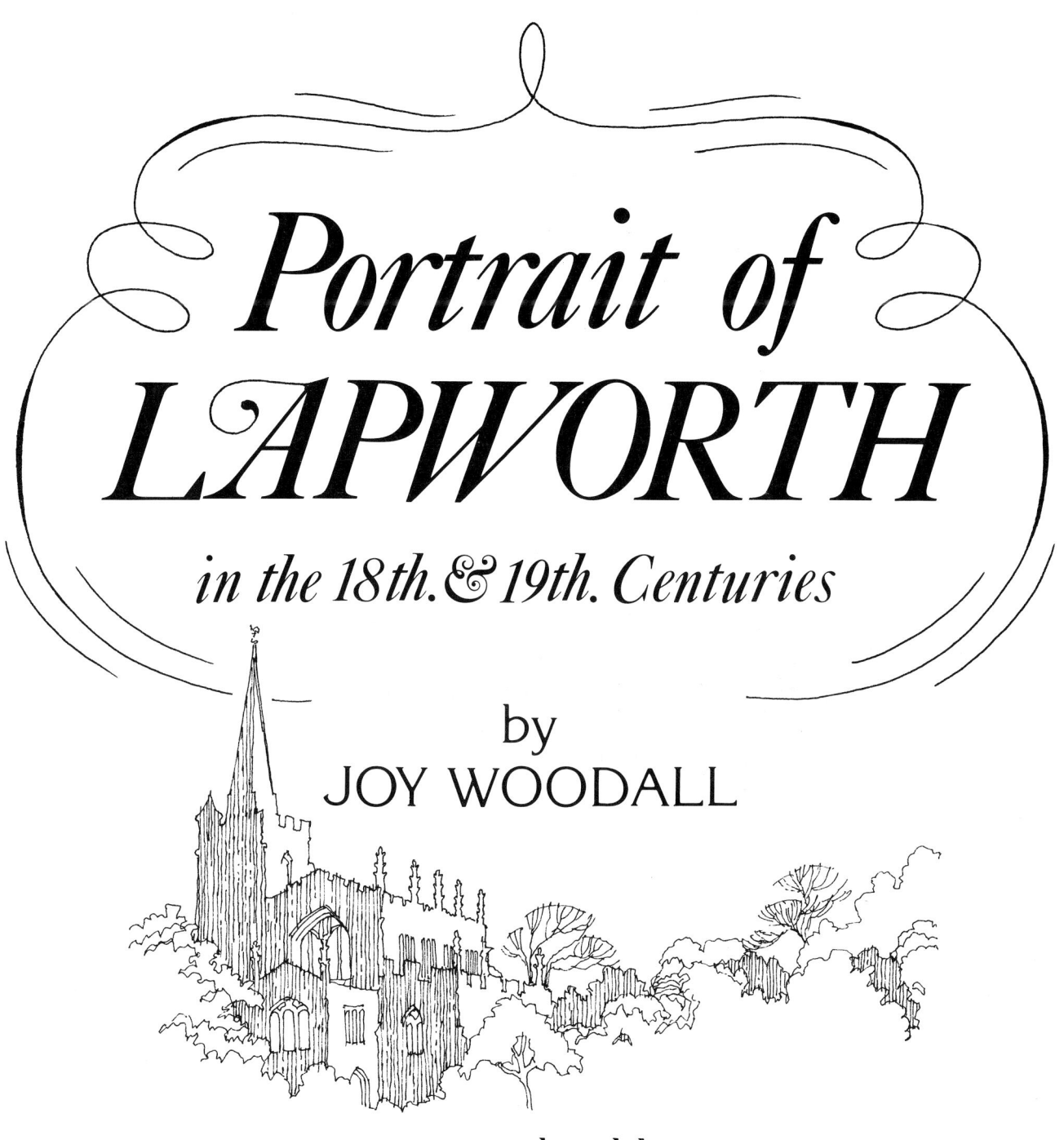

researched by
Dorothy Dagger Paddy Gaunt Annette Hardy
Mollie Varley Joy Woodall

illustrated by George Busby

To The Home Team
John, Penny and Jim

The Barn at Sands Farm

© Joy Woodall, 1986
ISBN 0-9504039 4 6
Published by Joy Woodall, Solihull
Printed by Louis Drapkin, Birmingham

Contents

Foreword			5
Introduction	—	Lapworth And It's Regional Setting	7

Lapworth 1750-1800

Chapter 1	—	The Coming of Owen Bonnell	11
		'Memoranda Parochiala' 1751-75	15
		'Memoranda Parochiala' 1776-1800	16
2	—	The Three Manors	18
		Lapworth	18
		Kingswood	24
		Brome	28
3	—	The Art of Husbandry	32
4	—	Along The King's Highway	40
5	—	'That Most Excellent Gift of Charity'	48
6	—	'. . . Unwillingly To School'	57
7	—	'To Be Provided By The Parish'	61

Lapworth 1801-onwards

8	—	'Memoranda Parochiala' 1801-50	69
9	—	'Horses To Be Unhitched'	73
10	—	A Living From The Land	79
11	—	The Church	84
12	—	'. . . How Many Poor I See'	91
13	—	Trades and Occupations	99
14	—	'Children Who Attend Regularly Do Well'	104
15	—	'Memorials of A Warwickshire Parish'	110
Appendix 1	—	Perambulation of Lapworth Manor Boundaries 1794	112
Appendix 2	—	Perambulation of Kingswood Manor Boundaries 1833	113
Appendix 3	—	Farms and The Land Tax	114
Appendix 4	—	Houses and Barns	116
Notes and References			117
Weights and Measures			120
Index	—	Lapworth Personal and Place Names	121
General Index	—		125

MAPS

One Inch Ordnance Survey 1895	Frontispiece
Lapworth Area Relief and Drainage	6
Sketch Map of Pre historic Sites in the West Midlands	8
Lapworth 1750	10
The Three Manors and Lapworth Demesne	19
Kingswood Manor 1807	25
Stratford-upon-Avon Canal — Hockley Heath to Lowsonford	75
Lapworth c1840: Field Pattern and Land Use	82

Lapworth Church, West, A. E. Everitt, c.1858.

    . . . . with livelier charms
Intent t'illumine Arden's leafy gloom.

    . . . . such as the moated hall,
With close circumference of watry guard
And pensile bridge . . . .

Lines from his poem *Edgehill* by Richard Jago, curate at Lapworth during the 1740's.

FOREWORD

Although I have had the enjoyable task of writing this book the research has been carried out by a group of five friends. We first came together, at Dorothy's instigation, in 1972 after I had given a talk on Local History to Lapworth W.I. We had no particular object in view simply a wish to know more about Lapworth's history and an enjoyment of the landscape, the buildings and the past.

During our regular fortnightly (and later weekly) meetings we walked the fields and the proposed Motorway route, visited several houses in the parish and spent hours in various Record Offices. On cold winter days we worked together at home transcribing probate inventories and collating our records. For several years we were a group of six, until Margaret Francis left us to give more time to her many other interests.

When in 1981 it was suggested that we might mount an exhibition for Lapworth History Group we were pleased to discover the extent of our records and we were able to display material from the pre-historic period to the 19th century. From that time we directed our efforts towards a book — the result is *Portrait of Lapworth*.

We have considered in detail the 18th and 19th centuries with occasional glimpses further back into the past. Throughout it has been the people who have interested us, and the material available, brought us closest to them in these two centuries than any other. We hope that what has been written will interest the general reader and help both the genealogists and the local historian. Our work has been greatly helped by the research undertaken, in the late 19th century, by Robert Hudson, a resident of Lapworth, and we have used his book *Memorials of a Warwickshire Parish,* extensively.

A great many people have assisted us in our research by lending photographs, deeds, and family archives, by inviting us into their homes, and by giving us the benefit of their expertise. For their particular help we would like to thank Mr. Tim Booth, Dr. Dorothy Gaunt, Mrs. Ann Hedley, Mrs. Mary Higgins, Mr. Richard Johns, Mr. Arthur Potterton, Mr. W. Seaby, Miss Kate Smallman, Lapworth W.I. and the Feoffees of Lapworth Charity Estate. For their professional help our thanks are due to Mrs. Sue Bates of Solihull Library, Mrs. E. Copson of Warwick Museum, Dr. Brian Gough; Mr. M. Farr, Miss M. Ory and the staff at Warwick Record Office, Mr. R. Bearman and his staff at the Shakespeare Birthplace Record Office, the staff at Birmingham Reference Library, and at Worcester and Hereford Record Office.

On a personal note I would like to thank the members of the group for their work and support over the years, and for the special contribution each of them has made to the team.

Without an excellent production unit the manuscript would never have become a book; for giving so generously and freely of their time and themselves I would like to thank Molly, Dorothy and Bob, David, and George who has enriched the book with his excellent drawings and delightful cover.

Joy Woodall
August 1986

Lapworth Area Relief and Drainage

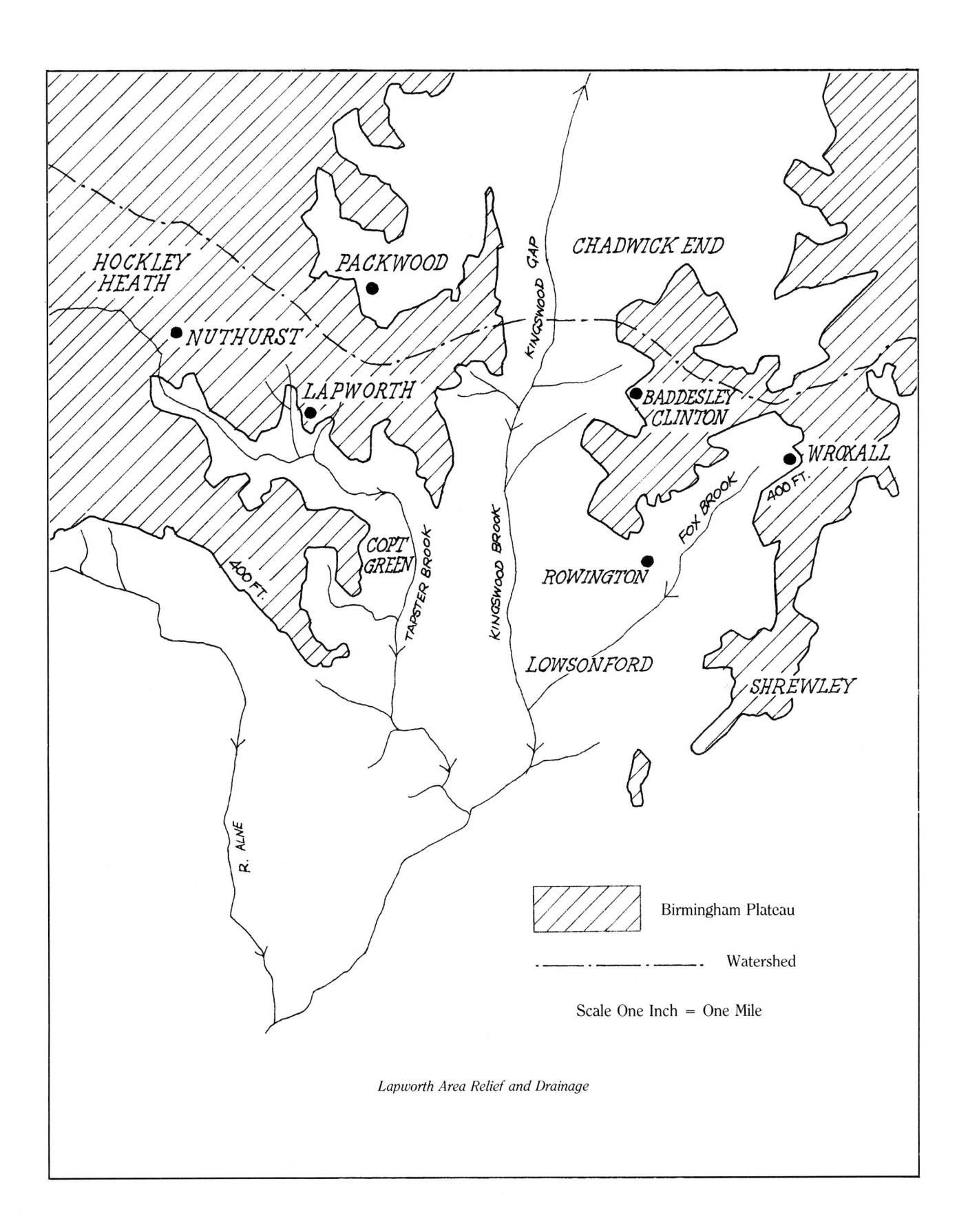

Introduction
LAPWORTH AND ITS REGIONAL SETTING

Situated in Shakespeare country, at the heart of the Forest of Arden, Lapworth is within easy reach of Birmingham (14 miles), Coventry (14 miles), Warwick (8 miles) and the Midland Motorway system. Geographically it lies at the south eastern edge of the Birmingham Plateau. The country is undulating, generally between 275 and 450 feet, the highest ground being in the northern part of the parish. The land slopes away eastward to the Kingswood Gap (formed by a depression in the Birmingham Plateau) and falls away more sharply southwards to the Alne and Avon valleys. In places, however, fingers of high ground extend from the plateau into the surrounding low land creating small, narrow, hidden valleys between them. The problem of finding a way off the Birmingham Plateau down into the Avon Valley was solved in the 18th and 19th centuries by taking a route through Kingswood Gap for the Birmingham-Warwick Canal, the Birmingham-Stratford Canal and the railway line to Paddington.

The northern part of Lapworth parish lies across the Trent-Avon watershed. The many springs and small streams which rise to the south of the watershed drain ultimately, via the rivers Avon and Severn, into the Bristol Channel. Lapworth Brook which rises in Tanworth-in-Arden enters the parish below Nuthurst Grange and makes the boundary with Nuthurst as far as the Stratford Road. After passing under the road the brook is joined first by an unnamed stream which rises in Spring Lane and then by Tapster Brook which rises near the church. They join at Tapster Ford and pass through Tapster Valley as Tapster Brook. After being joined by other small streams Tapster Brook flows southwards making the boundary between Lapworth and Bushwood. Kingswood Brook which rises in Kingswood Gap near Baddesley Clinton flows southward forming the boundary between Lapworth and Rowington parishes. Just south of Poundley End (in Rowington) Tapster Brook and Kingswood Brook meet and flow south to their confluence with the Alne approximately half a mile north of Wootton Wawen.

The underlying rock at Lapworth, as throughout the district, is Keuper Marl laid down in the Triassic period some 270-180 million years ago. The resultant soil is a heavy clay which drains badly and is difficult to work. In places, however, thin beds of grey Upper Keuper (Arden) sandstone and shale are found near the top of the clay, these give rise to a lighter soil less difficult in character. Where the sandstone outcrops it has been quarried for building stone,[1] this is the case not only at Lapworth but also at Rowington and Baddesley Clinton. In the medieval period Arden sandstone was extensively used in the building of local churches — Knowle, Rowington, Lapworth, Baddesley Clinton — and one or two of the more important houses — Baddesley Clinton Hall, Pinley Priory and the house of Sir John de Bishopsdon. Unfortunately the stone tends to be soft and does not always weather well.

Overlying the bed rock of Keuper Marl and Arden sandstone are patches of drift[2] — Boulder clay and sand and gravel. These were strewn across the landscape during the Ice Age by the movement of glaciers and ice sheets and by the melt waters of the retreating ice. Patches of Boulder clay occur in places throughout Lapworth, the largest areas stretching from Station Lane to near Bear House Farm, from Church Lane to Hockley Heath and from High Chimneys south west to Bushwood Wood. There are no extensive areas of sand and gravel but several small patches here and there. The largest is north east of Tapster Lane, and a long narrow strip of fluvioglacial sand and gravel forms a river terrace along the east side of Kingswood Brook from near Dicks Lane to Lowsonford. Material from this area was used by the Romans in the manufacture of tiles, at least two kilns operating here during the first half of the second century, c.125 AD.[3]

Illustration is of a Roman Box Flue Tile.

The natural vegetation of the Keuper Marl is deciduous woodland — ash, hazel and particularly oak. Much of Lapworth would have been covered with an abundance of such trees — the so called Forest of Arden. However where the Keuper gives way to the Arden sandstone or is overlaid with sandy drift the soil produced is lighter and of a more porous nature, the vegetation is thinner, there are fewer trees, more shrubs and bushes and many natural clearings. These may also have occurred on the Boulder clay which gives a sandy pebbly soil especially on high ground. Early man chose such clearings for his camps and later, colonists intent on establishing themselves permanently, chose the lighter and more easily exploited soils for their initial settlements and cultivated fields.

PRE HISTORY

It is clear from archeological work undertaken during the past thirty years that people of the Middle Stone Age were active in what is now Warwickshire. They moved about the forest in small nomadic groups gaining their living by hunting, fishing and gathering wild plants and made camps on the river terraces or on high ground where the soil was light and vegetation open. Evidence of their occupation has been found near the river at Baginton and Shottery, and above 500 feet at Corley, Packington and Meriden.[4]

During the Neolithic period man began to carry out a primitive kind of farming, 'ploughing' with forked branches and growing an early form of barley and wheat on the light soils of the river terraces and the uplands. Evidence of their settlements has been found in the Avon valley at Warwick, Charlecote and Barford.[5] A stone axe, of a type used by Neolithic people, was found in Lapworth in 1952 during the making of Kingswood Close.[6] It was probably made in Cornwall and indicates that a system of trade already existed. It does not mean, however, that Neolithic people lived in Lapworth, merely that they knew the area and passed through.

No finds of the Bronze Age have yet been discovered in the parish, but in 1971 a Bronze Age axe dated c.1300 BC was found at Norton Green[7] and previously a flanged bronze axe had been turned up at Arden Croft, Beaudesert.[8]

During the Iron Age man's ability as a farmer increased, his tools were of cheap and durable iron, a knowledge of smelting having been brought from the continent by the Celtic people who arrived in Britain from the 7th century BC. Numerous places, especially rivers, forests and hills, still bear Celtic names eg., Alne, Leam, Arrow, Cole, Cannock, Malvern and Kinver. Many of the newcomers were warlike and conflict often developed. Small bands therefore gathered together for self defence in or near forts which they built on strategically placed hills. Several earthworks suspected of being Iron Age exist in the Lapworth area. Those at Yarningale Common, Claverdon; Liveridge Hill, Beaudesert; and Harborough Banks at Lapworth have not been excavated but are probably Iron Age.[9] Those at Barnmoor Wood, Claverdon; and Beausale have been excavated and are confirmed as being Iron Age.[10] Regretfully Harborough Banks has been much destroyed especially in the last 200 years.[11] Until it is excavated its origins will not be known, but it is probably Iron Age later altered and re-used by the Romans.

In the Iron Age tribal boundaries became of paramount importance, the boundaries of the three great tribes of the Dobunni, the Coritani and the Cornovvii meeting in the region of the Midland triangle.[12] The Coritani rarely built forts and the cluster of camps in the Lapworth area may have belonged to the Dobunni or the Cornovvii, indeed the Lapworth district

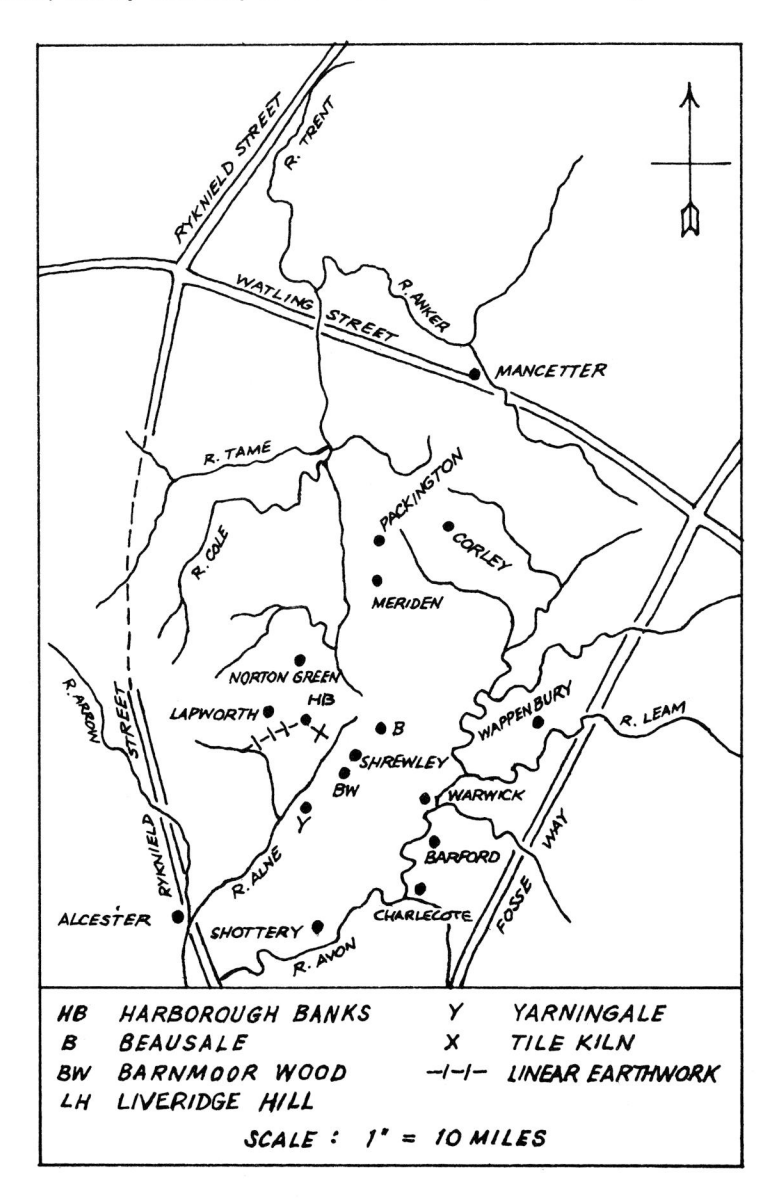

HB	HARBOROUGH BANKS	Y	YARNINGALE
B	BEAUSALE	X	TILE KILN
BW	BARNMOOR WOOD	–/–/–	LINEAR EARTHWORK
LH	LIVERIDGE HILL		

SCALE : 1" = 10 MILES

may have been a Celtic boundary area. This would go far to explain the linear feature which appears to be associated with Harborough Banks and can be traced by field boundary and some excavation over four miles of country from south of Tanworth-in-Arden to Lapworth.[13] Thought to mark the line of a boundary or trackway it may have been established in the Iron Age but was known and used through the Romano-British period. At the western end, at Botley, several sites have been found containing evidence of Romano-British occupation.[14]

From such evidence it would seem that the countryside in and around Lapworth was occupied in the late Iron Age by people who, when the Romans came, adopted those things which were convenient to them — pottery, tiles, and technical innovations such as road building — but continued to live as previously.

The Romans drove three roads through the Midland area, Ryknild Street, Watling Street and the Fosse Way, but their interest was not confined to the vicinity of the roads and there is evidence of industry in various places. Pottery was made at Wappenbury, pottery and tiles in the Mancetter area and there was an industrial suburb at Alcester.[15] At Lapworth, half a mile south of Harborough Banks on the fluvioglacial river terrace, two Roman tile kilns have been found.[16] Tiles were first turned up by the plough in 1935. A cursory excavation found slag, clinker and tile but no sign of a settlement. In 1968-9 a full excavation was carried out and two kilns of c.125 AD were discovered together with square, tegular and oblong tiles suitable for roofing and flooring, also box flue tiles. The tiles were heavy, tegulars weighing up to 14 lbs each, and needing careful transportation; their destination, probably a villa, can hardly have been more than five miles away. It has been suggested that Broomhall Lane, also known as Dicks Lane, which passes the kilns is Roman but this is not yet certain.

During 1977 traces of a considerable Roman building were found on Shrewley Common.[17] Excavation revealed a cobbled surface with postholes and pits, roof and floor tiles, nails, pottery of local Severn ware, and Mancetter *mortaria* fragments, all of which suggest late 3rd or 4th century occupation.

EARLY MEDIEVAL PERIOD

Lapworth is first mentioned in a written document in 816 when it was granted to Deneberht, Bishop of Worcester, by Coenwlf, King of the Mercians.[18] The Bishops of Worcester remained as the lords of Lapworth until 1036 when the then Bishop, Brihteah, granted land in Lapworth to one Herlwin. This was as a reward for Herlwin's companionship when the Bishop took Cnut's daughter, Gunnild, to Saxony for her marriage.[19]

Thirty years later, in 1066, Herlwin's son, Baldwin, was holding Lapworth; he also held Rowington and land elsewhere in Warwickshire and other counties. Baldwin was presumably killed at Hastings, all his lands passing to Hugh de Grentemaisnil of Normandy.[20]

There is no evidence to show when the first permanent settlement was made in Lapworth but it was probably quite late for in 1086, when the Domesday Survey was made, the total population was only three families.[21] Their settlement, probably on the sand and gravel patch beside Tapster Lane, the site of Church Field one of Lapworth's communally worked fields, was surrounded by woodland. The Domesday Survey measured the Lapworth woodland as being one league by two leagues in extent, the approximate equivalent of 2,880 acres, virtually the whole of the parish.[22] Only one ploughland — about 120 acres — of land was under cultivation, but even this was probably more than 20 years previously, the value of the manor having increased 100% during this period.

THE PLACE NAME

The name Lapworth in its earliest known form was written *Hlappawurthin* (816 AD) and *Lappawurthin* (11th century[23]). *Laeppa* or *Lappa* in Old English means 'a lap, skirt of a garment' which in a topographical sense means 'a border, boundary, edge',[24] whilst *worthign* or *wurthign* means 'an enclosure'.[25] Generally such an enclosure was small, the word often being applied to places which were single homesteads surrounded by a fence or hedge and often in remote places. Although there is no doubt that Lapworth was both isolated and sparsely populated in early times (which fits with the second element of the name) there has been much discussion about the interpretation of the first element *'Lappa'*.

Sir William Dugdale the 17th century antiquary thought that Lapworth was so called because it was a detached portion of Fexhole Hundred and was surrounded on three sides by land belonging to other Hundreds,[26] — Baddesley Clinton and Nuthurst being part of Hemlingford Hundred; Rowington, Preston Bagot and Beaudesert being in Fernecumbe Hundred; and Bushwood being a detached portion of Pathlow Hundred. Many places in this part of Warwickshire, however, were detached portions of other Hundreds or were clearly associated with other distant manors. Besides which the division of large areas of land into counties, shires and into smaller units known as Hundreds occurred from the 10th century onwards and we know that Lapworth was named long before this.

Rather it would seem that Lapworth had this boundary name for some other reason. Was it because of its position so close to the watershed which divides the water courses of England? Those streams rising to the north of the watershed flow via the Tame, Trent and Humber to the North Sea, whilst those rising to the south of the divide flow via the Avon and Severn to the Bristol Channel. Was it from its position close to the boundary between the Diocese of Lichfield and that of Worcester? When Worcester Diocese was created in c.680 AD carved out of the earlier vast Midland Diocese of Lichfield, its boundary followed the line of the ancient Saxon tribe of the Hwicce. Lapworth stands at the boundary of the lands of the Saxon Hwicce and the lands of the tribes of the South Mercian Angles. Or did this boundary name have its origin in the linear feature of the Romano-British period, or the boundary between the Celtic Dobunni, Coritani and Cornovvii tribes?

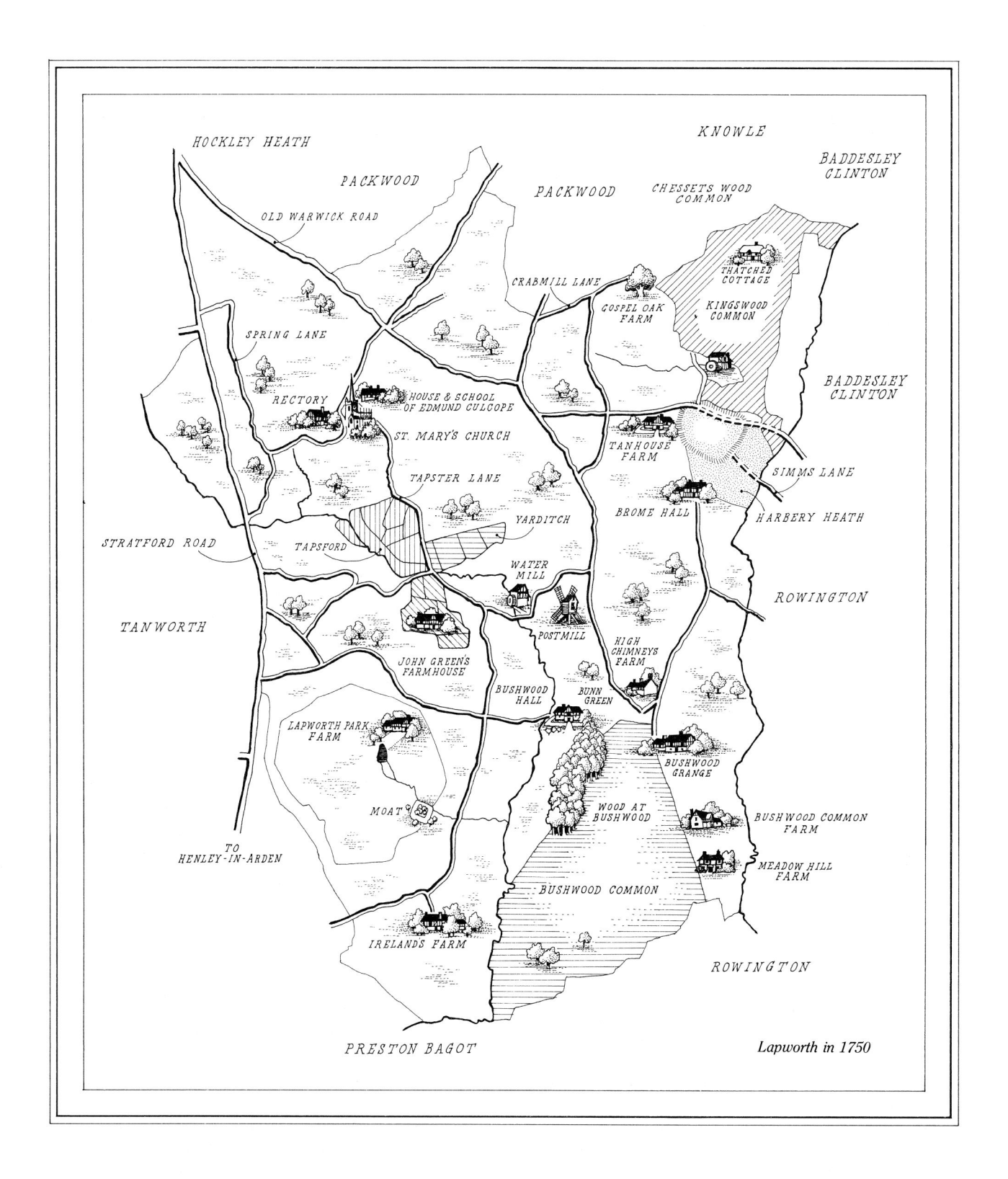

Lapworth in 1750

Lapworth 1750-1800
1
THE COMING OF OWEN BONNELL

* *In the summer of 1750 a young man, the Reverend Owen Bonnell, arrived in Lapworth to serve St. Mary's church as curate. Although he was only 24 years old and recently down from University*[1] *Bonnell found himself in sole charge of the parish, for the rector, the Reverend Charles Bean, was a pluralist, being also the vicar of St. Mary's church, Warwick,*[2] *where he preferred to live. He took very little interest in his Lapworth benefice and rarely visited the parish.*

The curate took up his duties at once, holding services, overseeing parish affairs, officiating at marriages, baptisms and burials and recording these events in the parish registers. The entries he made in his distinct, small handwriting give only essential details, no more, but at least the registers were kept in an orderly manner, which they had not been prior to his coming.

When he had time to take stock of his new home, Owen Bonnell found Lapworth to be a moderately sized parish of some 3,000 acres. The landscape was one of small fields, narrow winding lanes and isolated farm houses, most of which were timber framed, although here and there walls of a warm rusty coloured brick were to be seen. In spring and summer the countryside, abundantly endowed with great and ancient trees, was lush and green. In autumn the mixed hedgerows of hawthorn, hazel, blackthorn, elder and bramble glowed with colour and provided a prolific harvest of nuts and berries to be gathered and preserved against the winter.

Scattered through Lapworth were about 55 houses and perhaps 30 cottages[3] sheltering a population of approximately 330 people. In such a rural community most of the men worked on the land, but there were also those craftsmen who were essential in any 18th century village — the smith, the wheelwright, the carpenter and the cordwainer. In addition, at Lapworth, there was a mason, a tanner and a brick-maker.[4]

The farms were not large and each was owned, or more often tenanted, by an individual farmer and his family. The farms were generally mixed, the farmers investing similar proportions of their time and substance in both crops and animals. The larger farmers grew a variety of grains — wheat, barley and oats, as well as peas, hay and some vetches, — whilst the smaller men grew mostly barley and peas with a little wheat for their bread. There were no oxen in the parish, horses being used to work the ground, which *Bonnell, who was country bred, considered to be well husbanded.* The larger farmers each kept several horses and even the small farmers had one and often two. Much of the parish was on stiff soil which could be difficult to work, so good pulling power was essential.

Almost all the farmers had a small herd of dairy cows plus a few heifers and calves, and several of the larger farmers kept a bull. Some of the milk was made into butter but most of it was used to make cheese. The female members of the farm households spent long hours in their dairies and cheese rooms producing considerable quantities, which were sold in the local market at Henley-in-Arden and perhaps also at Warwick. The buttermilk and whey were fed to the pigs, most people keeping two or three. A number of farmers also had sheep which were useful for both their wool and their meat; the flocks were never more than 30 strong, 12 sheep being the average.[5]

Lapworth contained no Great House or grand land-owning family, although there were a number of good and honest men of yeoman stock. *Bonnell was perhaps disappointed to find no educated society within the parish to provide him with the stimulating friends and conversation he had enjoyed whilst at Oxford.* Those who might have asked him to dine, the Holte family, the lords of the manors of both Bushwood and Lapworth, lived in their magnificent mansion, Aston Hall, near Birmingham; and the Ferrers family, the lords of the manor of

**The use of Italics indicates a mixture of fact and fiction.*

Kingswood, were rarely in residence at Baddesley Clinton Hall. Without a resident rector, or other patron, to introduce him into local society it was virtually impossible for a young, unknown Welsh curate to make his way.

So Bonnell lived alone at the Rectory with a servant to care for his needs. This was a timbered house which had been much altered by a previous rector, Edward Welchman.[6] He had lived there from 1690 to 1739 and, as his extensive family grew, improved and added to the house until it was large and rambling.

Bonnell learned something of such past events from Edmund Culcope, the gentleman schoolmaster, who kept a private school at his home, close to the church. Although considerably older than Bonnell he was an amiable and interesting companion and the young curate was pleased to have his friendship.

It was Culcope who suggested enjoyable walks and who directed the curate's footsteps towards Kingswood Common, a large tract of unenclosed land in the north eastern corner of the parish. Covering approximately 155 acres, the Common was open and windswept, with few trees. The highest ground (420ft) was to the north, from where the land sloped gently down to a stream and disused water mill. The mill-house, small and timber framed, nestled at the south eastern edge of the Common. Above, on the high ground, were two or three natural clumps of pine trees, and here and there were rowans, yews and limes. Near the pines, quite isolated in a small garden enclosure, was a tiny thatched cottage. At the western corner of the Common stood a giant oak tree, known locally as the Gospel Oak. It marked the boundary of Lapworth and Packwood parishes, as well as the edge of the Common. Close by was an old farm house which shared its name with the tree.

In April the open ground of the Common was a carpet of yellow and blue flowers, dandelion, buttercup, crosswort, field forget-me-not and various speedwells. But during May and June the colours changed to include a variety of greens, pinks and lilacs as an abundance of grasses (Timothy cats tail, red fescue, crested dogs tail) and flowers (sorrel, common centaury, clover, tare, hoary plantain and many others) came into bloom.[7] The grasses provided excellent and nutritious grazing for the cattle which was used to full advantage by the people of Kingswood.

Running contiguously to the north of Kingswood Common but in the adjoining parishes of Packwood and Knowle was a similar waste — Packwood or Chessetts Wood Common — which seemed to stretch away as far as the eye could see.

To the south of Kingswood Common, being virtually a continuation of it, was a further, but smaller, area of open ground. Its extent was difficult to ascertain, for most of it was enclosed by a large and high embankment which described an irregular oblong across the land. The local people called the area Harbery Heath and the great mound Harborough Banks. They told many stories of ancient people, of hob goblins and weird events. Bonnell dismissed such tales as fantasy, but he could not but wonder at the size of the banks and ponder as to who had built them and for what purpose. He had heard that some 20 years or so previously, when the banks were dug for gravel, the spout of an ancient ewer had been discovered. It had been melted down and found to be of 'Princes' metal, a sort of Aurichalcum.[8] Bonnell regretted that he was ignorant of such things and only wished he understood their significance.

Culcope had told him that digging into Harborough Banks for gravel was common practice locally. The curate felt it was wrong that the earthwork should be despoiled in this way, but no one else seemed to care, not even Mr. Robert Basket, the lord of the manor of Brome, to whom he presumed the Banks belonged.

Close beside Harborough Banks, on the west side, was the moated house, tanyard and pits owned by Thomas Mason and once occupied by Humphrey Shakespeare and now by the Overton family.[9] Thomas Overton and his family lived simply and worked hard. The house was old and plainly furnished for all their substance was invested in the tannery. Some 20 years previously they had built a new tanhouse, tanyards and vats where they treated large numbers of hides and calf skins. The nearby stream provided a plentiful supply of water, and tree bark, another essential for tanning, was readily available within the area. The Overtons were also small farmers keeping a couple of cows, a pig, a dozen sheep and growing a few acres of wheat and barley, just enough to keep the household in basic provisions: milk, cheese, butter, meat, flour, beer and wool.[10]

On the other side of Harborough Banks, at the south eastern corner of the embankment, stood Brome Hall, another old, moated building and the manor house to Brome manor. Bonnell knew, from the tablets in the church, that this house was for many years the home of the Camden family, the lords of the manor of Brome. The last Camden had died in 1729 and the house was now occupied by a tenant, Thomas Buckle, a working farmer.[11]

Beyond Brome Hall, through the farmyard, was a lane leading to Lapworth Street, Lowsonford and Bushwood. About a mile along this lane was another farm house; it had fine tall chimneys, one of the stacks being quite ornate. Some people called the house High Chimneys, others Brommen Priory,[12] *and Culcope thought that it had once been known as Sorrells House. The lane turned away from the house and emerged on to a small green — Bunn Green — for at its edge, in a cottage, lived and worked the family of Bunn, the blacksmith. Beyond the Green was the hamlet and the common of Bushwood.*

Nestling between the two southern parts of Lapworth parish, Bushwood was a very small settlement with but seven houses.[13] *The largest of these, Bushwood Hall, was moated and the reputed birthplace of Robert Catesby, the instigator of the Gunpowder Plot. Although truly a part of Old Stratford parish the manor of Bushwood was always closely connected with Lapworth, the history of the two places being firmly intertwined.*

The natural vegetation of Bushwood was deciduous woodland and one of its earliest owners was the Bishop of Worcester. From the combination of 'Bishop' and 'Wood' the place gained its name. Throughout the centuries a portion of the ancient woodland remained as a wood, whilst 200 acres of the rest of the manor was used as common land by the people of the neighbouring manor of Rowington. The exclusive right to the use of Bushwood Common was negotiated by the lords of the manor of Rowington at an early date, probably in the 12th century. From that time it was well cared for, and jealously guarded by the Rowington people, for it was one of their most valuable assets. No encroachments were permitted to be made, the Common was closed to sheep from mid April to the end of October to preserve the fine grazing, and the number of animals, of any type, permitted to graze, was strictly limited.[14]

Having discovered Bushwood Common and the wood, Owen Bonnell returned to it again and again. It was such a delightful place with so many flowers and lovely trees, guelder rose, great sallow, small leaved lime and almond willow, quite different from those he saw at Kingswood. The ground was undulating, the highest land being occupied by the wood which dominated the landscape and made a wonderful backdrop for the rich flora surrounding it. Throughout the year the trees presented a kaleidoscope of colour, fresh green in the spring, mixed shades of green in the summer and russets and brown in the autumn. The Common, roughly triangular in shape, lay to the east and south of the wood, its most northerly part being close to High Chimneys Farm and its southern boundary stretching from Brookhouse Farm, in Rowington, to Lowsonford. On the east it extended to the very doors of Bushwood Grange, Bushwood Common Farm and Meadow Hill Farm. There were no made roads over the Common[15] *and Bonnell wandered as he wished, watching the birds, looking at the wild flowers and enjoying the distant views and the wonderful skies. He particularly liked to be there at sunset for the colours then were frequently spectacular.*

The grasses on which the animals grazed on Bushwood Common differed little from those at Kingswood; many of the flowers of the grassland were also similar. But in addition Bonnell found green, creeping parsley piert, rare heather bedstraw, red bartsia, and where it was moister, white lady's mantle and water pepper. At the edge of a pond were several types of sedge, toad rush, and floating sweet grass. In the hedgerow which divided the farm gardens from the Common were hawthorn, dog rose, blackthorn, wild plum, black bryony, wild hop, cuckoo pint, herb Robert and betony which the old men mixed with their tobacco. Occasionally Bonnell met women and children picking the leaves and digging up the roots of certain plants which were to be the ingredients of herbal cures. They told him that the juice of fleabane was useful against fleas, that a decoction of sanicle cured ulcers and ailments of the lungs and throat, and that the juice of burdock eased pain in the bladder. The seed of burdock, taken in wine, was they said, a helpful panacea against sciatica. They were especially anxious to find eyebright for its juice was good for all diseases of the eye, and also helped a weak brain and memory.[16]

Northwards, beyond the Common and Bunn Green, on a high knoll, stood Bushwood Windmill.[17] *Bonnell was delighted when he discovered it and frequently visited the miller and watched him at work. It was a post mill, made of wood; the design was simple, having changed hardly at all since windmills first came to England in the 12th century. The rectangular body contained all the corn grinding machinery, stones, gears, etc., access being by ladder at the rear. The sails were attached to this body, which could be rotated on a central main post to catch the wind. The base of the structure was supported by a trestle of quarter bars and cross trees. Working a windmill could be dangerous and Bonnell was fascinated by the expertise of the men who managed to tame and utilise the wind.*

The miller told him there had once been two water mills on Lapworth Brook, one being in Bushwood manor and the other in Lapworth. The mill-pool to the latter was in the valley below Lapworth Street. Neither mill could have been very efficient and they had been long disused, perhaps for fifty years.

Bonnell went to look for the Lapworth mill site. It was easily found for the mill-pool, half full of water, was still there. The pool was fed by Tapster Brook, the water entering at the north western corner. It was contained by a dam forming the south bank of the pool and across which ran the lane. Below the dam the ground fell away steeply; out of this a deep vertical channel had been cut to take the mill wheel. The water, when released by sluices in the dam wall, fell down on to the wheel forcing it to turn and grind. Having turned the wheel the water sped downwards towards Bushwood Hall.

The summer of 1750 was hot and sunny and Bonnell, anxious to investigate every corner of the parish whilst the good weather lasted, spent as much time as possible out and about. His way frequently led him down Tapsford Lane, which ran between the church and Edmund Culcope's house. It was deep and shady with fine trees; he had been told that in spring the banks were carpeted with violets and wild daffodils. Half way down the lane, on the right hand side, was the land called Tapsford which was owned by William Green. His uncle, John Green, having no children of his own, had left it to him in his will. Isaac Green, William's brother, farmed a group of fields on the other side of the lane; they were known as Yarditch.

A wide shallow stream crossed the bottom of the lane. This was Lapworth Brook, the same which fed the mill-pool, but just here it was called Tapster Brook. There had once been a bridge but since the mill ceased working it had fallen into decay and collapsed; now it was necessary to ford the stream. By the ford three lanes met, that to the left went towards the mill-pool, that to the right curved its way to the turnpike road which joined Birmingham with Stratford. Bonnell crossed the stream then took a fordraught across the farm of another of the Green family, John, brother to William and Isaac. The fields of John's farm were known anciently as Oldfield but now, divided into smaller acreages, were called Bridge Close, Gravelly Hill and the five Thistle Closes.[18]

Eventually Bonnell found himself in Bushwood Lane which skirted the edge of the Park, close to the homestead of Lapworth Park Farm. The house, set back from the road, was old, timber framed, but taller and grander than many of the other houses in the parish. The tenant of Park Farm was Benjamin Edkins, his family had lived and farmed here since at least the 1660's.

The land of Lapworth Park, some 400 acres in extent, resembled a slightly tipped shallow bowl in shape. The highest ground lay along the northern rim, which was bounded by Bushwood Lane. From here the ground sloped gently down to a central dip where an outcrop of local sandstone had, in the past, been quarried for building. The area was rough and overgrown with scrubby trees and bushes. At the centre was a pool fed by an unseen brook. To the south east the ground sloped away again, to the lower rim of the bowl. Here several small rivulets gathered to make a stream which fed an ancient moat; this was wide and very deep. The platform of the moat was large and square and covered with sapling trees. There was no sign of any building of any kind. The Park had ceased to be a hunting park long ago and the land had been divided up into large fields, now parcelled into farms and let to tenants. But there were still many magnificent trees which Sir Lister Holte, the lord of the manor and the owner, kept in hand and which Henry Cook, the woodman, looked after attentively.

Beyond the Park, some way along a narrow lane, was Irelands Farm the home of the Mander family. They had farmed here since the 1670's and also rented two other farms in Bushwood, all the property of Sir Lister Holte. Bonnell enjoyed his visits to the farm and was always welcomed warmly by Robert Mander. He and his young family had only recently moved there from the Hall Farm at Bushwood, Robert's father, also Robert, having occupied Ireland's Farm until his death in July 1749. The Manders, and other large tenants too, had fallen very much into arrears with their rent during the 1730's and 40's[19] *when corn prices had fallen. Robert was anxious to pay off all the debts and he liked to discuss with Bonnell how best, with his large acreage, he could make it profitable.*

After a wonderful summer and excellent harvest the late autumn of 1750 was very wet. The rain started in October and continued, it seemed almost every day, until December. The lanes were like quagmires and consequently Bonnell had to curtail his visits about the parish. His first Christmas at Lapworth was approaching, he had enjoyed these months as curate on the whole, and hoped he might stay for a few years at least. He missed his family, the sea, the fresh winds and open skies of his home in Carmarthenshire, but he was virtually his own master at Lapworth (if not very well paid), the people had received him kindly, and caring for the parish gave him much satisfaction.

'MEMORANDA PAROCHIALA' 1751-75

The years following Owen Bonnell's arrival in Lapworth were quiet and fairly uneventful. As season followed season it was the weather, the state of their crops and livestock and the well being of their families which concerned local people, rather than what was happening in the world at large. Not that Lapworth was cut off from the outside world — the Stratford Road had been turnpiked in 1726 and through the travellers on the road, coachmen and passengers alike, news of events in London and beyond filtered in.

A series of good harvests in the 1730's and 40's had produced nationally more grain than was needed. Some of the excess was made into gin (leading to much wanton drinking) but a great deal of it was exported, a million quarters being sent abroad in 1750. As a result the cost of living, including the price of corn, fell and for the first time people of all classes could afford to eat bread made from fine, white wheat flour. Unfortunately the profits of arable farmers were greatly reduced and many got into financial difficulties. Three or four of the larger tenants at Lapworth fell badly into arrears with their rent, but the majority were engaged in mixed farming and appear not to have been greatly affected.

There were six good summers and four poor ones in the 1750's.[20] The good years all produced excellent harvests and most were described as dry and very hot. The last year of the decade, 1759, was the third in a row to have a hot summer. Unfortunately, at Lapworth, it was also a year of high mortality. The parish's burial figures show no evidence of a fatal epidemic but there were more deaths through the year than usual. The following year, 1760, also had a dry, very hot summer and the burial figures were even higher. It seems probable that the cause was 'a throat distemper and miliary fever', similar to scarlet fever, which was widespread in other parts of the country at this time. Although infectious and very unpleasant it killed approximately only one in 30 of its victims. Adults were mostly affected in the throat, few having a rash. In children however, a rash similar to measles covered the body, there was a fever and a less severe sore throat. Such fevers and malignant sore throats prevailed in many parts of England through the middle years of the century. The throats described frequently as 'putrid' or 'gangrenous' appear to have been the worst part of the illness.[21] The mortality figures for 1762 and for the three years 1764, 1765 and 1766 were also higher than average and it seems probable that the illness was once more claiming some victims. The summers in two of these years, 1762 and 1765, were again hot and dry.

During the 1750's the population of the parish was virtually static, at about 330 people, and had been since the early 1740's. The next decade, however, saw a change and despite the years of high mortality the population began to rise and continued to do so for the rest of the century reaching approximately 500 in 1800.[22]

In 1767 the Old Warwick Road was turnpiked. It was a road which had been used by travellers since medieval times but now a regular succession of coaches would be passing through the village bringing more traffic and strangers than ever before.

In the same year the rector, Charles Bean, died. He had visited the parish occasionally, but not often enough for his passing to have caused any great sadness amongst his people. In November 1767 a new rector was appointed by Merton College, Oxford, who held the gift of the living. The Reverend Joseph Kilner was to be the rector of Lapworth for the next 26 years, but like his predecessor, he was an absentee parson preferring to live elsewhere. During the whole of his rectorship he appears never to have taken a service, or conducted a baptism, a marriage, or a burial at Lapworth. All such duties were left to Owen Bonnell who ran the parish for him, and was absent on very few occasions.

The fine summers of the 1760's were not repeated during the first five years of the 1770's for these were indifferent with mixed harvests. The winter of 1770-1 was at first very wet and then extremely cold, some thought as cold as the exceptional winter of 1740. It remained cold until April 1771 and the spring did not begin until warm rain fell during May. The winter of 1775-6 was similarly very cold with blizzards in January, frost in March and a cold April and May. From 1775-80 the winters continued cold but there were warm summers to compensate although the harvests were mixed — 1776 and 1777 average, 1775 and 1779 abundant and 1778 excellent.

In March 1771 Edmund Culcope, the schoolmaster, died. He lived at the house now called Broomfield,[23] almost next to the church, where he is thought also to have had his school. His family, who had lived in Lapworth for over a century, were farmers of good standing, his three nieces marrying leading farmers of the parish. Culcope had six children, two sons and a daughter who predeceased him, and three daughters; Elizabeth and Susannah married but the youngest, Mary, remained at home. His wife, Elizabeth, was probably an invalid and in his will Culcope instructed Mary to live with her mother, look after her well and make sure she had everything she wished.[24] Mrs. Culcope died two months after her husband and Mary, already 37 years old, married four months later. Her husband William Bond joined her at Broomfield and farmed the land to the house. Later they acquired more land and finally moved to Lapworth Park Farm.[25] They had one son, John.

In the winter of 1774-5 a Highwayman 'infested the road', presumably the Stratford Road near Lapworth. He appears not to have been caught, but Sir Charles Holte, the lord of the manor, gratified that one Wooldridge had assisted in an attempt to take him, gratefully rewarded him with a guinea.[26]

By the summer of 1775 Owen Bonnell had been curate of Lapworth for twenty-five years. Why he stayed on in the parish is a matter of conjecture; did he choose to remain because he liked Lapworth and the people and did not mind being the curate if he was free to run the parish as he wished? Or did he lack the influential friends or patron necessary in the 18th century to gain preferment in the church? Knowing the people with the right connections was essential; advancement then had little to do with ability.

'MEMORANDA PAROCHIALA' 1776-1800

The last quarter of the 18th century was a period of war and revolution abroad and of increased prosperity, population and industrial growth at home. During these years the population of Lapworth rose by about 25%, most of the increase taking place between 1785 and 1800. Such an increase appears to have been the result of families in the 1760's being much larger than previously. During the decade 1760-69 there were 67 reproducing families in the parish, of these 13 (19.4%) had five children or more. Not all these offspring survived to adulthood and of those who did, not all remained in the parish, but a good proportion stayed and married. By the mid 1780's and 1790's they were producing families of their own. The Parish Registers show that in the decade 1780-89 there were 66 reproducing families, 10 of which (15.5%) had more than five children each and, that during the 1790's there were 84 reproducing families, of which 11 (13.09%) had five children or more. Of these 11 larger families three were very large, Matthew and Lydia Bayliss having 11 children, William and Mary Bradbury 12 children, and George and Elizabeth Smith 15 children.

Large families were by no means the prerogative of the better-off but the Bradburys and the Bayliss' were certainly high in the village social strata. Both men were farmers, Bradbury occupying Lapworth Lodge Farm, one of the largest in the parish. George Smith was also a farmer but, as far as can be ascertained, he worked only the 15 acres of land around his house, Bredon House, hardly enough to keep 15 children; possibly he had a secondary occupation. Of the fathers of the other larger families one was a shoemaker, four were farmers (one in quite a small way) and three were probably wage labourers.

At Lapworth, as throughout the country, Friday 13 December 1776 was a Fast Day, so appointed 'against the rebel Americans'.[27] There were services and prayers for the support of the King (George III) in all churches, although they did little good. The Americans, who had declared their Independence five months previously on 4 July, continued to fight and win. In 1781 after the siege of Yorktown all the British forces surrendered and in 1783 America was recognised as independent.

The weather during the 1780's appears to have been fairly reasonable with generally warm summers but cold winters. The decade started with two warm dry summers but mildew attacked the wheat in both years and the harvests were light. The following summer (1782) was very wet, producing plenty of grass but a poor harvest; November was extremely cold. The death rate at Lapworth was raised slightly this year probably from the effects of influenza which was prevalent during the spring and summer, although the disease itself was not a killer.[28] The summer of 1783 was hot and stormy, of 1784 wet, and of 1785 warm but with a very late harvest. Gilbert White records that at Selbourne hay and crops were still being carried in November. Both 1786 and 1787 had warm summers with good harvests, unfortunately the latter was again a year of higher than usual mortality at Lapworth, but for no obvious reason. The last two years of the decade both had hot summers but the winter between them was long and cold, frost continuing into April 1789.

The decade ended with revolution in France after the storming of the Bastille in July 1789. Those who had been dismayed by the loss of America were now fearful of unrest at home. Two years later in 1791, on the anniversary of Bastille Day, there were commemorative meetings held by sympathisers in London, Norwich and many other places. In Birmingham, after such a gathering, a mob, purporting to be supporters of the King and the Church, attacked and destroyed four nonconformist churches and two Quaker meeting houses. They also burnt down the houses of several prominent citizens including those of Dr. Joseph Priestley and William Hutton, and ransacked many others. The rioting lasted for four days and spread as far as Kings North.[29] A group of rioters set out for Hatton where Dr. Samuel Parr, an eccentric, radical, Whig schoolmaster, was the parson. They intended to destroy his house and extensive library but fortunately the distance, 15 miles, was too far and they gave up and returned home before any damage was done.

During the early 1790's the idea of a canal passing through Lapworth was mooted and surveyors were about the parish studying the landscape and preparing plans. The Act of Parliament for the building of the Stratford-upon-Avon canal was passed in 1793 although the work in Lapworth did not begin until 1800. During the intervening years plans, and yet more plans, were made as a variety of routes were suggested, surveyed and discarded.

In June 1793 the absentee rector, Joseph Kilner, died and shortly after was succeeded by the Reverend Henry Anthony Pye. Kilner who had been supported by the tithes and revenues of Lapworth since 1767 for doing absolutely nothing, was said on his memorial stone in Cirencester church to have had 'a life of infirmity most graciously alleviated and wonderfully lengthened out to more than 72 years'.[30] The new rector was quite different. He was young, only 27 years of age, unmarried, and intent on living in the parish. It must have been with some relief that the ageing Owen Bonnell handed over the running of the parish to his new superior. For some time the curate's writing had been tremulous and at the end of 1793 entries in the Registers, in his hand, cease.

One of the Reverend Pye's first tasks in the parish was the rectory house. The old house was obviously not to his liking and in June 1794 plans were submitted by Thomas Johnson of Warwick for a new house on the site. They were quickly accepted and subsequently the old rectory was demolished and the new house built. It was an elegant three-storey house of red brick entered by a central door with an ornate pedimented door-case. It contained a dining room, drawing room, study, large kitchen and a washhouse. There were about nine or 10 bedrooms on the two upper floors.[31]

About 1796 Mr. Pye married and in October 1797 he and his wife, Frances Ursula, had their first child, Harriet. She was quickly followed by six further sisters and brothers before the family left Lapworth in 1806.

In July 1796 Owen Bonnell died, his memorial stone being placed on the chancel floor inside the altar rails.[32] He was 70 years of age and had been the curate at Lapworth for 45 years. It is not known whether he ever married, but in 1806 an Elizabeth Bonnell was buried in Lapworth. She was certainly not his sister but she could have been his widow or some other relative.

The weather during the 1790's was generally poor, there were good harvests only in 1791 and 1798, the rest being variously described as 'poor', 'average', or 'deficient'; that of 1799 was a disaster. The winter of 1794-5 was very severe with arctic conditions from December 1794 to 21 March 1795. The average temperature for January, one of the coldest on record, was 23.9°F. Parson Woodford in his diary recorded that on 23 January the temperature in his study, even with a fire, was only 46°F., that 'it froze apples within doors, tho' coverd with a thick carpet'. At other times the milk, cream and the chamber pots froze.[33] The summer of 1795 was also cold, there was frost in late June, the newly shorn sheep dying in the fields. The harvest of 1794 had been badly deficient and by June 1795 a severe shortage of wheat and increased prices led to scarcity riots in Birmingham and other towns. In September there were riots in Dudley 'at the dearness and scarcity of bread'.[34] Despite high hopes the harvest was again disappointing, in October Aris's Gazette advised readers that they 'must be careful with flour and not waste it' and a recipe for bread made partly with potatoes was given. Corn prices remained high through 1796 and the poor, who lived mainly on bread and cheese, suffered greatly. It has been estimated, that a white loaf which a short while before cost 6d., now cost at least 1s. 9d.[35] In 1797 corn prices fell and continued level during 1798, but by the end of 1799 they were rising again, and reached astronomical heights in 1800 and 1801, a bad omen for the start of the new century.

Bushwood Common Farm

2

THE THREE MANORS
Lapworth, Kingswood and Brome

Lapworth, Kingswood and Brome were the three manors which lay within the bounds of Lapworth parish. Each had its own lord, manor court and set of rules by which it was administered. Lapworth was the largest of the three, its boundary following exactly that of the parish except in the north and in the east. Here Kingswood manor was situated some 433 acres being under its jurisdiction, of these, 144 acres running contiguously, were in the adjoining parish of Rowington.

The smallest of the manors and the one with the most difficult boundaries to determine was Brome. Situated on the eastern side of the parish, adjoining Lapworth and Kingswood manors on the north, Rowington manor on the east, Lapworth manor on the south and west and Bushwood manor on the south west, Brome included Harborough Banks, and several farms within its bounds.

Bushwood was a separate manor altogether, although through the centuries Bushwood and Lapworth manors were often owned by the same person. In the medieval period particularly they are frequently mentioned together in deeds, leading to a great deal of confusion. But they were separate, and Bushwood Hall, although often wrongly called Lapworth Hall, was the manor house of Bushwood, never of Lapworth manor.

THE MANOR OF LAPWORTH

At the time of Owen Bonnell's arrival in Lapworth the lord of the manor was Sir Lister Holte of Aston Hall and Duddeston Hall, both near Birmingham. Lapworth manor, together with that of Bushwood, had been purchased about 1602 by Sir Lister's ancestor, Sir Thomas Holte, who had lived locally for a time in the 1590's and had two of his children baptised at Lapworth parish church.

Lapworth manor was managed for the Holtes at first by a Bailiff and later by a Steward. Until 1768 the Stewards were men of farming background but from this date they were gentlemen with legal training. It was the Steward's job to collect the manor rents, keep the accounts, record changes of tenancy, oversee repairs and the care of the woodland, and generally keep things running smoothly. Once or perhaps twice a year a manorial court would be called and presided over by the Steward in the lord of the manor's name. At Lapworth all those who lived within the bounds of the manor, whether manor tenants or not, were obliged to attend; those who failed to do so were fined. At such a meeting, known as a Court Baron, cases of misdemeanor and nuisance within the manor were heard and determined, and the offenders fined. By the late 18th century manor courts were held less frequently than previously and the proceedings were often quite short, even so a formal account of the business was written; this record was known as the Court Roll, the parchments traditionally being stitched together and rolled up, for safe keeping.

Based on ancient law and custom all the land of the manor was considered to belong to its lord, and any matter concerning such land, however small, was of interest to him. At Lapworth all the tenants were freeholders, none holding their land by customary service as at Rowington and Kingswood. Freehold tenants were at liberty to sell their property to whoever they chose, to lease or let it without being charged a fine or asking permission of the lord. As long as they paid their Chief Rent, attended the manor court when required, and kept the basic rules of good behaviour, they were at liberty to please themselves.

The first Lapworth manor court for which there is a Court Roll extant was that held on Tuesday 25th October 1768;[1] the Steward was William Sadler. Several tenants were absent and were marked as such on the Suit Roll, a kind of register of those who should have attended. In the Court Roll the names of the manor tenants were listed together with rents they paid. Known as Chief Rents, they were a kind of ground rent, and totally artificial

Illustration shows Coats of Arms of Brome, Ferrers and Holte families.

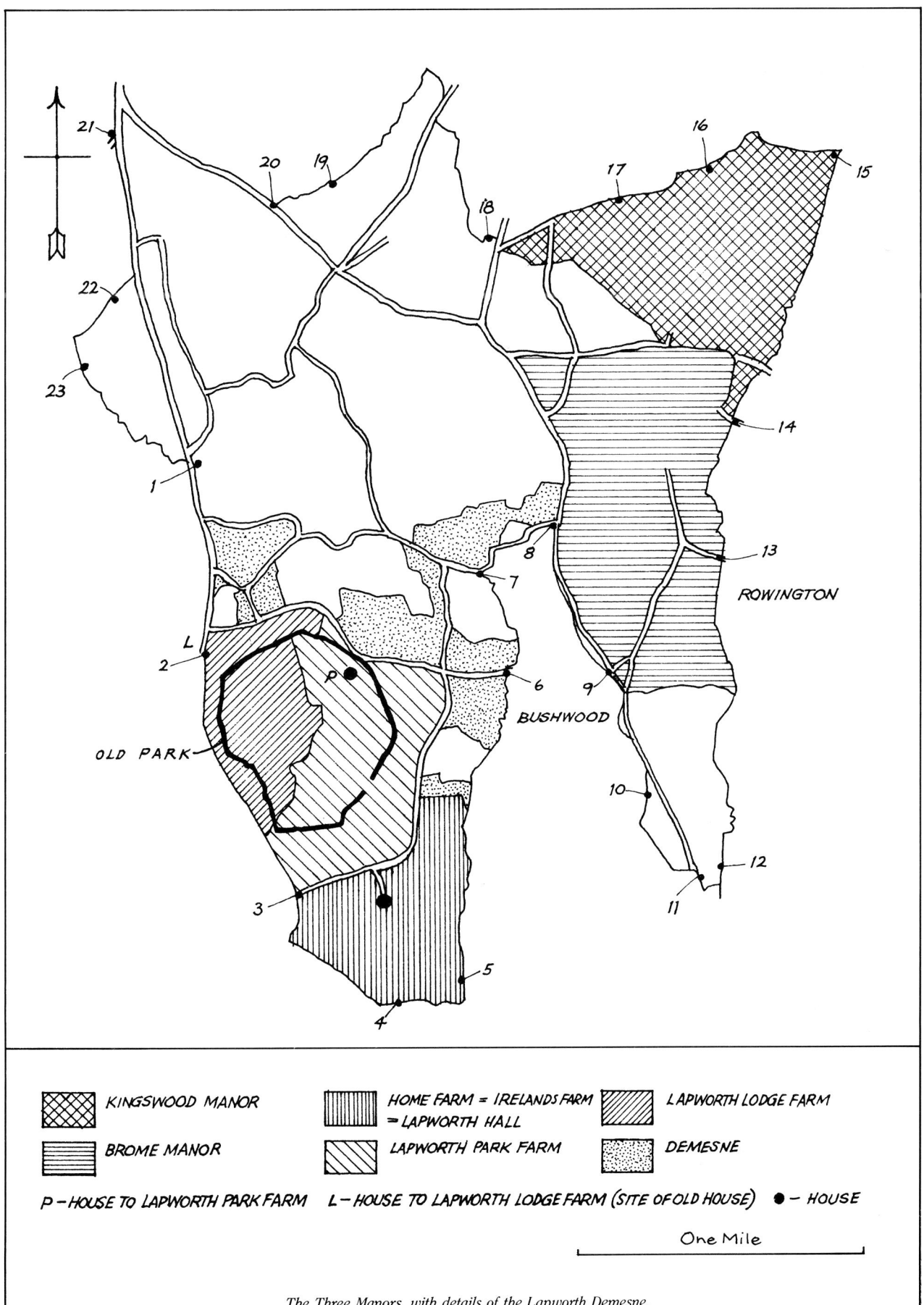

*The Three Manors, with details of the Lapworth Demesne.
For explanation of key figures, see page 112.*

bearing no relationship to the contemporary price of land, whether bought or rented. Altogether there were 16 manorial tenants listed and between them they had 18 properties, one of the tenants, William Green, occupying three holdings — Hole House Farm, a farm in Lapworth Street and another at 'Tapsters'.

Eleven of those who paid Chief Rent were not resident in Lapworth and they let their holdings to others. The under-tenants were expected to pay a wholly commercial rent for their property and the manor tenants, thus sub-letting, made a considerable profit whilst Sir Lister received the purely nominal Chief Rent; for 18 farms in 1768 this totalled £2 16s. 5d.

The main business of the 1768 court was concerned with the common land or waste and with those who, in one way or another, had illegally taken a portion of 'the Lord's waste' into their own possession. Very little common existed within Lapworth manor; and although they were so temptingly near, Kingswood and Bushwood Commons were not available to Lapworth tenants, being used exclusively by the manor tenants of Kingswood and Rowington respectively. The little Lapworth common land which remained was along the side of the Stratford Road and Lapworth Street. It was probably most highly prized by the poorer members of the community, particularly the cottagers, who found that being able to graze a cow or a few sheep, or even some geese on the waste made a great difference to their slender economy. The lord of the manor and his Steward however, appeared not to mind about this asset being diminished, as long as those who did it were fined, and later paid a rent for the land they had taken in.

Altogether 17 cases were heard at the court, fines of between 2d., and 6d., being imposed. Six of the offenders had built hovels on the common, a seventh man had erected a pig sty and an eighth man was occupying a stable previously illegally erected on the waste. Each was fined 2d., but the buildings were allowed to remain and were not pulled down. A rent charge of 2d., per annum per building was to be charged from this time onwards. The rest of the offenders had enclosed and taken for their own use small pieces of waste, the size of the enclosure being, no doubt, reflected in the size of the fine. Charles Clues had taken land near his house in Lapworth Street for a garden and was fined 2d. Robert Mander had taken soil and clay, and enclosed a piece of common land beside the Stratford Road, he too was fined 2d. Isaac Green had enclosed land by the side of Lapworth Street to make a private road leading from his barn to Barrs Lane, for him the fine was also 2d. John Greenhill had taken the lord's land beside and in the lane near his house, and John Warden had made a pleck (or small enclosure) by the side of Hockley Heath, they were each fined 6d.

A number of the poorer tenants lived in cottages which had been built on the waste sometime previously. Charles Horton, John Day, Henry Court and Edward Ekins paid between 2s., and 6s., per annum for their cottages but there were 10 others who were so poor that their rents of between 1s., and £1 per annum were paid by the Overseer of the Poor, the 18th century equivalent of social security.

Sir Lister Holte, the 5th baronet, died in April 1770 and was succeeded by his brother Sir Charles Holte. The first manor court of the new lordship and the first since 1768 was held on Tuesday 23rd October 1770,[2] William Sadler again being the Steward. The Court Roll reveals that many of the tenants were in arrears with their rent, some not having yet paid that of 1768. Very little business was conducted and most of it was concerned with rents.

Further courts for which records are available were held in 1772 and 1775. At the former held on 13th October 1772 three tenants and eight residents of the manor were each fined 6d., for failing to attend. It was recorded that all rents, except that of William Falks and a Mr. Wilcox had been paid. Falks, a cottager, was too poor to pay and was therefore excused all but 1d., of his rent, the penny being a token acknowledgement that he was a tenant and still liable to pay. Mr. Wilcox, of Bradnocks End, had claimed at the 1770 court that he was not liable to pay any rent for his land, and that it had been paid in error in 1768 by his tenant. The matter was left over until the next court (held in 1772) in order that Wilcox might prepare his case for exemption. Instead Mr. Wilcox simply ignored the court and neither appeared nor sent any explanation. At the following court, held on Friday 6th October 1775, Mr. Wilcox again failed to appear and the matter of his rent 'remained unsettled and unpaid'. Several tenants and residents again failed to appear at the court and were fined 6d., each for their absence.

By 1784[3] when the next manorial court was held the manor had passed into the hands of Heneage Legge a grandson of the first Earl of Dartmouth and the nephew of the late Sir Lister Holte. The court was held on Tuesday 19th October 'at the dwelling house of Mary Bott, widow, at the sign of the Boot'; she being the tenant of the inn at the time. Edward Sadler, probably William's son, was the Steward. The record of this court, the first of Legge's lordship, is more detailed than any previously, the new Steward being anxious, no doubt, that the new lord of the manor should be given as much information as possible about the manor and tenants. The court was well attended only one person failing to appear. The names of the 18 freeholders, the 44 residents, the 26 cottagers and labourers within the manor are all listed, as well as the 16 who paid Chief Rent and the sums they paid. Seven cottagers paid their own rent and seven others had it paid for them by the Overseer of the Poor. The total income paid to Legge, including rents and fines was £6 7s. 7d.

Attached to the end of the 1784 Court Roll was a perambulation of the 'anceinte meets and bounds of the manor and Lordship of Lapworth'. In it the boundary is described in great detail, starting at the bridge over Lapworth Brook on the Stratford Road. Using still recognisable points, such as barns, streams and houses, and some, such as trees and crosses in the ground, which have been long gone, the perambulation moves slowly round the edge of the manor, finishing where it began. The 1784 parish boundary and the manor boundary appear to be identical, most of Kingswood manor and all of Brome manor being clearly included within Lapworth manor. Yet this was not the true case; why then should the Steward claim that it was? After some investigation it seems unlikely that there was any ulterior motive and that it was a genuine error made by a new lord of the manor and a new Steward, the parish and manor boundaries being confused.

Heneage Legge had become the lord of the manor in 1782, under the will of his uncle Sir Lister Holte, who married three times but had no children. Sir Lister's first wife, Lady Anne Legge, was the daughter of the 1st Earl of Dartmouth, and Heneage Legge was her nephew. By Sir Lister's will, made in 1769, the Holte estate passed to his brother Charles, for his lifetime and then to Mr. Legge.[4] Sir Charles had only one child, a daughter Mary, and she was left fourth in line of succession, only coming into the estate if Heneage Legge, a Mr. Bagot and a Mr. Digby, (all Dartmouth relations) failed to produce heirs. Heneage Legge married in 1768 but had no children; Mr. Bagot (later the Bishop of St. Asaph) and Mr. Digby were also childless and it became clear that Mary Holte, who had married Abraham Bracebridge of Atherstone in 1775, or her heirs, would eventually enter into the estate. On the strength of inheriting the estate Mary Bracebridge's husband, Abraham, raised large sums of money which he put into a patent for making soap. Unfortunately it was not a success and he was unable to discharge his debts. An agreement was therefore made between Heneage Legge, Mr. Digby, and Abraham and Mary Bracebridge, (Mr. Bagot had died in 1802) under which the estate was to be divided into eight parts. Some of the parts, such as Aston Hall and Park, and certain land in Cheshire, were to be sold, whilst others were to be allotted to creditors and to Legge and Digby as compensation.

The Lapworth part of the estate was given to creditors involved in the soap débâcle — Sir William Paxton, Sir Charles Cockerill and Charles Greenwood Esq. Until the settlement was completed, from about 1813 to 1817, Mrs. Bracebridge appears to have been regarded as the lady of the Lapworth manor. Paxton, Cockerill and Greenwood acquired an estate of 1,014 acres 1 rood and 23 perches which included land in the parish of Old Stratford, Rowington, Preston Bagot, Beaudesert and Lapworth, a rental of £1,046 per annum, and the lordships of the manors of Lapworth and Bushwood.

Lapworth manor was retained by the three joint lords for a number of years and by Sir Charles Cockerill certainly until 1830 when it was sold to W.H. Cooper Esq., of London.[5] On his death his widow became lady of the manor, but some time after 1850 she sold Lapworth to George Miller of York. By 1863 Miller had also disposed of the manor, Richard Dolphin being the purchaser. Mr. Dolphin had died by 1876 and his widow retained the lordship for only a short time before giving it to John Edmund Watts who immediately mortgaged it. In 1892 the manor was sold by the mortgagees to a Mr. Weiss who retained it until his death in 1911.[6]

THE DEMESNE

In the south western part of Lapworth manor are the lands which were originally reserved for the use of the lord of the manor — the demesne. Established in the medieval period the demesne at Lapworth consisted of the manor house with the home farm and a hunting Park enclosed by a bank and palings. The Park entrance was protected by a moated gatehouse which may also have been used as a hunting lodge. The Park was in being by the mid 13th century and may have been created by the Marshall family, who were the lords of the manor of Lapworth from the end of the 12th century, or by Henry Pippard who succeeded them and died in 1258.[7]

The manorial descent of Lapworth during the middle ages is very complex, both the manor and the Park being frequently divided and held by different people. In 1313 Sir John de Bishopsdon, who through his grandmother, Cicely Pippard, was holding part of the manor and part of the Park, contracted with a mason and John de Pesham of Rowington to build a house of stone 'at his manor of Lapworth'.[8] William Hoese was the mason, the stone coming from the quarry situated in the centre of the Park. The contract[9] stated that the house was to be 40ft. long and 18ft. wide with the gable-end walls 3½ft. thick and the front and back walls 2½ft. thick. There was to be a central doorway with a room on each side; one with a fireplace and one without, each room was to have proper windows and doors and a wardrobe (garderobe). These rooms were to be 11ft. high, as was the principal doorway which was to have double doors, suspended on columns of stone, and surrounded by a porch. Above stairs there was to be a 'sovereign chamber' the length and width of the house with two fireplaces and two wardrobes projecting out, this room was to be 9ft. high. A parapet 2½ft. high was to be placed around the edge of the roof. The building was to be completed within one year, Sir John carrying the stone and providing the timber, the sand, the lime and a carpenter. The cost was 25 marks or £4 3s. 4d.

The quarry site, the best of the stone having been worked out, was subsequently made into a fishpool which Sir John de Bishopsdon leased in 1329 to William de Charindon and John de Pesham of Rowington[10] who had promoted the building of Sir John's house. William and John were to have all the fishing in the great pool between St. Gregory's Day (12th March) and Easter Monday (24th April) 1329, that is throughout Lent. They were to pay Sir John 20 marks (£3 6s. 8d.), reserving certain stipulated fish as stock for the pool. Sir John was also to have daily, for his own use at table, a pike, a bream, a great eel and four small ones, plus a dozen perch and roach. The rest were to be sold with the intention of making William and John a good profit.

It was Sir John's stone house which in 1369 was being physically divided, as was the Park and the manor lands, between Rose and Agnes, the then joint ladies of the manor, and the daughters and co-heiresses of Sir Hugh de Brandeston,[11] who had recently died. Rose Brandeston had married Sir Richard de Montfort and they were to have the part 'of the great park towards Liverycheshill' (Liveridge Hill) with the fishpond, the water mill, various farms, and part of the house, namely, 'la stonenechamber above the hall' (sovreign chamber), 'the chapel' (the lower chamber without the fireplace), 'the wardrobe, the brewhouse and stable, half the fountain' (the well) and 'half the dovecote'. The other sister, Agnes, had married Philip de Aylesbury and they were to have the part 'of the great park towards Bischopwod' (Bushwood), that is 'the half next the old gate', plus various farms and land. They also had 'half the dovecote', and 'half the fountain' as well as 'the hall with all the rooms below' (the lower chamber with fireplace), 'the kitchen', which was clearly detached from the main house, and 'all the rooms between the door and the new courtyard'. Despite some extra building the house is recognisable as Sir John's.

A century later, in the 1480's the whole of the demesne was held by William Catesby the then lord of Lapworth manor. Catesby, nicknamed 'The Cat', was a great favourite of Richard III who in May 1485 granted him 600 trees to make his new Park at Lapworth. This was in fact the old Park with a ring of extra land added, making it bigger. The new wooden boundary fence was to be made from 100 oaks taken from the old Park at Tanworth and the 500 trees to be used for rails were to be taken from Ladbrook Park, also at Tanworth.[12] Catesby did not enjoy his new Park for long for he was executed for treason in 1487, all his lands being forfeit. However, his son George managed to get all the family lands restored in 1495.

The chief seat of the Catesby family was at Ashby St. Leger in Northamptonshire, but they owned much land in other counties. When George Catesby died in 1505 he held locally the manors of Lapworth, Bushwood and Brome. In Warwickshire the Catesby's favourite home appears to have been Bushwood Hall, leading many people, including Sir William Dugdale. to believe mistakenly that it was the manor house to Lapworth. In fact the true manor house to Lapworth was the old stone house of Sir John de Bishopsdon, known in the middle of the 16th century as 'Lapworth Hall, commonly called Ireland's Farm'.[13] This name came from the family of Ireland who farmed the land and were tenants there in the early-to-mid 16th century. Robert Ireland died in 1559 and shortly afterwards his widow, Elizabeth, married George Walker who took over the farm until his death in 1566.[14] A new lease of the house and farm for 15 years at £20 per annum was granted in 1571 jointly to George Walker (possibly his son) and William Bott.

At this time the Park was being cared for by a custodian, John Clark. In the 1560's he was living at the Park, probably in the house now called Lapworth Park Farm. William Clark, perhaps his father, had married Dame Elizabeth Catesby the widow of William Catesby; she had an annuity of £40 per annum paid partly out of the Park income.[15] By 1586 Clark had gone, and the Park, Irelands Farm, the water mill and other land in Bushwood and Lapworth were leased to Edward Hedges for seven years. The rent for the Park was £66 13s. 4d., per annum, for Irelands Farm £24 per annum, for the water mill, let to Gibson the miller, £5 6s. 8d., per annum, for land at Bushwood £17 and for other land £15.[16]

Sir Thomas Holte purchased Lapworth and Bushwood manors about 1602. The Park was then still enclosed by a paling fence and is shown as such on maps of 1603, 1610 and 1648. However by 1656 it appears to have been disparked; it was then divided into fields, two farms — Lapworth Park Farm and Lapworth Lodge Farm — being formed out of its acres. Other land, outside the Park boundary but also part of the demesne, was farmed by various tenants. These men were direct tenants of the Holte estate to whom they paid a commercial rent.

Sir Thomas Holte, an ardent Royalist, was created a baronet in 1611, he started building Aston Hall in 1618 it being ready for occupation by 1631. During the Commonwealth all his estates were sequestered and only returned when he agreed to compound for them, his fine, set at £4,791 being paid in 1652. At this time the receipts from the Lapworth and Bushwood lands were estimated at £350 per annum.[17]

When Sir Thomas died in 1654 his grandson, Robert, inherited his property and also substantial debts. To help pay them he mortgaged the Lapworth estate in 1655 for £2,500 and for a further £2,500 in 1658. The original mortgagee sold out to Andrew Fountaine, a doubtful character who foreclosed in 1670. As a result the Holte's became involved in a complex legal tangle and the Lapworth lands were not retrieved until 1694. Sir Robert's son, Charles, spent much of his life finally settling the family's debts. He became extremely mean, only one of his six daughters marrying in his lifetime (when she was 36 years old) because he could not, or would not, provide marriage portions. Sir Charles died in 1722 and his son, Sir Clobery, in 1729. Lister Holte, Sir Clobery's son and heir was only nine when his father died and during his minority the estate was controlled by his grandmother and trustees.

During the 1730's and 1740's the rent roll from the Holte property in Warwickshire at Aston, Erdington, Bordesley, Lapworth and Bushwood should have been some £2,600 per annum but in reality, because it was a period of agricultural depression and many tenants were in arrears with their rent, the receipts were far less than this. The arrears at Lapworth were worse than for any other part of the estate.

Account books for several years between 1737 and 1780 survive and give a useful insight into the finances of the estate.[18] In 1737 the Lapworth demesne together with the Bushwood lands appear to have been divided into

15 units and held by 11 tenants. The rent due from these properties was £240 15s. 10d., plus £1 12s. 2½d., for the Chief Rents of the Lapworth freeholders, per half year. Unfortunately the receipts fell far short of this, only £52 14s. 11½d., being collected. The three tenants with the largest farms, Samuel Mander of Irelands Farm, Robert Mander of Bushwood Hall Farm and Benjamin Edkins of Park Farm, were unable to pay any rent at all and owed between them £715 12s. 4½d., the total Lapworth and Bushwood arrears this year being £751 0s. 8½d. By 1746 Sir Lister was controlling the estate but matters were no better, indeed at Lapworth they were worse than ever, the arrears totalling £1,160 4s. 11d.

Sir Lister kept a very keen eye on the management of the estate and was meticulous in overseeing the accounts. By 1753 he had managed to pull the estate round and the arrears of rent at Lapworth had been reduced to £278 without any tenants being evicted. The Mander family had managed to pay off all their outstanding debts and Robert, the head of the family, was the tenant of three farms — Irelands, Bushwood Hall, and Mill Farm. Generally a certain amount of consolidation seems to have taken place and there were now nine units held by seven tenants.

Sir Lister died in 1770 his heir being his brother Charles. The Lapworth accounts for 1771-2 show that although most rents had been increased since 1753, one by 233% and another by 111%, none were in arrears. The timber on the estate was being worked as an asset, Henry Cooks, who had 'hedged Bushwood' and taken care of it and the Common in 1746 for wages of £1 1s. 0d., was now engaged to look after Lapworth woods at a salary of £2 2s 0d., per year. As a tenant on the estate he was well placed for such a job. Some of the timber had recently been felled, £780 being raised by its sale. Certainly Sir Lister appears to have left the estate on a sound commercial footing. During the 1770's new leases of 21 year's length were granted to four of the tenants and some rents were again raised, but only slightly. From 1775 a gamekeeper was employed, shooting for sport becoming at this time a popular pastime with gentlemen. The Steward, William Sadler, was paid a salary of £100 per annum for administering the Lapworth portion of the estate.

Throughout all the Holte/Bracebridge troubles of the early 19th century and the change of ownership the Lapworth demesne remained the same size, no parts being sold away. When the parish was surveyed for the purpose of the Tithe Apportionment in 1839 W. H. Cooper, the owner, held the same lands that Sir Lister had in 1770. However by 1892[19] circumstances had changed considerably; the demesne had been broken up and the farms sold. Mr. Weiss, the new lord of the manor, owned only a few acres of land, Mr. Watts the previous lord retained the woods, the pool, and a few cottages; Irelands Farm had been purchased by Mr. Couchman, Lapworth Park Farm and Lapworth Lodge Farm by William Udall, and the remainder by various other people.

Irelands Farm

THE MANOR HOUSE

There is now no sign of Sir John de Bishopsdon's stone house at Irelands Farm. It is possible that the building was abandoned or used as a barn and that the stone was robbed for other purposes — building chimneys or house groundsills — a new dwelling being built on the site of the present house. Certainly there was a house suitable for a yeoman family on the present site in the 16th century when it was occupied by Robert Ireland, his wife Elizabeth and their five children.[20] Probably single storey, Ireland's house had four rooms — a hall which was used as the living/dining room, a parlour and a chamber, both used for sleeping, and a kitchen where the cooking fire was situated. Evidence of stone foundations and timber framing is to be found in the kitchen and service quarters of the present building and these may date from Ireland's time.

Since the 16th century the house has been much altered, the last major change being made about 1820 when a three storey section was added to the front of the house. This may have replaced an earlier part which was demolished, for its seems unlikely that the Mander family, who occupied the house for 200 years and were people of consequence in the parish, would have been prepared to live only in the old part of the present house.

Of red brick and with a very plain facade the 1820 section of the house consists of two reception rooms, each approximately 15ft. by 17ft., an entrance hall and staircase plus four bedrooms on two floors. A stone tablet over the central front door bears the date 1820 and the letters PCG. These are the initial letters of the surnames of the three men who had recently acquired the manor and were the joint lords — Sir William Paxton, Sir Charles Cockerill and Charles Greenwood. Sir Charles' brother, Samuel Pepys Cockerill was an architect and he may have been involved with the design. When the new front was added the old part of the house containing the kitchen, dairy and other service rooms was encased in brick giving the whole of the exterior a uniform appearance but hiding any useful dating evidence.

The present farm buildings offer no evidence as to the fate of the stone house either, for these are 'new', a completely fresh start having been made, probably in the 19th century, all the old buildings having been swept away. They were replaced by an extensive range of barns, stables, cowhouses etc., arranged around three sides of a square yard and set well away from the house.

THE MANOR OF KINGSWOOD

The manor of Kingswood was partly in Lapworth parish and partly in that of Rowington. In total it consisted of 433 acres; 289 acres being in Lapworth and 144 acres in Rowington, Kingswood Brook making the division between the two parishes. Anciently Kingswood was a detached portion of the royal manor of Wellesbourne,[21] south of the Avon. It is probably from this royal connection, as the 'King's Wood' that the place derives its name. By the early 16th century Kingswood manor was in the ownership of Nicholas Brome of Baddesley Clinton. Through the marriage of his daughter, Constance, it passed with the Baddesley Clinton estate to the Ferrers family who retained both lordships. From this time much of Kingswood's history marched with that of Baddesley Clinton, but it remained manorially independent.

The manor played a much more important role in the life of ordinary farming people at Kingswood than it did at Lapworth. An 18th century list of rules and guide lines for conducting Kingwood manor[22] and its courts shows that it was a very important and serious business. Instructions on how to call a court, the correct oaths to be taken by the Foreman and the jurymen and the various types of defaulters to be expected are described in great detail. The rules of the manor were very strict and any tenant convicted in the King's Court of a felony lost his land and all his possessions in Kingswood. Not keeping buildings in repair, subletting land without the lord's permission also resulted in the forfeiture of land and goods. Even a tenant's birth could tell against him — a person born a bastard who acquired land in Kingswood had it confiscated at his death if he did not leave lawful issue.

The Customs of the manor were also very detailed:[23] these were further rules, basically medieval but adapted over the centuries, setting out the terms upon which the lord of the manor permitted his tenants to hold land. Most of the Kingswood Customal dealt with the rules for customary tenants, that is those who held their land by copy of Court Roll and were tenants of inheritance. Unlike free tenants they could not sell their property to anyone they chose, instead it passed by inheritance to their eldest son, or failing sons, their eldest daughter, brothers, sisters, etc. A simplified version of the basic rules is set out below:-

1) All tenants hold land by rent, attendance at the lord's court, and pay heriots and fines when due.
2) Those not attending the court will be fined.
3) A heriot (that is the tenant's best beast or goods) is payable at a tenant's death or when a farm is given up. If the tenant has no beast or goods his next heir or tenant to pay.
4) Every new tenant entering a farm to pay a fine.
5) Only the first wife allowed to carry on the property after her husband's death. Second wives obliged to leave.
6) Land may be leased to sub-tenants for two years without licence.
7) Land leased to sub-tenants for more than two years requires a licence.
8) Land passes only by inheritance, to eldest son, eldest daughter etc.

Although many people must have considered such rules out of date by the 19th century they were still being used, having been adapted to the world of legal charges and mortgages. When Thomas Buffery died in 1833 his brother, David, was admitted to his property in the customary way and in the same words as would have been used two or three hundred years previously.[24]

> 'At this court the homage present the death of Thomas Buffery, late of Rowington, farmer and that he died seized of a copyhold estate within this manor and they furthermore present that David Buffery is the only brother and heir at law of the late Thomas Buffery and ought to be admitted tenant. Now at this court came the said David Buffery and desired to be admitted tenant to all that his copyhold or customary messuage, barns, stables, wharfs, buildings, yards, fold yards, backsides, and several pieces of meadow and pasture land containing six acres or thereabouts in the occupation of John Garston, and also all those several small tenements with gardens and appurtenances belonging and now in the occupation of George Sanders, Samuel Williams, George Sherwood, Joseph Smith, William Hardin, John Hainse and Thomas Hunt. To hold the same to David Buffery his heirs and assigns forever and to be paid a fine for his admission. Being admitted as heir at law of his brother, Thomas Buffery, at whose death there fell to the lord a heriot for which composition was made at £5 and did fealty.'

	£	s	d	
Presenting Death		13.	4.	
Drawing admittance	1.	5.	0.	[these were the charges
Ingrossing		10.	0.	and legal fees]
Parchment and Duty	1.	5.	0.	
Fealty		10.	0.	
	4.	3.	4.	

In this way David Buffery acquired ownership of the Navigation Inn, the adjoining wharf, two small meadows and seven cottages, being the row of five 'Kingswood Cottages' plus two, now demolished, which were adjacent.

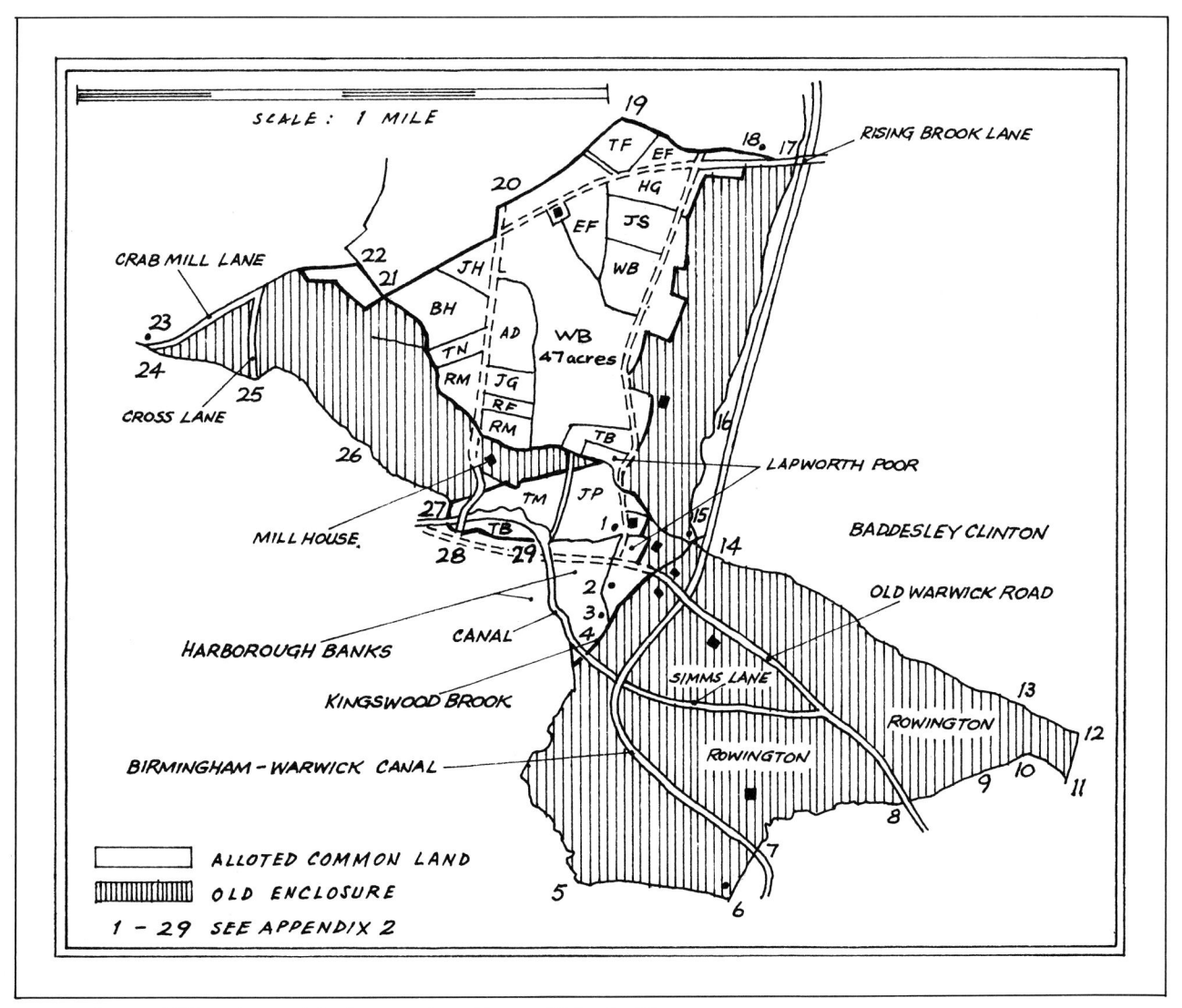

Kingswood Manor 1807, enclosure of the Common. (See table page 26 for details).

KINGSWOOD COMMON

At the centre of Kingswood manor was a large tract of open common land some 162 acres in extent. The Customal said that this land was especially for the use of the tenants of the manor who could graze their animals on it 'sans number', the lord of the manor and outsiders being excluded. In practice, in order not to over burden the Common and thus diminish it, the tenants agreed amongst themselves to stint or limit the number of animals they each grazed — in proportion to their holding of land. This permitted a tenant with only a small amount of land to keep animals of some kind — a cow, or a few sheep, or perhaps some geese, thus augmenting their income considerably. The tenants were also permitted to cut and take thorns, ferns, furze and gorse, to dig turf or take earth from the Common as they wished. The soil and trees of the Common were also considered to belong to the tenants for their own use by agreement; enclosing pieces of the Common away from the use of all, however, was greatly condemned and not allowed.

In 1807 several of the manor tenants decided that it would be better for them if the Common was enclosed and divided into fields, each tenant receiving an allotment of land in proportion to his existing holding. There was some discussion and disagreement at first but finally in March 1808 Decimus Slatter began the job of surveying and valuing the land, and Robert Smith drew a detailed map of the manor, showing the houses, the fields and the Common.[25] Slatter as the Commissioner, allocated the land as he thought fairest and the Act of Parliament for the Enclosure of Kingswood Common was finally passed in September 1808.

There were 19 manor tenants and each received a share of the Common, approximately half the size of their existing holding. William Bellamy was given the biggest allotment as the largest tenant of the manor. He already had 108½ acres of old enclosure and he received 47 acres of new enclosure. This was enough to make a new farm, and in this way, Common Farm (now the site of Kingswood Grange) was created out of the Common. The smallest allotment was of 13 perches to William Wheeler who had 1 rood 17 perches of old enclosure. The extra 13 perches could have been of little use to him except as garden land and it was certainly not enough to support any animal. Fortunately Wheeler did not depend on this land for his living as he had a farm in Rowington, but the loss of common rights — to graze, to cut furze etc., take soil, sand and gravel for repairs, to take wood, herbs, wild flowers etc., could reduce a day labourer, living in a cottage and using the Common to the full extent allowed, to penury. At Kingswood very few, if any, of the smaller tenants with under 10 acres of old enclosure were wholly reliant upon their Kingswood holdings for their livelihood. Some like Wheeler and Thomas Buffery also had farms in Rowington. Samuel Parsons was a carpenter, John Grafton a farmer and tanner in Lapworth, and Charles Horton, Richard Field, Thomas Newberry, Thomas Fetherstone and Hester Green all lived and had land elsewhere. Such absentee tenants obviously sub-let their holdings, but records do not always reveal to whom. Both before and after 1808 Richard Field's and Thomas Fetherstone's holdings were let to farmers in Lapworth, the others were perhaps held by wage labour cottagers.

Those wholly reliant on farming in Kingswood were William Bellamy, John Smith, Ann Dolphin, Benjamin Hildick, Thomas Moore, Richard Martin and Joseph Parsons; some of these also had land in Lapworth as well.

Name	Old Enclosure A. R. P.	New Allotment A. R. P.	Total Acreage after Enclosure A. R. P.
Edward Ferrers Lord of the Manor of Baddesley Clinton	In right of being Lord of the manor	10. 0. 38	10. 0. 38
Thomas Buffery of Rowington	7. 1. 32	5. 0. 39	12. 2. 31
Lapworth Feoffees	1. 0. 32	2. 0. 36	3. 1. 28
Joseph Parsons of Lapworth	13. 3. 22	10. 1. 24	24. 1. 06
John Grafton of Lapworth	7. 3. 34	4. 2. 25	12. 2. 19
Charles Horton of Lapworth	0. 0. 35	0. 0. 16	0. 1. 11
William Wheeler of Rowington	0. 1. 17	0. 0. 13	0. 1. 30
Thomas Moore of Solihull	11. 0. 34	5. 3. 11	17. 0. 05
Richard Martin of Campden	10. 3. 25	6. 1. 19	17. 1. 04
Richard Field of Tanworth	2. 0. 04	1. 1. 00	3. 1. 04
Thomas Newberry of Eastcote	5. 0. 20	1. 3. 21	7. 0. 01
Ann Dolphin of Kenilworth	20. 2. 07	8. 2. 05	29. 0. 12
Benjamin Hildick of Birmingham	24. 2. 27	11. 3. 21	36. 2. 08
Joseph Harding of Solihull	15. 0. 25	7. 3. 11	23. 3. 36
Thomas Fetherstone of Packwood House	6. 0. 10	2. 3. 35	9. 0. 05
Hester Green of Aston	7. 2. 05	3. 3. 38	11. 2. 03
John Smith of Lapworth	17. 1. 32	8. 1. 00	25. 2. 32
William Bradbury of Lapworth	19. 2. 18	10. 3. 06	30. 1. 24
Samuel Parsons of Lapworth	0. 0. 04	0. 2. 03	0. 2. 07
William Bellamy of Rowington	108. 2. 27	47. 0. 13	155. 3. 00

THE ROADS

The enclosure of the Common meant that proper roads had to be made in place of the old footpaths and trackways. At Kingswood these were not so much new roads as the confirmation, by straightening, aligning and the planting of hedges, of existing well used tracks. Like most enclosure roads they are very straight and easily recognisable as such. The Enclosure Act stipulated that the Old Warwick Road between Mill Lane and Kingswood Brook was to be set out properly at a width of 60ft. between hedges. Mill Lane, from the canal bridge to Rising Lane, was to be set out at 40ft. wide as a public carriage road, as was Rising Lane (then called Rising Brook Lane) from Mill Lane to what is now Station Lane. The latter was to be a public bridle road and only 28ft. wide. Many private carriage roads were also set out giving people access to houses and old enclosures otherwise cut off by the making of new fields. A final note stated that trees, which might be planted in the new hedges beside the roads, were to be at least 50yds. apart.

Punch Bowl Inn and Cherry Trees

THE HOUSES

After the enclosing of the Common and the making of the new roads several new houses were built in Kingswood. Common Farm was created out of William Bellamy's allotment and a house built to serve it. Later, after the making of the railway line had taken a slice of the land, the farmland was made into a mini-park and the house, possibly rebuilt, was renamed Kingswood Grange and occupied by Mr. William Gerrard, a manufacturer, and his household. By 1881 the land had been divided and a second large house, The Terrets, built adjacent to Kingswood Grange.

Almost opposite Kingswood Grange Thomas Newberry's six acres became a smallholding, a charming red brick house, now called Dingley Dell being built to it. A house of similar style was built at Kingswood Cross, the Rising Lane/Mill Lane/Chessetts Wood cross roads. By 1841 this small house had become a beer-house known as *Cherry Trees*. Later the licence was transferred to the house on the opposite side of Rising Lane which took the name of the *Punch Bowl Inn*. The age of the *Punch Bowl* building is uncertain, it is not shown on the 1808 map and so may be presumed not to have existed at that time. Yet the building contains 17th century timbers and a wide fireplace; if these are original it must be pre-1808 in construction and was probably an encroachment on the Common, erected illegally at a much earlier date. Situated at the very edge of the parish and at the junction of Kingswood and Chessetts Wood Commons, it is possible that the house was not actually in Kingswood but came to be so after the roads were made and the commons enclosed.

Other houses built on previously common land after 1808 were Grove Cottage, a cottage at the end of Cross Lane, and the *Bird in Hand* building which was erected by 1841 but was not used as a beer-house until 1871.

As at Lapworth a perambulation of Kingswood manor bounds took place from time to time. That made in 1833[26] is given on page 113.

THE MANOR OF BROME

The manor of Brome appears to have come into being during the medieval period. In 1296 Robert de Brome held land, said to be about a carucate, in Lapworth parish of the Earl of Lancaster by a knight's service.[27] This estate became Brome manor.

The Brome family was still involved with the manor in 1501 when Nicholas Brome of Baddesley Clinton sold it to the Catesby family. They retained it for about a century. In 1585 Elizabeth Catesby, the widow of Edmund Catesby of Brome, was living in the manor at Sorrells House on Harbery Heath.[28] Brome Hall, the manor house, was occupied by Nicholas Sly, his family having lived there for most of the 16th century although during this time their social standing seems to have deteriorated. Roger Sly who died in 1527 was undoubtedly a wealthy gentleman[29] whilst Nicholas Sly was described in 1585 as a 'turner'.

The manor then appears to have passed through various hands. In 1657 it was owned by Sir Richard and Francis Lucy. Soon after this the Camden family became the occupants of Brome Hall. They were living there in 1662 and remained until 1729 when Elizabeth, the widow of the last Camden died. For many years the family were also the lords of the manor of Brome but the date of their acquisition is unknown.

By 1730 Mr Francis Chernock of Wedgenock Park was the lord of the manor, and was quickly followed by Timothy Stoughton in 1743, and Robert Basket in 1750. To the latter a legend is attached.[30] Basket is said to have been a foundling child, discovered in a basket on the doorstep of High Chimneys Farm, hence his name. He was brought up at the farm and had a very happy childhood. His wish in life was to succeed and buy the manor and the house which had been so kind to him; this he did in 1750. Benjamin Parnell acquired the manor in 1785 and it remained in his family well into the second half of the 19th century, although the name changed from Parnell to Ross and later to Divett.

There are no references to manorial courts being held at Brome or of customs and rules. The exact extent of the manor is not easy to determine but it seems to have consisted of Brome Hall sometimes called Bromeham Hall and now Broom Hall, High Chimneys Farm also known as Bromeham Priory[31] and possibly as Sorrells House, Harbery Heath including Harborough Banks, Tan House Farm, Catesby Farm, Tudor Farm and the Chain House. Indeed it would seem all the land on the east side of Lapworth Street from its junction with Old Warwick Road to High Chimneys Farmhouse.

Brome Hall

THE DEMESNE

The demesne lands of Brome manor consisted of the manor house — Brome Hall — and the home farm. The house, timber framed and once much larger than today, was originally moated. A little distance from the house are the remnants of medieval fishponds used during the middle ages to breed and keep fish for the numerous meatless days in the calendar.

The last resident lord of the manor was John Camden who died in 1724.[32] At that time the home farm consisted of 60 acres of land which he worked as a gentleman farmer, the fields being under peas, oats, wheat, barley, rye grass, plus 13 acres of mowing grass. His stock consisted of 11 dairy cows and a bull, four horses and a few sheep and pigs. Cheese and some butter were made from the milk, cheese making utensils being recorded in the dairy and cheese to the value of several pounds in the cheese chamber. Wool was also stored in this room and as there were four spinning wheels in the house it would seem that the home grown wool was spun on the premises.

The house was quite large, comfortable and very much the house of a well-to-do farmer. There was a parlour, furnished with two tables, 11 chairs and a carpet, but the hub of the house was the kitchen. Here were the only clock in the house, plenty of tables and chairs and the cooking equipment of the period. The large open hearth had a jack, a spit and a grate, the fuel used for cooking probably being coal. There were several other service rooms — a dairy, buttery, pantry, backhouse and a cellar. Upstairs was the cheese room and four bedrooms. The 'best chamber', Camden's own, was furnished with a feather bed, a chest of drawers, six chairs, a looking-glass and a chest. There was a fireplace, window curtains, and in the chest 11 pairs of fine sheets plus a quantity of other linen. The servants probably slept in the 'chamber over the pantry'.

After the death of Mrs Camden in 1729 the manor passed through various hands, the manor house and lands being occupied by working tenant farmers. From this time no major structural alterations appear to have taken place and the house today is thought to be much the same as in Camden's time.

By the 1760's the house and land were owned by Samuel Cook and his wife together with several other people possibly relatives.[33] They sold it in 1768 to John Mander and his wife Elizabeth who lived in the house and farmed the land until 1792. Mander had mortgaged the property in 1783 for £650 and in 1792 he decided to sell. Robert Hildick, a box iron maker from Wolverhampton and Benjamin Hildick, a steel toy maker from Birmingham, paid £2,000 for the house and 14 closes of land. The whole was still subject to the will of the lord of the manor and each year the Hildicks paid Benjamin Parnell 20s 0d., Chief Rent.

The Hildicks had bought the land as an investment for the family. They did not take up a residence but let the house and land to Francis Fetherstone who remained until about 1808. The next tenant was John Grafton who also owned and farmed the neighbouring Tan House Farm where he also had the tannery. Grafton gave up the tenancy about 1814, a member of the Hildick family — Moses — taking over the house and farm.[34]

Benjamin Hildick was by this time the sole owner of the property and Moses Hildick was his nephew. In February 1824 Moses, then aged 44, married Martha Hildick, presumably a relative and possibly Benjamin's daughter. They had two sons, Benjamin and Joseph Robert, who were born in 1830 and 1833. Unfortunately in November 1834, Moses was killed in an accident involving a stage coach[35] and about the same time Benjamin Hildick senior, also died.

For some years the family had also owned Gospel Oak Farm and a couple of small farms, all in Kingswood, the whole Hildick estate being administered by trustees. The Kingswood farms were let and as Martha was clearly competent to run Brome Hall Farm she took up the reins.

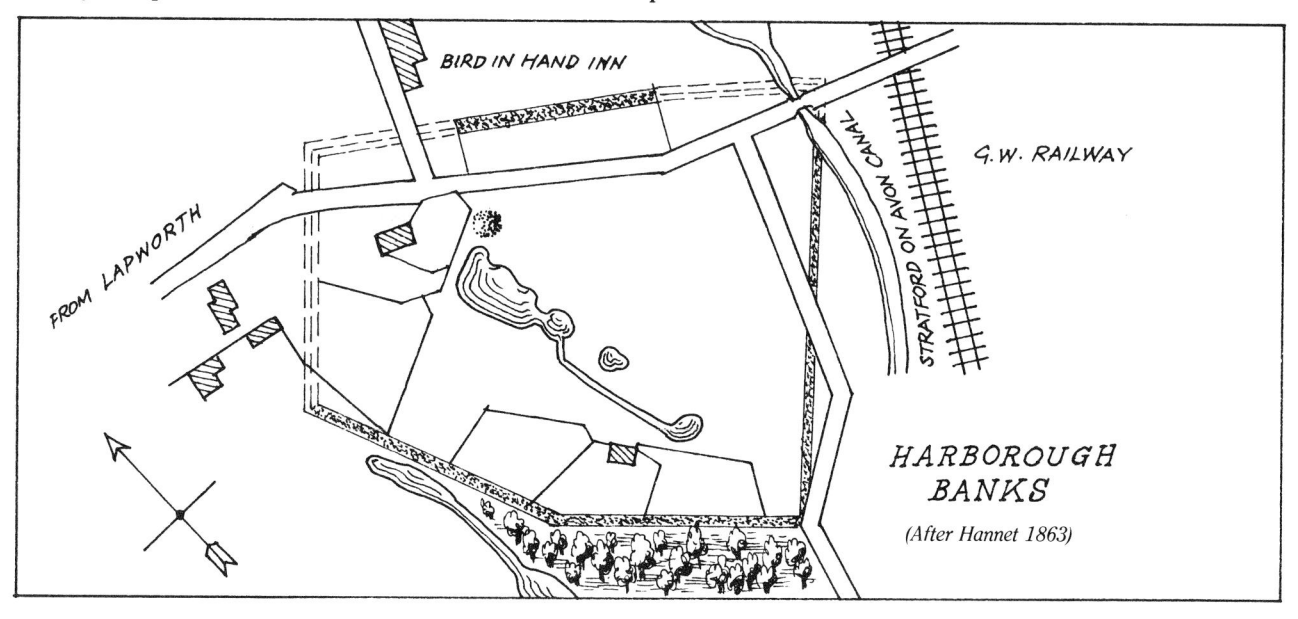

HARBOROUGH BANKS

(After Hannet 1863)

During the 1840's Martha decided to leave Brome Hall and move to Gospel Oak Farm.[36] She farmed the land of both farms, some 120 acres, with the help of farm labourers and her boys, Benjamin being in his teens. At some point the old timbered house was pulled down and the present Gospel Oak house built: probably this was Martha's purpose in moving — a new house on a healthy hill top site. The family remained together at Gospel Oak until after 1861; by 1871 Joseph was living alone there, Martha and Benjamin having either died or moved elsewhere. By 1880 Joseph was also dead.

When Martha Hildick left Brome Hall in the 1840's John Needle, a farm worker, and his family moved into the house. He probably worked for the Hildicks for he was still there in 1871. By 1881 the Hildick family had sold Brome Hall and the farm to J. E. Watts of Edgbaston and he let it to a tenant farmer William Taylor.[37]

Over the years the acreage of the farm remained much the same, a few acres being added at the enclosure of Harborough Banks in 1863.[38] In deeds it was continually given as 'approximately 65 acres', although by accurate measurements it was certainly more. In 1839[39] it was 73 acres, 3 roods, 20 perches. Benjamin Hildick purchased three fields equalling 15 acres, 3 roods, 8 perches in the 1850's and these were probably included in the sale to Watts, the acreage in 1880 being given as 89 acres, 1 rood, 10 perches.

HARBERY HEATH

This is an area of open common ground lying south of, and adjacent to Kingswood Common. Its original extent is unknown but it was certainly much larger than the 21 acres remaining in 1863, when it was enclosed by Act of Parliament. Over the centuries the Heath had been gradually eaten away as people made small encroachments or enclosed areas.

Known at various times as *Erdbyr* (1220), *Erbury* (1343), *Harbery* (1586), and *Harborough*,[40] the Heath acquired its name from the great earthwork which once dominated this section of the landscape, the Old English *eord-burgh* meaning 'an earthwork' 'a fortification built of earth'. At what date the earthwork, known as Harborough Banks, was erected and by whom is not yet determined for it has never been excavated. Late 19th century archeologists thought it was Roman, later it was thought to be Iron Age. Current opinion is that probably it is Iron Age, later altered and re-used by the Romans; only excavation will reveal the truth. Unfortunately only a small section of the once massive earthwork now remains but it probably originally consisted of a fosse and rampart of irregular oblong shape, enclosing about 25 acres.

During the early 18th century the Banks started to be eroded by gravel digging. Thomas Featherstone of Packwood was digging in this way in 1730[41] when he found a metal spout-shaped object which was melted down and thought to be of 'Prince's metal', a form of brass. The Banks continued to be quarried and were further destroyed by the making of the Stratford canal, road making, and some building. A plan of about 1860 shows the shape of the ramparts, at that date a considerable portion of them still existed although probably much damaged and reduced in height. Judging from the present remaining sections the Banks must have been some 20ft. high. By the middle of the 19th century all that remained of Harbery Heath was Harborough Banks and the immediate area; this was enclosed in 1863.

THE ENCLOSURE

The land was divided up, proportionately, between the six holders of land in the manor of Brome. A seventh portion was allotted to the Churchwardens and the Overseers of Poor of the parish for the use of the people for recreational purposes. There were 21 acres 2 roods 21 perches of land to enclose, most of it being within the earthwork.

The area of land allotted to each landowner was quite small and the process of acquiring an Enclosure Act quite expensive. Usually the cost was shared by all the landowners and for the smaller ones this could bring financial ruin. More sensibly the cost of the Harborough Bank Enclosure was met by selling off approximately a third of the land available. Extending to 7 acres 1 rood 35 perches, this was split up into 11 parcels, the smallest being approximately a quarter of an acre and the largest 1¼ acres. All the parcels lay alongside the Old Warwick Road and were a good buy as potential building plots. They were sold for about £80 per acre and raised £585 to defray the expenses. In later years Devon House, Harborough House, The Mount, and 'Harborough Banks' were built on these plots.

The remaining 14 acres 0 roods 26 perches were split into 16 parcels and allotted to seven recipients. One of the largest parcels was 1 acre given to the people of the parish, via the Churchwardens and Overseers of the Poor, presumably in lieu of their loss of the area as an open space. The allotment was beside the Old Warwick Road and is the site now occupied by The Village Hall, the car park and the children's play area. Thus it is still being used, as intended, for the benefit of the people.

The other six recipients were Jane Taylor who owned a house on the site of the present Fairview, Richard Smith who owned a cottage lying within the earthwork, Lapworth Charities and the Stratford Canal Company, respectively, for their land and for the part of the canal within Brome manor. Edward Divett received three parcels of land, one as lord of the manor, and one each for the Tan House and High Chimneys which he owned.

Benjamin Hildick, the largest landowner in the manor, was allotted eight parcels for his ownership of Brome Hall Farm, Tudor Farm, Catesby Farm, the Chain House, fields called Long Lands and three other holdings without names which together totalled 6 acres 3 roods 27 perches.

BROME MANOR LAND OWNERS AND THEIR ALLOTMENTS AT THE ENCLOSURE OF HARBOROUGH BANKS

Name	Allot No.	Acreage A. R. P.	Property in Right Of	
Edward Divett	8	0. 3. 2	Lord of Manor being 1/15 of land to be enclosed	
do do	19	2. 3. 22	High Chimneys	5. 1. 13
do do	22	1. 2. 29	Tan House	
Benj Hildick	12	0. 3. 12	Catesby Farm	
	17	0. 1. 2	Long Lands	
	18	0. 1. 13		
	21	0. 0. 13	All part of Brome Hall Estate	6. 3. 27
	27	2. 1. 8		
	24	0. 2. 35	land once James Bradbury's	
	25	0. 3. 13	Tudor Farm	
	26	0. 2. 11	Chain House	
CW and O/P	15	1. 0. 0	Recreation of the people	
Lapworth Charity	16	0. 1. 13	Charity Land	
Richard Smith	23	0. 1. 21	His Cottage	
S/C.C	11	0. 0. 18	Canal	
Jane Taylor	20	0. 0. 14	Fairview site	
		14. 0. 26		

Land Sold To				
Geo Sheldon	6	0. 1. 12	£ 22	
do do	7	0. 2. 15	56	
Benj Hildick	10	1. 0. 33	100	
do do	13	0. 3. 35	70	Benj Hildick exchanged
do do	14	1. 1. 15	110	his allotment 10
Wm Parsons	5	0. 2. 9	33	with Lapworth Charity
Jos Osborne	9	1. 1. 2	57	allotment 16
Thos Smith	1	0. 1. 17	29	
do do	2	0. 1. 11	35	
do do	3	0. 1. 11	35	
do do	4	0. 1. 25	38	
		7. 1. 35	£585	

Total Acreage 21. 2. 21

FOOTPATHS

The Enclosure Act was an opportunity to officially regulate the position of certain footpaths in the manor and in the parish. These appear to have been surplus to requirements and probably rarely used. Two zig-zagged across the fields of Tudor Farm and two others across Catesby Farm and Brome Hall Farm for no apparent reason. Similarly several short footpaths wandered across Lapworth Farm in Lapworth manor, across Gospel Oak Farm in Kingswood manor and across various fields once part of Kingswood Common; at least one of these had led from Mill Lane to Station Lane but the cutting of the railway had blocked it. All these were closed but new footpaths, giving access to Harborough Banks and the newly allotted fields and plots, were made. In addition a footpath from Mill Lane to the station, across the fields and the railway line, was agreed. This path, a short cut to the station, is still used daily.

3

THE ART OF HUSBANDRY

THE MID 18th CENTURY

Elsewhere in this volume reference has already been made to the mixed type of farming which the majority of Lapworth farmers undertook in the middle period of the 18th century.[1] Such an economy, growing a small acreage of the most common crops, wheat, barley, oats, peas, and hay, and keeping horses, cows, sheep, pigs, poultry and bees — a proportion of everything — appears to have suited local land conditions, the size of the holdings and the family based farming unit. The detailed information about the farms, and the crops and animals they supported, comes from a number of inventories, made for the purpose of probate, and dated between 1722 and 1760.[2] These records, made shortly after the occupant's death, itemize the rooms in the farmhouse and their contents, the farm implements, crops and livestock and give an illuminating insight into the houses and lives of the local people at this period.

Compared with modern farms those of 18th century Lapworth were, with a few exceptions, small — 65 acres or less. Correspondingly their herds and flocks were also small, 18 cows and 30 sheep with their lambs being the maximum recorded.[3] Usually the farms were worked by a farmer and his family with the help of wage labourers if necessary. Farming at this time was, however, very labour intensive for there was no machinery to lighten the work. About one acre of land could be worked by one man a day. Ploughing and harrowing were assisted by horse power, but sowing, reaping, mowing and threshing were all done by hand and were hard back breaking work. Because everything took such a long time to complete the weather was crucial, not only at haymaking and harvest time but throughout the calendar, and could make the difference between profit and hard times.

The soil at Lapworth is in many places heavy clay, elsewhere, on the Boulder clay and the limited patches of sand and gravel it is somewhat lighter, but everywhere it required all the farmer's skill. Knowledge of his land, of local weather conditions and of his stock and seed were essential so that he might gauge how to marry them together for the best results. As yet there was little except his own resourcefulness to help him.

By the mid 18th century there were no open fields at Lapworth, the area of the parish which had once been communally worked having been divided up into enclosed fields. Thus each farmer was his own master; he did not have to grow (as the common field farmer did) what was the choice of the majority, but could follow his own inclination and experiment with new crops and new ideas if he wished.

Some farmers were very conservative and suspicious of anything 'new fangled'. Others were interested in improvements but were cautious, for few could afford to fail. However in an age with no artificial fertilizers to sustain the soil and little to supplement the animals diet of grass and hay some successful new ideas were slowly adopted.

Convertible husbandry also known as ley-farming and up-and-down farming had been adopted by a number of farmers in the parish of Rowington[4] — Lapworth's neighbour — by the early years of the 17th century, and was gradually taken up generally in parts of Worcestershire, West Warwickshire and the Arden area, including Lapworth. It consisted of a cycle of grain crops followed by a grass-ley of variable length, to rest the soil and support the stock. The system was highly flexible, the arable succession could last from two to nine years (but was usually three or four) and the ley from six to twenty years (but was usually seven to twelve years).[5]

Up-and-down farming was a satisfactory way of producing mixed crops — wheat for bread, barley for malt and beer, oats for the horses, peas and the newly introduced vetches for winter feed — in varying quantities, for subsistence or for sale, on a rotation to suit the farmer and the land. It greatly enhanced the structure and productivity of the soil, the yield of arable crops being increased and the quality of grass nutrients improved.

The system fitted in well with butter and cheese production, hemp and flax growing, cloth making and malting.

The cycle of ley-farming meant that about a quarter of a farmer's land was under crops and pulses at one time. All the land was ploughed regularly but not so often that the heart was ploughed out of it. The first year of the cycle the pasture was ploughed up in the spring by tearing up the turf and turning it over. It was immediately planted with either oats, barley, peas or beans but usually oats. After harvest the field was left fallow throughout the winter and in the spring sown with barley or another spring planted crop. After this second harvest the land was ploughed, well manured and sown with winter wheat or rye. This third crop sheltered the new sward of grass and after harvest it was left to grass over naturally. On well manured ground in good heart the grass soon came again. It was essential that the ground was not ploughed too much and only fallowed in the winter. It had to be clean of weeds and pests and this needed to be dealt with when initially converting to ley-farming. The secret of the system was that the old turf was preserved during the tillage years, the grass roots being kept alive the whole time, the new ley rising from the ruins of the old.[6] In the Midlands, particularly, this preserving of the grass roots seems to have been religiously observed and to have given quite satisfactory results.

Tan House Farm

Adopting convertible husbandry required a considerable investment of both time and money. The fields needed to be fairly small thus large fields had to be divided. Each farm required a variety of implements — ploughs, harrows, carts, wagons, and the horses to pull them. A range of outbuildings, and a good yard in which to fold the stock and so collect the precious manure, was also necessary. Old pasture, previously unploughed, was often rank and full of wireworm and cranefly larvae which would eat the roots of the corn and destroy the crop. These had to be destroyed during the conversion period either by rolling and crushing them or by starving them by long bare fallows. An alternative was the planting of woad which they would not eat.

The benefit of all this investment and hard work was that convertible husbandry produced better crops, including more winter feed and more nutritious grass so that more animals could be kept on the same acreage. The output of manure was thus larger and this was used to fertilise the fields. More fertilisers were always needed, however, especially on the impervious clay soils. Marl, dug out of the ground, was used as were any waste products locally available — soot, ashes, saw and malt dust, tanner's waste, and lime which became increasingly available when it could be burnt with coal.

At Lapworth up-and-down farming was probably being practised by the majority of farmers by the 1720's. The inventories of all but the smallest farmers show that they had numerous outbuildings — barns, stables, cowhouses and cart hovels — and that most had at least two ploughs and pairs of harrows, as well as carts, tumbrels, sleds, rollers and wagons. Their wheat and barley almost certainly went to market, although a quantity of each was retained for home consumption. The wheat would keep the household in bread flour and the barley in malt for brewing into beer. The inventories show that numerous farmhouses had malt stored in the upper rooms, but it is doubtful if many farmers made their own, for malting required a fair amount of equipment and a special malthouse. Most people at this time probably sent their barley away for malting and it was then returned to them for brewing at home. Only one Lapworth inventory records a malthouse, that of Thomas Sly who died in 1722.[7] He was described as 'Innholder' and his pub was possibly *'The Boot'*. He was also a farmer and may have malted not only his own barley but that of his neighbours. The ale and beer sold in the inn was home brewed for there was also a brewhouse on the premises. Many farmers had brewhouses where large quantities of beer for their own domestic use was brewed, small beer, and ale made without hops being the common beverage of all age groups.

The rest of the farmers' crops — peas, oats, vetches, rye-grass, and hay — were used to feed the animals through the winter. In many areas clover and turnips, both newly introduced crops, were grown to supplement the winter feed, but neither are recorded at Lapworth at this time. There was, of course, some natural clover in the pasture grass but clover as a separate crop was not grown. Instead, at Lapworth, rye-grass was cultivated as a fodder crop and several inventories record it either in the field or stored in the barns. The turnips grown at this period were of a hard variety (not swedes which came in later) and they did not do very well where the ground was heavy and damp. In addition they did not fit very well into a farming cycle where the roots of the turf were so carefully preserved.

With regard to the livestock — all the farmers, even the smallest, had at least one horse, some doing a little horse breeding. Cattle were kept solely for dairying and there is no evidence of beef farming. The milk produced, a considerably smaller yield per cow than is given to-day, was made into some butter but mostly into cheese. In almost every farmhouse, a dairy, cheese making utensils and a cheese chamber for storage were to be found. Cheese was worth about £1 0s. 0d., per hundredweight and some cheese rooms contained 10 to 14 cwt. of cheese. Warwickshire cheese was sold widely, labourers as far away as London and the surrounding district reputedly living on it. The local grass, as grown at this time, had a sour taste which apparently made a good cheese. Clover, which was grown generally in England by 1718, was said to spoil the cheese and was thus not cultivated in dairy areas.

Almost every Lapworth farmhouse had a pigsty with at least one pig in it. The pigs were fed on skimmed milk and the whey from the cheese and butter making, barley mash, malt waste, ale dregs, kitchen waste, indeed almost any edible waste. Flitches of bacon and meat salted and smoked, were stored in many houses, every bit of a pig being useful.

The refinement of specific breeding was not yet established and the animals kept — cows, sheep and pigs — were of a type rather than a breed. The sheep at Lapworth were of a type generally referred to as pasture sheep.[8] They were white faced, big boned, polled animals with long thick legs and large loose frames. They had heavy fleeces weighing up to 15 pounds each. The wool was long and was combed (not carded) for the making of jersey which was used by hosiers and clothiers. The sheep were kept for both meat and wool, although the wool was far superior to the meat, a coarse grained mutton which took at least two years or more to be ready for the market.[9]

The damp clay lands were not very suitable for sheep, hence the small size of the flocks. Even so a few pasture ewes, with their good cut of wool, were able to provide a useful income and most farmers had spinning wheels and wool, jersey, woollen yarn and/or woollen cloth stored in their house. In later years when definite breeds were developed the ancient pasture sheep were referred to as the 'Warwicks' or 'Old Leicesters' to differentiate them for the 'New Leicester' breed which replaced them.

The cattle kept were probably a type of Longhorn which were common in the Midland Counties. They were large big boned animals useful for meat, milk and pulling power. Although some selection of the best milkers must have taken place, the excellence of the butter and cheese produced from their milk probably depended more on the quality of the grass which they ate than on the refinement and breeding of the cows. Much later, when the breeding of specific strains was developed, the importance of milk production was for a time somewhat lost sight of in the attempt to produce bigger and better beef cattle.

THE SMALLER FARMERS

Although the majority of Lapworth farmers adopted convertible husbandry there were a few who had only a small acreage which would not allow of such a system. Many of these men were also craftsmen who fitted their work into the keeping of a few animals and producing a small quantity of corn and hay.

William Overton [10] the tanner of Tan House Farm had 13 acres of land which provided the household with basic foods and drink — flour, meat, butter, cheese, milk, and ale. Joseph Smith [11] was a carpenter by trade but he also kept a mare, presumably for transport, and 33 sheep. Their fleeces provided him with additional income, some of the wool being carded by the family and then spun into yarn on the two spinning wheels in the house. William Baker, the brickmaker, had two horses, two cows, a pig and a few crops. The milk, too much for domestic needs, was made into cheese and a quantity of it sold to supplement his income. Robert Wilkes was a hatcheller or flax dresser, in his house he had flax, and hempen and flaxen yarn valued at £18 11s. 0d. He kept a horse, two cows and a pig.

THE LARGER FARMERS

At the other end of the farming scale were a few Lapworth men with larger than average acreages; amongst them were the Mander family of Irelands Farm (about 150 acres), the Edkins of Lapworth Park Farm (about 200 acres) and the Green family of Lapworth Lodge Farm (about 140 acres).[12] These three were tenant farmers their land being part of the Lapworth manor demesne, Park Farm and Lodge Farm having once been part of Lapworth Park. By the 1730's they were all having financial problems and in 1737 the Manders and the Edkins were well in arrears with their rents of £104 0s. 0d., and £63 15s. 0d., respectively per annum. The Green's rent of £42 0s. 0d., per annum was paid, but by 1746 all three owed money to Sir Lister Holte, their landlord.

The cause appears to have been a fall in the price of wheat due to over production brought about by a long series of good summers and excellent harvests. With their incomes drastically reduced but facing the same overheads, including a labour force to pay, (approximately one man was employed for every 20 acres worked) many larger farmers throughout the country were in dire straights. Sir Lister appears to have helped and advised his tenants, and by 1753 the situation was much improved, the Manders' and Edkins' rents had been reduced and the arrears cleared. There is nothing to show how this was achieved but it was perhaps by a change of emphasis in their farming pattern.

THE LATE 18th CENTURY

After mid-century the population nationally began to rise, slowly at first but with increasing momentum. The demand for wheat was revived and the market for cheese and meat began to grow. A number of farmers, Robert Bakewell of Dishley, Mr. Webster of Canley near Coventry, John Fowler of Rollright and others, experimented with stock breeding to improve specific qualities in sheep and cattle. Bakewell ultimately produced a new breed of sheep, the New Leicester, and Webster and Fowler made improvements in the Longhorns. It was a long time before definite breeds, such as we know today, were to be found on ordinary farms but with the benefits of up-and-down farming — an increase in the quality, variety and quantity of grass and food plus improved stock breeding — the size and weight of all cattle and sheep rose by something like 150% in the period 1700-1850.[13]

In the years to the 1790's there was no run on seasons when the harvests were consistently good (which reduced prices by a surplus) or consistently bad (which raised prices, but had other unwanted effects). The weather and the harvests fluctuated, prices rose gradually and on the whole were favourable to the farmer. The benefits of the improved farming techniques were now being felt, thus some farmers had a little money to spare and they used it to improve their standard of domestic living. The fine regular brickwork of a number of Lapworth houses, *The Boot Inn,* High Chimneys, Lapworth Hill Farm, Hazelwood, The Chain House and Malthouse Farm, Kingswood, probably dates from this period when some small houses were extended and a few older houses were refronted or possibly rebuilt. About the late 1780's a new house to Lapworth Lodge Farm, large and proclaiming prosperity, was built on a new site. The contemporary outbuildings, of equally fine brickwork, are set round three sides of a large fold yard, cow ties to one side, stables and a variety of storage buildings on the other with an enormous barn at the head. Elegant, high roofed and approximately 90 ft. long the barn has central double doors and a threshing floor.

RENTS

Landlords also wanted their share of the prosperity and during the 1770's rents[14] started to rise. The Mander family who in 1753 had paid the Holte estate a rent of £149 0s. 0d., per annum for their three farms — Irelands Farm, Bushwood Hall Farm and Bushwood Mill Farm — paid £200 0s. 0d., per annum in 1772 and £205 0s. 0d., in 1775. The rents of Lapworth Park Farm and Lapworth Lodge Farm were also raised from £55 0s. 0d., per annum in 1753 to £116 0s. 0d., per annum in 1772 for the former and from £42 0s 0d., per annum to £140 0s. 0d., per annum for the latter, although both may have had their acreage slightly increased. About this time the estate started granting leases for 21 years and fixing the rent for the duration of the term.

THE WOODLANDS

During the early 1770's a great deal of tree felling appears to have taken place on the old Park lands at Lapworth, considerable sums being earned by the sale of the timber. Plantations and coppices, established in corners unsuitable for crops, could provide a useful source of additional income. The trees were farmed as a crop, albeit one which took a long time to mature. In the meantime the underwood was cut at regular intervals and sold for faggots, brooms, hoops, rakes, stales and hurdles. Copse woods were cut approximately every 15 years and white poles used for ladders, rails and hoops, after 24 years growth.[15] About 1773 the trees on the land of High Chimneys Farm were valued.[16] There were 524 trees — oak, ash, elm and alder — round the house and in the 22 adjacent fields valued at £51 8s. 6d. The majority, 297, were oaks; surprisingly there were only 22 elms.

Large landowners with several tenant farmers usually kept copses and plantations in hand, for they were ideal sites for the breeding of game; shooting for sport being increasingly popular with the gentry. A gamekeeper, William Butwell, was employed on the Holte estate at Lapworth by 1775 and it may be that the new leases, agreed about this time, reserved the right to the game to Sir Charles Holte.

Lapworth Lodge Farm

THE 1790's

The population of Birmingham more than doubled in the 40 years after 1750 reaching 60,000 by 1790. Such an increase must have affected farms within a wide radius and Lapworth cheese, wheat, and barley probably found a ready market. Meat was also much in demand and cattle were driven on the hoof to market. In 1798 two Lapworth farmers, John Soden and John Cotterill, were described in the Land Tax Returns as 'graziers' — men who grazed and fattened cattle ready for the market — the rest of the parish taxpayers being described as 'farmers'. Soden had approximately 40 acres of land and Cotterill about 80 acres in two farms. All three, Lapworth Farm, Blockbury House (later Lapworth Grange), and Lapworth House Farm, were close to the Stratford Road, along which the cattle would be driven to market.

An indication that more corn was being grown at Lapworth than previously, probably with the Birmingham market in mind, is the building of a windmill at Tapster Farm some time in the late 1780's or early 1790's. A brick tower mill, it was worked by Samuel Canning who was both miller and farmer.

The weather during the 1790's was generally poor with few adequate harvests. Throughout the decade it rained a good deal, the damp causing foot rot in sheep and there was a shortage of fodder for cattle. Moderate seasons did occur but the bad weather came in runs, thus there were no reserves of supplies, flocks and herds were reduced in size and prices rose accordingly. The wheat yield in 1794 was very low, perhaps only half of what was possible in a really good year. The following winter was very harsh, and the spring and summer of 1795 cold, resulting in another poor harvest. Wheat and flour were in very short supply and everyone was asked not to waste it. Restrictions were imposed on using grain and flour for the production of starch and hair powder and people were encouraged to eat rice and potatoes. Wheat prices[17] at Birmingham market between October 1794 and May 1795 varied from 22s. 6d., to 30s. 0d., per bag (three bushels = one bag), the higher prices occurring in the spring as the remains of last year's harvest were used up. In October 1795 when it was realised that the harvest had again been poor, prices in the market started at 30s. 0d., per bag and rose steadily reaching 46s. 0d., per bag by the end of March. Corn prices fell considerably during 1797 and 1798, but rose again rapidly in 1799.

The situation was not helped by England being at war with France, the French Government having declared war early in 1793. Quantities of corn were still imported from abroad but war conditions, the poor weather and harvests, the demands of a rising and increasingly urban population plus the need to feed the army brought great shortages.

The effect of the food crisis, on prices and people is eloquently recorded by William Johns, a native of Lapworth. He kept a 'Memorandum Book'[18] from 1797 until 1804, which was used by his son, Thomas, from 1804 to 1843 for similar notes.

THE JOHNS' FAMILY BOOK

In 1797 William Johns started his 'Memorandum Book'. In it he jotted down notes on the weather, the cost of living, the sums of money lent to neighbours and details of his financial affairs. About himself Johns wrote 'I believe I was born in March in the year 1728. I was married the 15 day of July in the year 1756.' He was probably married twice, his first wife being Mary Culcope, a kinswoman of the schoolmaster. He had seven children and died in 1804.

Johns' property, a farm of about 50 acres, which he described as 'the estate near Lapworth Brook', was inherited from his uncle, John Green, 'that left me what I had', who died in 1742. Later, about 1781 Johns bought another farm in Lapworth Street of about six and a half acres, which he called 'Street Farm'. Johns appears to have worked Street Farm and part of his original farm himself, but the remainder was leased to John Cotterill, a kinsman by marriage and close neighbour at Lapworth Brook.

About seven acres of Johns' land was in strips, the last remnants of the Lapworth communal fields. As they adjoined Lapworth Brook these were not arable but meadow strips. The Charity Estate also owned five acres of similar strips which were interspersed with Johns; in the interest of efficiency he rented their strips (at £3 5s. 0d., per annum) and the meadow was worked as one field.

John Cotterill paid £40 per annum for the land he rented from Johns which included the whole of the strip meadow (known as 'Cleycrofte'). Cotterill paid the Charity rent and the Land Tax which Johns deducted when the rent was paid, thus Cotterill in fact paid only £33 12s. 0d., per annum. He was invariably behind with his rent '£84 due this Lady Day 1800 for rent without tax or town rent from Mr. Cotterill'. In May 1801 Cotterill paid £120 arrears leaving half a year behind, and in April 1803 he paid £80 leaving him still half a year in arrears. However all was paid in full by Lady Day 1805 when his lease expired.

In his book Johns records that in 1794 the house, only, of Street Farm was let to Isaac Mortiboys at £3 10s. 0d., per annum rent. After a year Mortiboys started to fall into arrears. He paid £7 in 1798, then nothing more till '30th day of March 1803, received of Mr. Isaac Mortoboys the sum of seventeen pounds and ten shillings being a full five years rent for the house they live in, due and ending the 25th day of June in the year 1802'.

Much of Johns' land was close to streams and was good meadow and grazing land. He appears to have concentrated on dairy farming and producing hay, some of which he sold. In September 1797 he sold a rick to 'John Jones of Islanton near Birmingham, coal dealer' for £28 10s. 0d. Two years later in April 1799 two ricks sold to Mr. Hildick of Birmingham realised £45. Prices then rose sharply and in May 1800 Mr. Soden a neighbour and grazier, paid £58 for a rick, the money to be paid at midsummer. The atrocious weather of the 1790's led not only to a shortage of bread and flour but also of fodder for animals. In August 1802 four ricks of new hay were sold for £122 'the money to be paid before they take the hay off the ground. They are allowed to let the hay stand on the ground till Lady Day 1803'. £42 was paid in December and the rest in April 1803. Comparing prices Johns comments that, in the past hay fetched £1 10s 0d., per ton, but in 1800 'it sold at seven pounds a ton'.

Johns also sold the lattermath, or late grass, each October for sums varying between £3 3s. 0d., and £10. The grass might be cut or grazed, but no cattle were to be put on the ground after 1st March. Much of Johns' milk production was made into cheese; six cwt., of cheese (70 cheeses) was sold in February for £2 14s. 6d., per cwt. In December 1800 a similar quantity fetched £3 9s. 0d., per cwt., the going price. Johns compared these prices with the past when cheese sold at 12s. 0d. per cwt; in the shops in 1800 cheese cost 10½d., a pound.

On Lady Day 1802 William Lea, who had taken the lattermath for several years, took a three year lease of fields called 'Brockshires', about 10 acres of the Lapworth Brook farm, for £25 per annum. The lease stated that he was 'not to plow any part of it nor cut down any timber, but to have the liberty to sell some of the hay, and I am to allow him 30 shillings the first year to buy lime with, to lay on the land'. Many landlords put such restrictions on land for they did not want their good grass land broken up by the plough.

William Johns seems never to have been pressed for money although his tenants were often late with the rent; many of his transactions had deferred payments, and he was willing to lend sums to neighbours and others. In December 1801 he lent Mr. Cotterill 10 guineas and another five guineas in August 1802. The following March Mr. Cotterill borrowed 9½lb. of bacon. In 1796 Mr. Field of the *Boot Inn* borrowed £20 'on a note of [h]and that is in the chest'. This loan was at interest but in 1801 Mr. Field was three years behind with it; in 1802 a fresh note had to be given 'because a note of hand will not stand good but for six years unpaid': only one pound of interest had been paid. Some loans were never repaid. 'master Butterell' who borrowed a guinea in 1798 was written off as a bad debt, as was John Jones, the coal dealer, who never paid for his hay.

When the canal was about to be built land was purchased from owners along the route. Johns had such land; of his dealings with the canal commissioners he wrote 'It was reckoned half an acre, but [they]made no more than a quarter of an acre and 6 perch on it. It was valued at 75 pounds an acre. The commissioners promised very faithfully I should be used well, but their promises are not to be depended upon, for they have had the pleck a year and a half and I have never received a farthing . . . nor for the damage they did and I am afraid I never shall. The commissioners had a man of their own choosing to value the land and according to their own valuation it comes to £21.11.3.' 'January 1802. Received of Mr Porter the sum of £13.8s for the pleck . . . their canal goes through. The land comes to £21.11.3, but they stopped £5 for the use of the Lord of the Manor in lieu of the 5s a year it paid him, and £3.3s for making the writings so that I received no more than £13.8.0.'. This same Mr. Porter was not above borrowing from Johns who lent him half a guinea in May 1803 and a further 12s 0d., a few days later.

William Johns enjoyed observation and comparison, he wrote 'My curiosity has led me to set down in my Pocket Book some remarkable things that have happened in my time and if it should happen to be seen in another age people may wonder, but let them wonder as long as they will, they are very near the truth'.

'In the year 1799 hit had bin a very severe winter an the spring was uncommonly cold. There fell a big snow on the third day of April very deep in some parts and the grass so backweir that Hay was sold for seven pounds a tunn, and in July following the heavy rains began and continued for a long time with great floods that swept a great deal of hay away and it was shocking to see in what a miserable condition the harvest lay in for a long time for the biggest part was not got in till October or November and then in such bad order that people were faint to dry their corn on malt kilns before it [w]ould grind'.

'It is astonishing to think on the onerous payments that fall on the midling class people for it has been computed that the Rents of the whole parish of Lapworth in . . . 1800 amounted [to] 2364:10: pounds a year and the taxes . . . paid by the farmers and the Land Owners . . . to 414:17 pounds a year . . . the parish rates . . . to £623.5.7 and the tythes . . . to £200 a year. A person that lives on his own Estate of 40 or 50 pounds a year . . . by means of these hevey payments his estate is redust to les than half the valey'.

'The account that's set down in this book was the common price of things in this neighbourhood'. 'It is surprising to think the time should vary so much in a man's age, for I remember grain so cheap that —

[Prices 1799 — 1800 — 1801]

wheat was sold at 2s.4d a strick (bushel) —	sold at	£1 5s a strick
	,, ,,	£4 a bag — so said
	Wheat flour	£1 8s a strick
barley ,, ,, ,, 1s.2d ,, ,, ...	sold at	14s.6d a strick
	Barley flour	17s a strick
peas ,, ,, 1s.3d ,, ,, ...	sold at	12s a strick
oats ,, ,, 10d ,, ,, ...	sold at	8s a strick
Malt ,, ,, 2s.4d ,, ,, ...	sold at	15s.6d a strick
Second butter sold at 2½d a pound	Butter sold at	1s.8d a pound
A good cow and calf five pounds	Middling cow and calf twenty pounds	
	Field beans	13s a strick
	Garden beans	6s 8d a peck
	Beef, mutton, veal	9d a pound
	Bacon	1s.4d a pound
	Potatoes	1s.4d a peck
	Fat goose	5s.6d
	Hops	4s a pound
	Apples	5s a peck

'April 1801   It may be supposed that the poor people have been in a very bad situation and suffered very badly these dear times for I don't know how anybody can be in a worser situation than them that want bread'.

'In the middle of May 1802 it was so uncommonly cold and there was hard frost and snow for several days together — very uncommon'.

William Johns

William Johns died on 2 May 1804 and was buried five days later. His second son, Thomas, who took over the farms and also the 'Memorandum Book', records that he bought to give as mourning gifts at his father's funeral, 6 crepe hat bands, 8 pair of mens and 5 pair of womens gloves and a suit of black, presumably for himself.

Thomas Johns was 22 years old when his father died. His elder brother Richard is reputed to have had only one arm and to have become a famous stage-coach driver. His younger brother William, with his wife, started a school at Kineton, which in 1806 was flourishing. Thomas continued to farm and when the leases arranged by his father expired he did not renew them but worked the land himself.

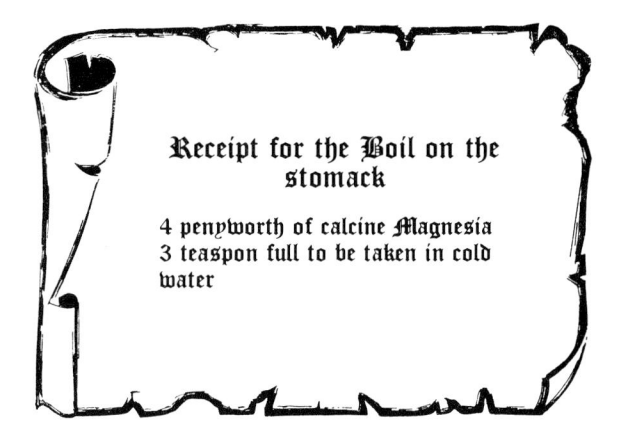

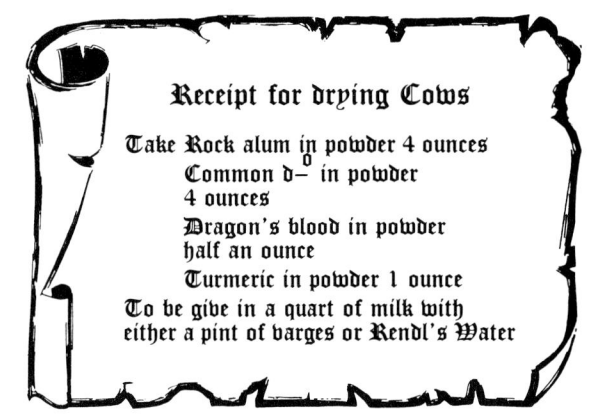

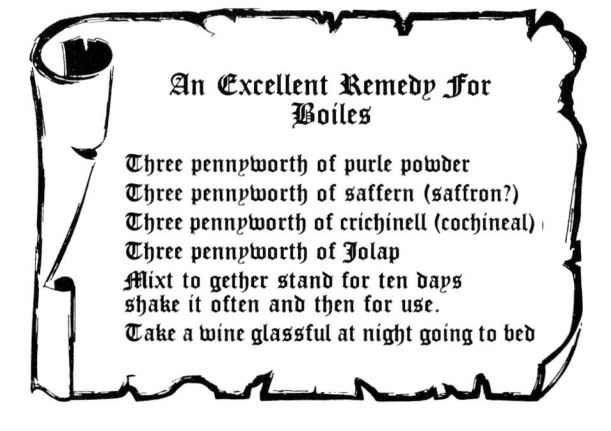

Receipt for the Boil on the stomack

4 penyworth of calcine Magnesia
3 teaspon full to be taken in cold water

Receipt for drying Cows

Take Rock alum in powder 4 ounces
Common d⁰— in powder 4 ounces
Dragon's blood in powder half an ounce
Turmeric in powder 1 ounce
To be give in a quart of milk with either a pint of barges or Rendl's Water

An Excellent Remedy For Boiles

Three pennyworth of purle powder
Three pennyworth of saffern (saffron?)
Three pennyworth of crichinell (cochineal)
Three pennyworth of Jolap
Mixt to gether stand for ten days shake it often and then for use.
Take a wine glassful at night going to bed

Extract of Recipes from William Johns' Book

4

ALONG THE KING'S HIGHWAY

During the medieval period two roads of some importance passed through Lapworth. The first was the Stratford Road, which travellers from Birmingham via Shirley, or via Solihull, used on their way to Stratford, Oxford and London. The second road was the Old Warwick Road which, as its name indicates was the old way to Warwick from Birmingham and also from Solihull.[1]

The medieval Stratford Road passed just within the western edge of Lapworth parish but on a different line to that which it follows today. The old route ran across Hockley Heath,[2] at that time almost certainly open heathland, then passed down Spring Lane. At its southern end Spring Lane joins Church Lane and the old route followed this lane down to Lapworth Brook and a ford. The stream crossing, known as 'Essenford', was then some 60 yards east of the present Stratford Road. Later a wooden bridge was built beside the ford, but this may have served for foot passage only. Across the stream the old road climbed the hill, through what is now a field, passing behind the site of 'Sunnybank' which did not then exist. A little distance along from the top of the hill the old and the present routes converged before passing out of Lapworth parish.

Early travellers upon the Old Warwick Road had a choice of ways. Some followed the road via Kingswood, Rowington and Hatton to Warwick described in 1646 as 'the great road between Warwick and Birmingham',[3] whilst others followed 'Warwick Wey'.[4] This route left the Old Warwick Road and went via Lapworth Street, Bushwood, Lowsonford, High Cross, Pinley Green and Hampton-on-the-Hill to Warwick.

Until the late 17th century and the introduction of the first Turnpike Trusts, the upkeep of all roads, whether lanes or part of the King's Highway, were the sole responsibility of the parishes through which they passed. Parishes like Lapworth, with two well used highways passing through them found the expense of keeping the roads, even barely passable, a great burden. In the Quarter Session Records of the late 17th century the inhabitants of Lapworth were continually before the courts for 'not repairng the highway from Hockley Heath to Liveretts (Liveridge) Hill',[5] the portion down Spring Lane and through the stream being the hardest to keep up. It must have been a great relief, therefore, when in 1726 an Act of Parliament was passed for the turnpiking of the road between Birmingham and Stratford.[6] Although the parish still had to make a financial contribution for the upkeep of this road, the responsibility for the repairs and the burden of finding the materials and the parishioners to undertake the work, was lifted. However, the many other lanes in the parish, including the Old Warwick Road, still had to be maintained by the parishioners, who by law were obliged to give their time and labour and to lend carts and teams for this purpose.

The Turnpike Trust surveyors re-aligned the Stratford Road along its present route and Spring Lane became a quiet country lane instead of a busy highway. The new road was wide and as straight as the gradient on the steeper parts would allow. A brick bridge was built over Lapworth Brook with a causeway at either end to lift the road above the marshy ground.

Yet, despite the turnpiking and the improvement of roads generally, the road surfaces still left a great deal to be desired and travelling remained slow, hazardous and expensive. The importance of the construction of the roads was not at first understood and the surveyors were mostly untrained. Making the road was particularly difficult where, as at Lapworth, the ground was clay. In such places it was usual first to lay a foundation of either timber or brush or faggots or heather or ling, and to cover this with layers of gravel or stone. Large quantities of such material, unprepared and unsorted, might be used, raising the road high above the surrounding land, the water draining away into deep ditches on either side; to encourage it to do so the surface was convex. Because no thought was given to how the road was laid, the materials to make a surface usually just being dumped on, when wet weather set in the stones began to sink under the weight of the vehicles, forming ruts which grew deeper and deeper. The answer to this problem was thought to be weight limits and wheel width restrictions upon the traffic, particularly wagons and carts which did the most damage. A succession of Acts and statutes were formulated but they were too complex and too difficult to enforce; the true answer was better made roads. Indeed it was by trial and error and experience that the surveyors, aided by a number of gentlemen trustees who studied the problem scientifically, slowly learned the art of road making. Generally however the improvements were overtaken by the great increase in traffic and it continued to be a struggle to keep the roads in repair.

The heavy traffic along the three routes out of Birmingham - the Stratford Road, the Warwick Road via Solihull and Knowle, both turnpiked in 1726, and the Coventry Road, turnpiked in 1724 - made them very difficult to maintain. In 1745 all were said to be 'ruinous' and the two former were described in 1781 as 'much used and neglected'.[7] Because the bad roads were having a deleterious effect on their carts and wagons, the carriers between London and Birmingham, in 1763, increased their charges. By 1765 it cost about 10s. 0d., per ton to carry goods 10 miles.[8]

In 1766-7 an Act of Parliament for the turnpiking of the road between Hatton and Hockley Heath,[9] that is the Old Warwick Road, was passed. The road formed part of the turnpike planned to run from Hatton to Bromsgrove via Kings Norton and Belbroughton. The Hatton to Hockley Heath section was completed but it is not clear what happened on the next part. The road seems to have been turnpiked for some distance west of Hockley Heath to a place called Gannow Green, near Rubery, but not as far as Bromsgrove.

In preparation for its new status the line of the road through Lapworth, Rowington and Hatton was tidied up and improvements made at such problem places as the ford over Kingswood Brook, the hill by Rowington church and the ford at Foxbrook. Bridges were undoubtedly much needed in place of the fords but they were not constructed until 1842. The route crossed several small areas of common and heath at Harbery Heath, Rowington Green and Shrewley Heath; at such places the road was probably a well marked track rather than a made road, for it is shown on contemporary maps[10] as open and unfenced. A toll house where the toll keeper lived and collected the monies was built on the Old Warwick Road south of Hockley Heath, just past the junction with Wharf Lane. A turnpike gate was placed across the road as a barrier where even local people would have had to pay tolls. The Toll House has been long demolished but its approximate position is marked by the gate of a newer house called 'Turnpike Close'. The Turnpike Act for this piece of road was renewed, as was usual after 21 years, in 1789 but subsequently appears to have lapsed.

As the 18th century progressed and the high period of the coaching era was reached the stage coaches improved greatly. They had better springing, were lighter in weight and therefore needed fewer horses to pull them. The days of winded worn out horses and rotten harness were past, instead, a special type of horse, strong and light, was bred to pull the coaches. These animals were cared for, changed frequently along the routes and not allowed to overwork. The job of the coachman increased in status, and the earlier loud-mouthed bullies who ill-treated the horses and yelled at the passengers were replaced by men who were skilled and careful drivers and who took responsible care of all their charges. Even so, conditions inside a coach carrying six passengers were cramped and uncomfortable and at times could be objectionable. On the outside it might be cold and wet or even too hot and it was often frightening for there was little to hold on to.

The Mail Coach

Not surprisingly some people preferred to travel by post-chaise which was lighter than a stage coach, and could be hired to carry one or two people and their luggage from one posting house to another along the road. Each was painted yellow and had two or four horses, one being ridden by a post-boy in a yellow jacket. The post-chaise was faster and more expensive than the stage, Dr. Johnson paying between £70 and £80 for the journey from London to Edinburgh via Newcastle in 1773.

The Post Office which had held the monopoly to carry letters since the reign of Henry VIII used neither the stage or post-chaise. Instead the post was carried in canvas bags by Postboys riding horses from town to town at, in theory, not less than six miles an hour. They were frequently delayed by the weather and, being unarmed, were no match for the highwaymen. Robbery was so common that the Post Office actually advised people to cut bank notes in half and await news of the safe arrival of one half before sending off the other. All this was changed however by the introduction of the Mail Coach service.

Throughout the 18th century the chief coaching route between London and Birmingham continued to be via Oxford and Stratford and it was by this route that the London — Shrewsbury Coach travelled from 1784,[11] carrying letters and parcels for the Post Office safely and in record time. An armed guard sat with the driver and only four passengers, travelling inside, were permitted. Stops were of the minimum time, only five minutes being allowed to change the horses, and a timetable was, for the first time, strictly adhered to. The fast and safe transportation of the post was all important; the passengers were secondary and those who were late or slow to get aboard were left behind. All the other vehicles on the road had to give way to the Mail Coach which paid no tolls and did not stop at the turnpike gates. When approaching, the guard blew loudly on his post horn and the gate was quickly opened by the gate keeper for the coach to pass through.

From 1808 the London — Holyhead Mail Coach travelled via Oxford, Stratford, Wootton Wawen, Birmingham, Wolverhampton and Shrewsbury[12] passing along the Stratford Road through Lapworth, the condition of the road being as usual 'pretty bad'. In 1810 Thomas Telford a road surveyor who, like his contemporary John Macadam, had learned his trade through practical experience, was asked to survey and later reconstruct the London — Holyhead Road. He began by looking at the northern section.

Telford believed in engineering roads. First he dealt with the terrain by lowering hills, filling in valley bottoms and removing awkward corners as required. He then laid a foundation of large stones and overlaid them with smaller material. Macadam had a different method, he was much concerned by the under drainage of his roads. He laid a 10in. depth of broken stones, each weighing six ounces straight on to the natural soil, if this was possible. Such a road was elastic, cheap to make — all the material from the existing road being re-used after screening and breaking up.

The roads made under the supervision of Telford and Macadam were good and long lasting, on them both speed and regularity were maintained. In 1811 the Royal Mail from London to Birmingham via Oxford and Stratford left London at 8.00 p.m., and reached Birmingham at 11.30 a.m., next morning, 116½ miles in 15½ hours, an average of seven and a half miles per hour.[13] On a Macadam road it was possible to do an average of 10 or 11 miles per hour; but the limiting factor, from this time, was the horse.

After Telford completed the northern section of the Holyhead Road he turned his attention to the southern part. But in 1817 the route was changed and instead of going via Stratford and Oxford the Holyhead — London coaches went via Meriden, Allesley, Coventry and Dunchurch. This was the route ultimately surveyed and reconstructed by Telford; in 1821 the Turnpike Trust earmarked £5,500 for the lowering of Meriden Hill.

Hockley House

Quite where the coaches stopped along the local roads to change their horses and rest and feed their passengers is not exactly known, for today many hostelries claim to be 'old coaching inns'. Generally horses were changed about every eight miles but hills such as Liveridge Hill and Lapworth Hill may well have caused more frequent changes. Henley-in-Arden had many inns but the *White Swan* was the largest and the most frequented. From Henley to Hockley Heath was four miles and in this space there were six inns — the *Bird in Hand,* the *Wheatsheaf* now Wheatsheaf Farm above Lapworth Hill; the *Royal Oak* now rebuilt; and at Hockley Heath the

The Boot Inn

White Lion which stood behind the present *Wharf Inn,* the *Nags Head* and *Hockley House.* The *White Lion* and the *Nags Head* both kept post horses but it was *Hockley House,* now demolished, which was *the* coaching inn. A large square Georgian building, it was in its heyday, very busy and much patronised. The horses taken on at Henley were almost certainly changed here.

The Navigation Inn

Several ostlers and post-boys, most of whom probably worked at *Hockley House,* appear in the Lapworth Parish Registers in the 1820's and 1830's, having brought their children to St. Mary's to be baptised. The presence of post-boys implies that it was possible to hire a post-chaise at one of the local inns.

Along the six and three quarter miles of the Old Warwick Road from Hockley Heath to Hatton there were five inns. The *Bell* at the corner of Wharf Lane, the *Boot,* the *Navigation* at Kingswood, and the *Elephant* and the *Cock* at Rowington. None of these inns was very large or had extensive stabling and residential facilities for the traveller, but as the road ceased to be turnpiked about 1810 and before the high peak of coach travelling, this is not surprising.

In 1788[14] there were four stage coaches and one mail coach passing daily between Birmingham, Oxford and London. By 1817 this had increased to seven coaches daily and by 1830 there were 10 coaches each day and 12 on Thursdays. The coaches called at the *Swan* at Henley-in-Arden at the following times and at Hockley Heath a little before or a little after, depending on the direction of travel:-

Birmingham to London
The Oxonian at 7.00 a.m.; The Triumph at 7.30 a.m.; The Union at 5.00 p.m.; The Prince at 8.30 p.m.

London to Birmingham
The Union at 5.00 a.m.; The Prince at 5.00 a.m.; The Oxonian at 1.00 p.m.; The Triumph at 7.00 p.m.; All went through Oxford and Uxbridge.

Birmingham to Oxford
Oxford Day Coaches: To Oxford at 12.00 noon; To Birmingham at 4.00 p.m.

Birmingham and Stratford
The Paul Pry: To Stratford — Thursday evening 8.00 p.m.
                To Birmingham — Thursday morning 8.00 a.m.

In addition there were coaches from Beaudesert (W. Johns) to Birmingham on Monday and Thursday morning at 7.30 a.m., and to Warwick every morning at 8.00 a.m. All were called 'The Shamrock'.

The most prosperous years of the Turnpike Trust were the early 1830's when there were numerous coaches and people travelled extensively. Then the railway arrived. Coach routes which competed with the railways were devastated, almost overnight, and many Turnpike Trusts were made bankrupt. The railway line from Birmingham to London via Hampton-in-Arden opened in September 1838. Prior to its opening 22 coaches left Birmingham daily for London, by the end of 1838 this had been reduced to four and it was expected that these too would soon disappear. This despite the difference in the fares of 20s. 0d., inside and 10s. 0d., outside by stage coach and 30s. 0d., inside and 20s. 0d., outside on the train. The Turnpike Trusts could not survive such a situation and although the Stratford Road Trust was said in 1841 to be financially sound and the road satisfactory, they expected to be hit by the railway competition and ultimately they were. The Trust was finally dis-turnpiked in 1872[15] and the responsibility for the upkeep of the road passed to the local Highway Authority which now cared for lesser roads instead of the parish.

A coach leaving the White Swan Inn, Henley-in-Arden c.1830

TURNPIKE TOLLS

BIRMINGHAM, WARWICK AND WARMINGTON

BIRMINGHAM TO STRATFORD-UPON-AVON AND EDGEHILL

	1725-6; 1744	1757-1810	1830
Coach etc. (passenger carriage) drawn by 6 horses or more	1s.0d.	1s.0d.	
,, ,, ,, ,, ,, ,, 4 ,,	6d.	9d.	
,, ,, ,, ,, ,, ,, Less than 4 horses	3d.	6d.	
Wagon, cart etc., (goods vehicle) ,, ,, 5 or more horses or oxen	8d.		
,, ,, ,, ,, ,, ,, ,, 4 horses or more		8d.	
,, ,, ,, ,, ,, ,, ,, 4 ,, ,, less	6d.		
,, ,, ,, ,, ,, ,, ,, 3 ,, ,, oxen	4d.		
,, ,, ,, ,, ,, ,, ,, 2 ,, ,, ,,	3d.		
,, ,, ,, ,, ,, ,, ,, 1 ,, ,, ,,	2d.		
Horse not drawing	1d.	1d.	1d.
Cattle per score	10d.	10d.	10d.
Sheep, pigs etc., per score	5d.	5d.	5d.
Horse drawing any coach etc., 4 wheels			4½d.
,, ,, ,, curricle 2 ,,			4d.
Wagon with wheels 6in., or more ,, ,, 6 horses or more, each horse			3d.
,, ,, ,, 6in., ,, ,, ,, ,, 5 horses, each horse			3¾d.
,, ,, ,, 6in., ,, ,, ,, ,, 4 ,, or less, each horse			5d.
Horse drawing wagon with 4½in., wheels			5¾d.
,, ,, ,, ,, less than 4½in., wheels			7d.
,, ,, cart ,, 6in., wheels			3d.
,, ,, ,, ,, 4½in., ,,			3¾d.
,, ,, ,, ,, less than 4½in., wheels			4½d.

BIRMINGHAM TO STRATFORD-UPON-AVON BRIDGE ONLY

	1770; 1800	1821
Coach etc., drawn by 4 horses or more	1s. 6d.	1s. 6d.
,, ,, ,, ,, 3 ,, ,, ,,		1s.1½d.
,, ,, ,, ,, 2 ,,	9d.	9d.
,, ,, ,, ,, 1 ,,	4d.	4d.
Wagons	1s. 0d.	
,, with wheels less than 6in.		1s. 6d.
,, ,, 16in., roller		9d.
,, ,, 9in., ,,		1s. 0d.
,, ,, 6in., ,,		1s. 3d.
Cart drawn by 3 horses or more	9d.	
,, ,, ,, less than 3 horses	6d.	
Cart with wheels 6in., or more drawn by 3 horses or more		10½d.
,, ,, ,, 6in., ,, ,, ,, ,, 2 ,, ,, ,,		8d.
,, ,, ,, 6in., ,, ,, ,, ,, 1 ,, ,, ,,		6d.
Horse, cow not drawing	1d.	1d.
Sheep, pig, per score	5d.	5d.
Ass drawing any cart		1½d.

LANES AND BY-WAYS

As far as the outside world was concerned the two most important roads in Lapworth were the Stratford Road and the Old Warwick Road, but the people of the parish, going about their daily business, moving between their farm and fields, visiting neighbours, used the lanes, and it was the condition of these minor roads which concerned them.

The lanes were kept in repair by the parish. In theory a highway rate was levied each year to pay for the materials; the labour and transport being supplied by the parishioners themselves. Under an Act of 1555[16] each farmer who kept a team of horses or oxen was supposed to lend it free, with a cart and two able men, for four days each year. Every other householder was supposed to give four days labour free; later this was increased to six days per annum. Those unable to work in this way had to send a substitute. As the centuries passed most people commuted their share of the work to a money payment, and workmen were hired.

Whoever did the work, it being the Surveyor of the Highways' job to organize such matters, the system was not satisfactory. The 'repairs' usually consisted of tipping stone and gravel into the pot-holes and ruts and allowing the farm carts and wagons to roll them into a 'surface'. There was no proper drainage and it is not surprising that the lanes were often described as 'foul ways' and were a continual source of complaint. In winter they squelched with mud, were full of puddles and were often impassable. In the summer they became hard, deep rutted tracks.

At Lapworth there were two Surveyors of the Highway, both were chosen by the parishioners and approved by the magistrates. For one year they had the task, unpaid, of caring for the local roads. They did not make a levy but bought stone, gravel, etc., and hired men to do the work with money provided by the Charity Estate, and later by the Overseer of the Poor. None of those involved knew anything about road making, indeed some Surveyors of the Highway thought it best to leave the roads alone and simply scour the ditches.

In 1835[17] the statutory obligation demanded by the 1555 Act was at last abolished and the old system of road care abandoned almost everywhere. Parishes were formed into highway districts, Lapworth coming under that of Henley-in-Arden. In most districts a general highway rate was levied and a professional, paid, surveyor appointed. In some places, however, the parish, still using the old system, continued to manage the roads for a further few years, and this seems to have been the case at Lapworth.

The highway accounts for the year April 1845 to March 1846[18] have survived and they show that the traditional method of maintenance, filling in the pot-holes and dips with loads of stone, still pertained. There were two Surveyors of the Highway, Joseph Osborn of High Chimneys Farm for 'the Street side' of the parish and John Mander of Irelands Farm, who cared for the roads on 'the Park side'. Both employed men, by the day or week, to labour on the roads.

John Mander employed two men only, Edward Sprag who did most of the work, and John Gilbert. Both were paid 10d., per day, Sprag giving 234 days work and Gilbert 12 days during the year. Gilbert worked only in December whilst Sprag, who worked throughout the year, did the least road work in July, August and September and none at all in October. Possibly during these months he also worked as a casual farm hand helping with the haymaking, harvest and other field work.

The roads under Joseph Osborn's care were more heavily used than those on Park side and cost more to keep up. Osborn employed six different men, John Reeve and William Bishop who worked regularly throughout the year, and William Horton, Thomas Young, James Parsons and one Barnet. Reeve who gave 157½ days work on the roads was paid 10d., per day until December 1845 and then 1s. 0d., per day. Like Sprag he worked most during the winter. Bishop was paid by the month earning £1 2s. 0d., every four weeks or 11d., per day. The others, who worked only an odd few days received more pay — William Horton had 1s. 2d., per day, Young and Barnet 1s. 6d., per day, and James Parsons 3s. 4d., per day but only for five days. Both sides paid men to load and cart stones for one day at 1s. 6d., each per day. Altogether Park side labour costs were £10 9s. 8d., and Street side's £22 15s. 8d.

The material used to repair the roads was stone or rather stones. Various people in the parish, mostly women but some men were paid for tons of stones, probably picked out of the fields by children or perhaps by the women themselves. On Park side three women, Mrs. Sprag, Mrs. Fanthom, Mrs. Jelphs, and two men Edward Sprag and Henry Sanders, provided the stones. Mrs. Sprag was the largest supplier with 46½ tons, for which she was paid £1 11s. 0d., i.e., 8d., per ton. The two other women also recieved 8d., per ton (34 tons together), but the men received 10d., per ton for the 25 tons they supplied. Altogether 105½ tons were used on Park side.

On Street side three women and four men provided stones, 10d., per ton being paid to everyone; 108½ tons being used. Little else was bought to maintain the lanes — a few drain tiles and some tools — a hammer, a scraper and a tomahawk for 7s. 0d., and a shovel for 2s. 0d., — plus a few administrative expenses. At the year end Park side had spent £14 0s. 6d., and Street side £30 17s. 5d., a total of £44 17s. 11d. Unfortunately only £35 0s. 0d., was available and the Surveyors had to be owed the remainder.

Some of the men who worked on the roads are to be found in the census records of 1841 — Reeve, Sprag, Bishop, Barnet, and Horton were all agricultural labourers, Reeve, Sprag and Bishop being well over 65 years of age. James Parsons was a farmer, the tenant of Catesby Farm, not the usual type of road labourer and no doubt too expensive to employ for long at 3s. 4d., per day. The women stone collectors were all poorish women, often with several children who may have done most of the stone picking. Mr. Billings was the landlord of *The Boot*, Richard Smith was a farmer from Bredon House, Henry Sanders the parish clerk, and Thomas Palmer a labourer. Most of them had two or three children, for it is unlikely that Billings and Smith would have had time, or been willing to collect stones themselves.

By 1872[19] the Lapworth roads were under the control of the Henley highway district, the Charity Estate making an annual contribution of £60 towards road maintenance.

In 1872, under the Public Health Act, Lapworth and its roads passed into the control of Solihull Rural Sanitary Authority. There were still complaints about the roads in winter, the headmaster of the village school frequently commenting in the log book that the roads were flooded, extremely wet, or blocked by snow and that attendance was affected, the children being unable to get to school.

In 1896 the Solihull Rural Sanitary Authority was superceded by the Solihull Rural District Council, Lapworth still being in its control. In the same year there were complaints about Station Lane at Kingswood being in poor repair. It was described as narrow, hollow in the centre, and surfaced with unsuitable material painful to horses and pedestrians. Some people thought that the roads had been better looked after under the parish!

The following year Solihull agreed to make Station Lane properly all the way along. A large pond close to Malthouse Farm, which took up half the road, was to be partially filled in and the road was to be widened. The rest of the pond was to be fenced off. All the ditches were to be filled in, 9in. diameter drainpipes having been inserted, and a footpath made on the station side of the road.[20] Such attention to one road was undoubtedly because the gentlemen commuters of both Lapworth and Rowington used it daily on their way to and from the train.

The Old Warwick Road early this century. On the left is the entrance to Catesby Lane.

A Vers

For mee dear Husband don't repine
Because I left you in my prime
But patiently thy loss sustain
Thy hopes in heaven to meet again
And let my tender babes find still
The joyful offspring of thy will

From William Johns' Notebook

5

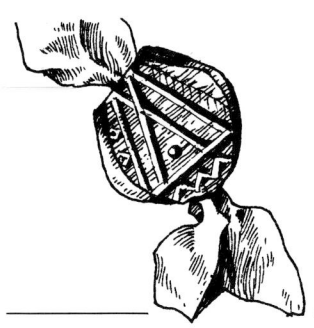

'THAT MOST EXCELLENT GIFT OF CHARITY'*

During the medieval period it was common practice for those who had been reasonably successful in this life to leave land or money for charitable purposes at their death. Some left small sums to be distributed to the poor at their burial, others left an annual payment for the upkeep of a certain piece of road, usually that between their house and the church, and a few left money for candles and masses for the repose of their soul. A small number bequeathed land, possibly a field or two but occasionally more, for the upkeep of the church, the roads and the poor, or a combination of all three. When Roger Sly of Brome Hall died in 1527 he left, in his will,[1] 20d., 'yerely to ye myndyng [mending] of ye hye wayes be twene Harbere hethe & Lapworthe cherche'. He also left 3s. 4d., to be given to poor people 'a pone good fryday', as well as money for masses to be said and candles to be kept burning 'be fore owere lady' and elsewhere in the church. These annual gifts were to be paid for out of the rent of a cottage and a considerable amount of land. They were meant to be of benefit not only to his family, but to the whole community.

A fine set of medieval deeds,[2] very small and beautifully written in medieval Latin, still survive. They relate to lands given to Lapworth for charitable use and lay for centuries in the parish chest. The earliest dates from c1190 and records the transfer of land called 'Ulelega' (later in 19th century known as 'Hullies') from Luke Sorel to William le Oiselur. Described as being close to the road from 'Bellu Desertu to Burmigeha' the land was given to the parish by Thomas Prat in 1479, but the donors and the dates of other gifts are not always so easy to determine.

By the reign of Henry VIII Lapworth had a considerable amount of such charity land. There was also a chantry, founded in 1373, by a group of Lapworth men including Richard de Montfort the husband of Rose, co-lady of the manor.[3] The chantry was founded, and a special chapel added to the church, for the purpose of praying daily for the souls of all the founders and their families plus numerous other people, including the Earl of Warwick. About 200 acres of land was given to support the chapel and the special priest who was appointed to serve it.

In 1547 King Henry swept away all chantries confiscating the lands which supported them. Some chantry chapels and altars were richly adorned with ornaments of silver and gold and were often encrusted with jewels. All such items, relating to 'supersticious uses', were taken away. If similar valuables existed in Lapworth, and they probably did in some measure, they were lost at this time. In addition, a further 106 acres of land in Lapworth and Nuthurst was confiscated, the income having been used to keep a mass lamp burning within the church.

16th AND 17th CENTURIES

It was usual for charity property to be administered by trustees, known as Feoffees, the donor appointing several men of good repute at the time of the gift. As the original group grew older or died, other men of similar standing replaced them. In most parishes by the 16th century, one set of trustees administered all the charity lands, but at Lapworth different sets of trustees looked after different gifts of land and this continued until the Commonwealth.

*Book of Common Prayer. Collects. Quinquagesima Sunday.
Illustration depicts Seal of Deed, 1435.

The Chantry Chapel

Occasionally, charity lands were lost usually because the Feoffees were lax, but at Lapworth corruption was the problem. In the 1570's a trust of 23 Lapworth Feoffees went to the Court of Chancery against Thomas Grimshaw of Packwood, an ex-Feoffee.[4] He with 'crafty practices and untollerable corruption' had attempted to steal Charity land by leasing it out as if it were his own. Grimshaw naturally denied the charges and cleverly explained his actions, but there was little doubt of his guilt and the land was rescued for the parish.

Some 40 years later, in 1615, William Askew, a man of apparent standing and importance in the parish, was accused by certain parishioners of 35 cases of stealing Charity property.[5] Askew was said to have appointed his sons and sons-in-law as co-Feoffees of a Charity trust and to have had them, and the other co-Feoffees (who did not resign) under his thumb. He used the property for his own profit, moving field boundaries, chopping down valuable trees, pocketing rents and taking over parish lands etc. He did this for 30 years until the parishioners could stand it no longer. One of his major acts of vandalism was to remove from the churchyard a large stone cross which had an arched canopy large enough for 12 men to have 'stood dry' under. This he carried away and used as the groundsill or base of his house. Some sort of commission of enquiry was appointed to look into the allegations, and evidence was given against Askew by many parishioners. Regretfully there is no indication of the final conclusion, but Askew appears to have survived without a stain on his character.

In 1668 the parishioners asked for another commission of enquiry[6] this time to sort out the administration of the Charity Estate which, since 1652, had been in the hands of a single trust. The commission decided that the existing trustees were incompetent and ordered that new, named, Feoffees, all landed gentlemen of the county, but no one from Lapworth, should be appointed and a new management scheme begun. The parish, somewhat shocked at the idea of outsiders running their affairs, ignored the commission and did nothing for nine years. Then, in 1677, Thomas Sly, the last of the old Feoffees, appointed 12 Lapworth men to be his co-trustees in running the Charity Estate.

The first survey of the Charity lands was made in 1699 by William Avern. The actual document has long since disappeared but the then rector, Edward Welchman, made a rough copy on the fly leaves of the Parish Register. The survey records the names of the 14 tenants, the fields they held, and the acreages. The smallest holding, of two fields = 2¼ acres, was held by Thomas Luckman and the largest, Millbourne Farm (also known as Drawbridge Farm) of 34 acres 3 roods 31 perches, by William Court. Amongst the holdings were three farms — Millbourne, already mentioned, a very small farm at Tapster Brook occupied by Richard Jennings and a larger unit (close to the present *Royal Oak*) of 29 acres 1 rood 36 perches, let to William Wedge, but most of the holdings were small, nine being of under 10 acres. The total acreage of the estate in 1699 was 175 acres 2 roods 16 perches.

The Charity Farm at Tapster Brook

It was the policy of the Feoffees at this time to divide the lands into three approximately equal portions and allocate each for a specific purpose — one part for the upkeep of the church, one for the maintenance of the roads and one for the support of the poor;[7] each being administered by the relevant parish officer. The only records to survive are those pertaining to the poor's portion of land and these are sparse, but they show that the poor received the rents of just over 43 acres of land plus that of a property in Banbury being a house and shops in the Market Place. The Overseer of the Poor received the rents of the poor's portion of the land which amounted to £21 6s. 0d., in 1688 and £22 17s. 0d., in 1701.[8] Out of this any buildings had to be kept in repair, then the residue was for the poor. Even if very little was spent on maintenance what was left was not enough to wholly support those in need. Therefore a levy of the householders of the parish was taken (as was usual in all parishes) to make up the deficit and meet the Overseer's disbursements. In this way £18 4s. 4d., was raised by levy in 1688 and £27 11s. 3d., in 1701. Thus, at the end of the 17th century about half the money spent by the Overseer of the Poor came from the Charity land rents.

THE LATE 18th CENTURY

Until 1775 the Feoffees kept no accounts but from this time it is possible to follow the rise and fall of the parish rents. In 1775 the income was £104 0s. 0d.; by 1795 it had risen to £127 0s. 0d.[9] In the latter year the parishioners, who always appear to have kept a very sharp eye on the Charities, expressed discontent over the uneconomical rents being charged. The Feoffees therefore asked for counsel's opinion regarding their difficulty in organising the Estate. As a result in 1797 the first Minute Book[10] was started, but the contents are a sad disappointment. The Annual Meetings were most perfunctory and the minutes record little more than the names of those present and a bare outline of the business. For some years (1814-1822) there is no record of any meetings being held at all. One of the problems was the quality of the Feoffees; only those who were both freeholders (roughly those men with a parliamentary vote) and inhabitants of the parish, were eligible to officiate. This reduced the number available considerably, and they seem to have had little interest or enthusiasm for such duties.

By the 1790's all the income from the Charity Estate rents — £127 11s. 6d., per annum was paid to the Overseer of the Poor[11] who, contrary to accepted practice, was paid £10 0s. 0d., a year to administer the Charity property and also look after the demands of the needy. He received the Charity rents out of which he paid the Charity doles, for repairs to the Charity houses and cottages, all taxes and dues on Charity land, church repairs and expenses, repairs to the stocks, the accounts of the Churchwarden, of the Surveyors of the Highway, and the Constable. He also paid the schoolmaster's salary (£20 0s. 0d., per annum) and for the school coals (£1 0s. 0d., per annum). Any residue after these payments, and there was never very much, was put 'towards the poor' accounts. In 1794-5 the residue was £2 15s. 6d., in 1795-6 £13 18s. 1½d. To supplement these meagre sums and raise the £300 0s. 0d., plus needed each year to support the poor, several levies of all the parish householders were made.

It is clear that the Feoffees felt that they needed a larger income in order to maintain their property properly and still have more than a few pounds residue to help support the poor. In August 1797 therefore, they decided to appoint Thomas Harding to value the lands let to the 14 tenants at a yearly rent and raise them at Lady Day 1798 if so advised; leases of seven to 21 years were to be offered.[12]

A start was made by surveying the land of seven of the 14 tenants, after which they 'should be acquainted and asked to answer whether they will accept the valuations and new rents and answer before Christmas Day next in writing'. By 29th December four tenants had agreed to the new rents; Mr. Ingram, who had the largest holding, taking a 21 year lease at £30 10s. 0d., per annum (an increase of 50%). The others remained yearly tenants, Mr. Cotterill with an increase of 49.8% and Mr. Edwards of 40.7%. William Smith had his rent reduced a few shillings; as he was always half a year in arrears he must have been very pleased. Two other tenants had their increases deferred, the land having been mis-measured. John Butwell had his rent increased by 38.5% from £6 10s. 0d., to £9 0s. 0d., although it was valued at £2 0s. 0d., more, 'but Butwell is poor and if his premises are let at a higher rent he would become a burden on the parish'. This was a problem the Feoffees had continually with their poorer tenants who could not always pay the rent. They were, after all, running a Charity Estate and it looked bad to evict those who were poor!

By Michaelmas 1798 the rents of nine tenants had been increased and four had agreed to leases, three to 21 year leases and one, Widow White, who was elderly, to a 10 year lease or term of her natural life. The income from the Chairty Estate for 1798 was consequently raised to £143 4s. 6d., and it was possible to give £40 15s. 10½d., towards supporting the poor.

Another result of the increase in income was that orders were given for more barns, gates etc., to be put in good repair.

THE REPAIR OF THE CHARITY PROPERTY

During the years between 1794 and 1799 considerable sums were spent on the repair of the property.[13] Brickwork using 300 bricks (cost 6s. 6d.) was carried out by Henry Parsons, the mason, on the house of Rogers, the cost of the whole being 33s. 9d. Work costing £15 12s. 3d., was done at the house of Isaac Mortiboys who rented the Charity farm near the *Royal Oak;* included was a new stone floor for his barn (£4 6s. 8d.).

The thatched roof of the row of cottages occupied by the poor at the Pound (Pound Cottages, now demolished) was repaired by Thomas Maids, who lived in one of them, 10cwt. of straw being purchased from Mr. Green at 2s. 8d., per cwt. Work was also done at John Butwell's house at Tapster Brook (cost £3 8s. 3d.) and at Williams' house to which 4700 bricks (£6 11s. 7d.) were carried (charge 2s. 6d.). They had been bought from Mr. Bradbury who had a brick-kiln in one of his fields at Lapworth Lodge Farm.

The largest expenditure however was on Barnbrook's house. This appears to have been completely re-built, perhaps on a new adjacent site. The Barnbrook family lived at Kingswood in a Charity cottage, (long demolished) which stood approximately behind the site of the Will Power Garage. This was apparently the house on which so much was expended in the 1790's, the total being £62 7s. 2½d. The timber was bought from Mr. Bott, who was connected with the woodland of the Holte estate, and cost £7 0s. 0d.; it was felled by Barnbrook himself. The nails (£1 13s. 9d.) were made by James Bunn the blacksmith at Bunn Green; James Leeson and Henry Parsons both worked on the house. The carriage of everything to the site was a considerable expense, 20 quarters of lime, bought for £2 15s. 0d., cost 13s. 6d., to load and carry. The timber cost £1 7s. 0d., to 'draw' and the brick and tile 8s. 6d. Glazing the house cost 17s. 0d., and a lock for the door 2s. 0d.

A fair amount of work was also done at the church at this time particularly to the roof. 700 tiles and 3 cresses (crest tiles) were purchased from Mr. Bradbury for £1 1s. 10d., including carriage. New timber and lath cost £2 14s. 10d., and the nails 14s. 1d. A variety of people submitted bills for work done — Henry Parsons (£7 17s. 11d.), John Smith (£1 15s. 0d.), Mr. Edwards (£2 10s. 0d.), Mr. Hobday for work at the bells and a new gate, Thomas Smith for repairing the bells (£5 10s. 8d.) and Mr. Lench (£20 17s. 9.) for plumbing (leadwork) and glazing.

Inside the church new mats were provided (5s. 3d.), and Mr. Eades repaired and cleaned the clock (15s. 0d.). The church linen was washed a few times (2s. 6d., per time), bread and wine for the sacrament was bought (2d.), as were new bell ropes (18s. 0d.). The bell ringers were paid 10s. 6d., several times, always in November when traditionally they would ring on Bonfire Day. Possibly they were only paid for ringing on special occasions for they were also given 10s. 6d., for ringing after Nelson's victory at the Battle of the Nile in August 1798.

Charity rents were paid half yearly at Lady Day and Michaelmas. Some poor people could not pay and then Charity funds helped them out paying the whole or part. Rent day was also a social event, drink, and usually food, being offered to the tenants when business was completed, at least £1 0s. 0d., being spent on 'Eating and Drinking, Rent Day'.

THE CHARITY ESTATE IN 1814

Due to the great increase in profits made by farmers generally during the Napoleonic War the Feoffees decided in February 1814 that the Charity properties should again be valued, this time by Mr. Joseph Armishaw who was also to estimate the cost of putting all the houses in good repair.[14] Mr. Armishaw, a lawyer and the Land Agent to Heneage Legge, did the valuation and measuring whilst Ebenezer Robins, the principal land surveyor in the neighbourhood, drew a set of beautiful plans. These — one for each tenant's property with an adjacent schedule of the acreage and rent — were bound together into a fine volume, which fortunately still survives in pristine condition.[15] The cost of the survey including the book of plans was £73 10s. 6d.[16]

Altogether there were 38 tenants of which 18 were poor cottagers. The 20 other tenants paid a fully economic rent for their land which varied between 14s. 0d., and 70s. 0d., per acre, but was mostly 30s. 0d., to 45s. 0d., producing an income of £471 0s. 0d., per annum from just over 185 acres of land. The holdings were the 14 existing in 1794 plus six new ones; the majority of the tenants were the same as in 1794 but their rents had increased considerably.

THE HOLDINGS

1) Millbourne Farm (also known as Drawbridge Farm) of 33¾ acres was let to Joseph Hobday at a rent of £63 1s. 8d., per annum; in 1794 he had paid £24 0s. 0d., per annum. There were 11 fields plus the house. The Stratford-upon-Avon canal had sliced through the farm in 1800 and

2) the land taken for the canal (2 acres 1 rood 20 perches) was let to the Stratford-upon-Avon Canal Company for £8 5s. 0d., per annum.

3) A small area of land — 3 perches, once common land, on the side of the road beside Millbourne Farm, had been recently taken in and enclosed by Mr. Hobday. The Feoffees claimed it for the Charities, built a house on it (now called Bumblebees) and annexed it to John Green who rented it for £6 0s. 0d., per annum.

4) A short distance from Millbourne Farm was land held since 1799 by Mr. Fowler, and then by his widow, Rebecca. The house stood on the corner of Warwick Road and Packwood lane, the fields being behind it. In addition there were two other fields in Tapster Lane, the whole being nine acres at a rent of £26 13s. 3d., per annum.

5) Four fields = 10½ acres near Packwood held by Thomas Featherstone, tenant since 1798 at a rent of £21 10s. 7d., per annum, on a 21 year lease.

6) On the ground where Lapworth School now stands was the house and garden of William Kendall, the parish clerk. Until 1805 he occupied the house and three fields rent free 'in consideration of his poor emolument as clerk'. From this time, however, he was asked to pay 1s. 0d., per annum rent to secure the property in the parish's ownership. In 1814 Kendall was expected to pay the full rent of £12 0s. 6d., for the house = 0 acres 1 rood 1 perch plus 2¾ acres of Charity land.

7) Beyond Church Lane, adjoining Lapworth Brook, were eight strips of land, four of meadow and four of pasture = 5 acres, being a remnant of the Lapworth open field system. They were interspersed with similar strips owned by Thomas Johns. Mr. Johns rented the Charity strips for £12 15s. 3d., per annum and thus had the use of the whole field. Mr. Cotterill, Thomas Johns' father-in-law, was the tenant in 1794.

8) Another Charity owned farm, tenanted by Isaac Mortiboys since at least 1794, was situated beside the Stratford Road opposite Lapworth Hill Farm. It consisted of buildings and six fields = 30¼ acres, the rent being £59 12s. 1d.

9) Just out of Lapworth in Nuthurst were five fields let to William Ingram of Lapworth Hill Farm. The 32 acres, which Mr. Ingram had held since 1794, were let for a rent of £57 14s. 3d.

10) Another property close to the last — a house and three fields = 7¼ acres — at Lapworth Hill also in Nuthurst was let to Edward Eborall for £24 5s. 10d., per annum.

11) Across the Stratford Road from Eborall's land was one very large field of 9¾ acres called Big Hullies and owned by the Charity estate since 1479. William Bradbury was the tenant at a rent of £15 12s. 4d., per annum being 32s. 0d., per acre.

12) A third small farm owned by the Charities was in Hole House Lane. The house and five fields = 9½ acres were occupied by the Butwell family who had been the tenants since at least 1794. Despite being given notice to quit in 1796 Joseph Butwell was still there in 1814 paying a rent of £23 5s. 9d., per annum.

13) In Tapster Lane were two fields = 6½ acres let to John Edwards, another old tenant. His rent was £11 15s. 7d., per annum.

14) Two fields = 5¼ acres rented to William Smith of Bear House Farm at £10 16s. 9d., per annum. They were situated opposite his house beyond the canal.

15) Fields and a garden = 6¾ acres let to Isaac Green at a rent of £15 4s. 11d., per annum. One field and a garden was at the junction of Old Warwick Road and Lapworth Street behind Pound Cottages. The second field was at Copt Green not very far from Bushwood Hall.

16) Two fields adjacent to Catesby Farm = 7¼ acres were let to Joseph King at £14 11s. 0d., per annum. These had been occupied in 1794 by Mr. Frankton and later in 1803 by Mr. Cattell.

17) The enclosure of Kingswood Common gave the Charity Feoffees an increased holding of land close to Kingswood Brook (where the garage and a new house stand). Two small parcels = 1¼ acres were let to John Grafton at £4 16s. 8d., per annum, and

18) Two slightly larger parcels = 2 acres were let to Samuel Parsons for £2 17s. 9d., per annum.

19) The property at Banbury was let to William Cockerill who paid £26 0s. 0d., per annum.

20) A new Charity property since the making of the canal was a portion of the branch canal which ran parallel to Wharf Lane and connected the main canal to Dowdeswell House, Stratford Road, where there was a coal wharf. The canal was used by the Stratford and Henley Coal Company who paid the Feoffees 9s. 6d., per annum rent for that portion of the canal which ran across the Charity land.

THE COTTAGES

These were let to poor or labouring families at various rents. The cottages were in four lots spread around the parish at Kingswood Brook, at Copt Green, The Pound and Warwick Road.

1) Kingswood Brook:- Three cottages under one roof set well back from the road and let to Thomas Barnbrook,* John Reeve† and Elias Carpenter.* This was 'Barnbrook's house' which had been rebuilt in the 1790's. There were three garden plots for the tenants to share, one round the house, one near the road and a third close to Malthouse Farm in what is now Station Lane. The rent of £8 10s. 0d., per annum for the three averaged at £2 16s. 8d., per cottage.

2) Copt Green:- Four cottages, together under one roof, set down a narrow side lane off the road from Copt Green to Yew Tree Farm. They were occupied by William Fantham,† William Heritage,*† Elizabeth Phipps† and Thomas Kendall.† There was half an acre of shared garden divided into three parts where vegetables could be grown. The rent was £8 15s. 0d., per annum, averaging £2 3s. 9d., per cottage.

3) The Poor's Houses at The Pound:- Demolished and replaced by bungalows and flats in the 1960's, there were five cottages under one roof here in 1814. They occupied a site on the corner of Old Warwick Road and Lapworth Street and were let to Mary Maids,* Thomas Ward,† William Saunders, Thomas Nash,*† and Thomas Maids*† the thatcher. The garden of half an acre was divided into five unequal portions. The rent was £16 0s. 0d., per annum which averaged out at £3 4s. 0d., per cottage.

4) Warwick Road Cottages:- Along the road opposite Millbourne Farm were six cottages in three lots. The first was a detached cottage and garden = 21 perches let to Thomas Dee† at £3 10s. 0d., per annum. Adjacent were a pair of semi-detached cottages and gardens = 27 perches let to Thomas Townsend† and Sarah Brookes*† at £3 0s. 0d., and £3 10s. 0d., per annum respectively. Further along the road, close to Packwood Lane were three cottages under one roof, having a quarter of an acre of shared garden. These were let to William Long, William Luckman,* and William Bate at £3 10s. 0d., £2 10s. 0d., and £4 0s. 0d., per annum respectively.

*Names appear in the poor records in receipt of assistance in 1790's.
†Names appear in the poor records in receipt of assistance, 1816-18.

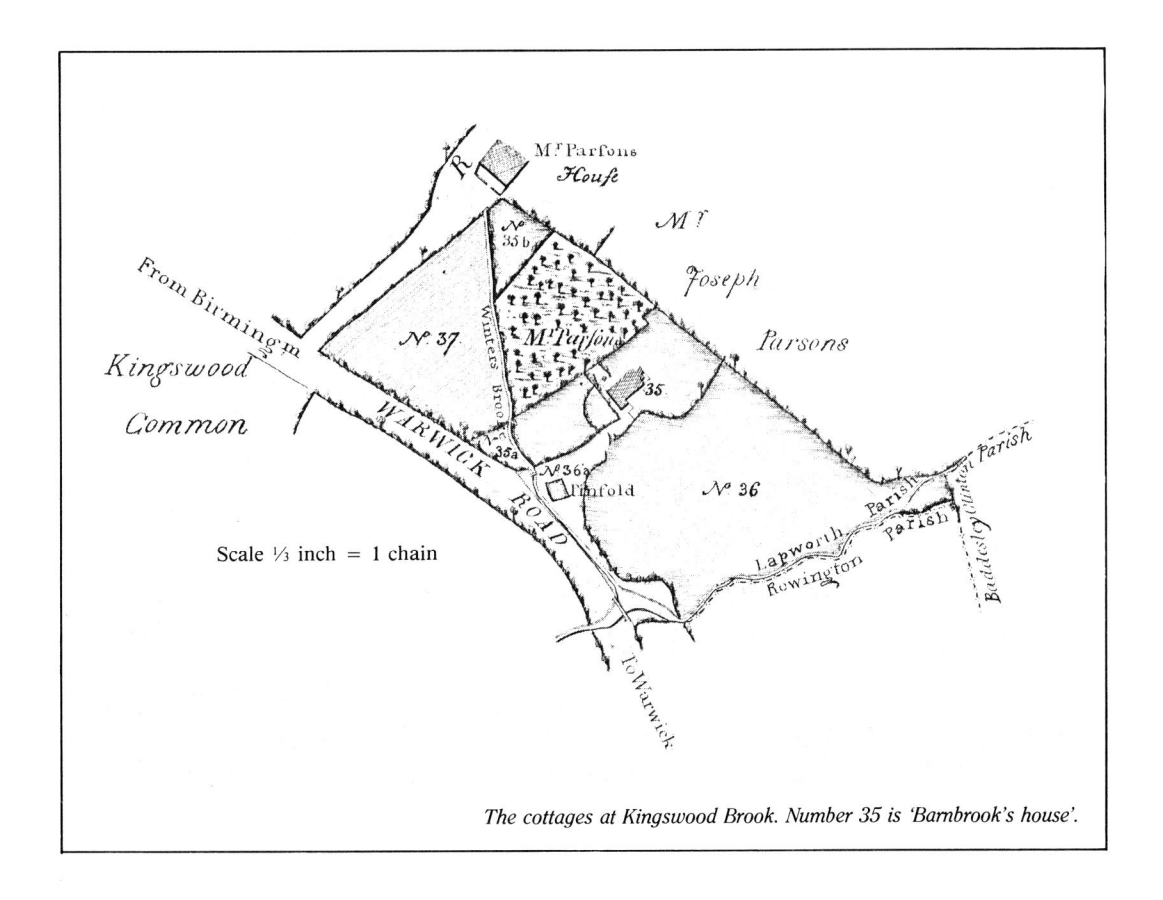

The cottages at Kingswood Brook. Number 35 is 'Barnbrook's house'.

1817 - 1875

In 1817 there was again discontent in the parish at the way the Feoffees ran the Charity Estate and a lawsuit was filed by a number of the inhabitants for mismanagement and misapplication of the funds.[17] In particular they complained of corruption in the granting of leases. All the papers with the details are now lost but defending the suit in the Court of Chancery cost the parish over £400 0s. 0d.

THE CHARITY COMMISSIONERS' REPORT

During the 19th century the Charity Commissioners produced a 32 volume report on the charities in England. In 1826 their inspector visited Lapworth as part of the county of Warwickshire survey. His report,[18] listing all the land, farms and cottages controlled by the Lapworth Feoffees, shows no major differences from the 1814 survey. There were a few new tenants, most of whom were paying slightly higher rents than had been asked in 1814. Many of the old tenants, however, were paying less rent; as a result the income of the Charity was reduced to £412 5s. 3d., per annum. The inspector reported that this was because 'a temporary abatement of £10 per cent upon the rents was allowed' during the agricultural slump of the post-Napoleonic war period. He thought that 'this should now be removed and the proper rents received'. All the rents were considered to be fair except that of Edward Eborall — 'no explanation has been given why Eborall pays so low a rent'. Other minor changes were the division of two Charity houses — Bumblebees and one near by — to make three extra cottages for poor families making a total of 21, most of which were occupied by paupers who lived rent free.

At this time a new school was in the process of being built, the old one, in the churchyard, being in a very poor condition. The new building was expected to cost £800 0s. 0d., a considerable outlay on such an income. The house and garden of the parish clerk had been appropriated as the site of the school.

In an attempt to discover the origin of each property the inspector studied the Charity board which then hung in the church and listed the dates and donors of 10 gifts made between 1440 and 1729.[19] He also saw the documents in the parish chest but nothing, apparently, earlier than 1563. He made no reference to the corruption problem of the 16th and 17th centuries and it seems unlikely that he discovered anything of them. The Chancery suit of 1817, however, is mentioned and it is clear he knew all the details.

With regard to the contemporary management, the report records that an Annual Meeting, open to all parishioners, was held about Easter when the accounts were produced and handed round for individual inspection, before being approved. By this time a change had been made in the way the Charity income was used. As always the estate property was maintained, the schoolmaster's salary paid and those of the treasurer (£5 0s. 0d., per annum) and the parish clerk (£8 0s. 0d., per annum). Another charity school, for girls, also existed in the parish and this too was supported by Charity funds. Doles were paid to the poor of Lapworth and Rowington, and of Nuthurst, the former dole of £1 0s. 0d., per annum, often given in the form of meat, was in respect of money left to both parishes by Humphrey Shakespeare in 1729. The poor of Nuthurst received 18s. 0d., per annum in respect of Collett's Charity. The land given by Collett in 1568 was that farmed by Edward Eborall who paid the dole each year; possibly a reason for his low rent.

The Charity still helped with repairs to the highways and the church. The inspector thought that the parish was especially responsible for the repair of the chancel (although usually this was maintained by the rector) and for the church 'ornaments'. After all these payments what was left over was no longer given to the Overseer for the general support of the poor but kept by the Feoffees. They used it as they thought best, giving coal, linen, flannel or clothing to those who were most needy. They gave small amounts of money at Christmas (not exceeding a total of £4 0s. 0d.) preferring, in all their gifts, to give to those 'were shy at asking for ordinary parish relief'. Annually on All Souls Day (2nd November) 12 loaves were distributed amongst the poor of Lapworth, the gift of John Shakespeare (died 1627) and paid for in 1826 by William Cox the tenant of Tudor Farm, which Shakespeare had owned.

'THE LAPWORTH CHARITIES'

After the inspector's apparent approval of the Feoffees management in 1826 it is hard to believe that 15 years later further discontent within the parish would be expressed, but this was the case. In 1841 headed by the rector, the Rev. George Tyndall, a group of parishioners petitioned the Court of Chancery for the formation of a new scheme for governing the Charity Estate.[20] It took seven years for the scheme to be formulated and the cost, £921 0s. 0d., crippled the Estate funds for a long time. However, it proved to be a success and the Estate, from this time known as The Lapworth Charities, is still largely governed by the rules then promulgated. Briefly these were:-

1) A sum, not exceeding ⅛ of the annual income of the Estate, to be laid out for insuring and repairing the church building.
2) £10 0s. 0d., to be invested each year towards a fund of £200 0s. 0d., for 'extraordinary' repairs to the church.
3) £65 0s. 0d., per annum to be paid for the repair of the roads.

4) A master and mistress to be engaged to teach the children at the school. The house to be occupied rent free. £90 0s. 0d., per annum to be set aside to pay the two salaries and all other expenses connected with the school, the school building and the master's house.
5) The parish clerk to live rent free in the house adjoining the school.
6) The houses owned by the Estate to be kept in repair.
7) The residue of the Estate income to be used to help the aged, impotent and other poor of Lapworth who do not get parish relief, for medical aid and attendance to them, for apprenticing poor children and to help the poor occupy cottages at low rent or rent free.
8) Leases were not to exceed 21 years.
9) Suitable land might be set out as cottage allotments.
10) Trustees must not themselves rent Estate property.
11) Trustees must not live more than seven miles from Lapworth.
12) Trustees must not be bankrupt.
13) Trustees to meet annually on the Tuesday in Whit week.
14) Trustees to be advised of the annual meeting 10 days previously.
15) A notice re the meeting to be placed on the church door for two Sundays prior to it being held.
16) A treasurer to be appointed at the annual meeting. His pay not to be more than 5% of the Estate income.
17) A chairman to be elected for each annual meeting and he to have the casting vote.
18) The rector to be an ex-officio trustee.
19) When the number of trustees reduced to seven only, more to be elected within six months making a total of 15.
20) No trustee to receive remuneration.
21) No Estate money to be spent on dinners or entertainment.
22) Vacancies to be filled on death, removal or dismissal of a trustee.

THE NEW POOR LAW

In 1834 the Poor Law Amendment Act completely changed the way assistance was given to the poor. Outdoor relief, via the Overseer of the Poor was discontinued for the able-bodied poor and their families, those who really could not manage ending up in the workhouse. Under the new system several parishes were joined together into a Union, and all the poor were sent to a central workhouse. Lapworth was in the Solihull Union, and it was to Solihull Workhouse therefore that the poor of the parish were directed.

From 1834 onwards the Feoffees tried to help poor families in various ways. Rewards were 'offered half yearly to those labourers (able-bodied) who have large families and try to keep them'.[21] How the families were chosen is not revealed, nor are the names known of any who were rewarded.

The rector started a Clothing Society to help people buy clothes on the instalment plan and to this the Feoffees made an annual contribution of £5 5s. 0d. In addition they took on the task of relieving the poor and needy, sometimes with the odd pair of shoes, pair of sheets, pair of trousers, bushel of flour or round frock. At other times they gave coal, and to some, regular payments of 2s. 0d., 2s. 6d., or even 4s. 0d., a week; when a large number asked for help the sums given were reduced. But however hard it was for the poor to manage it was better than being sent to Solihull Workhouse, where life in the fine, new building in Union Road was harsh and lonely.

THE ACCOUNTS

The accounts of the Charity Estate were kept very precisely from 1856 with details of rents, taxes, arrears, and necessary repairs being carefully noted.[22] Rents were paid half yearly usually at the *Boot Inn* but also at the *Bell Inn*.

During the 1850's Charity rents fell slightly to below those of the 1820's, but during the 1860's were restored to their previous level. Mrs. Bellamy had paid a rent of £60 0s. 0d., per annum for Drawbridge Farm in the 1820's, the next tenant, Thomas Baldwin, was paying £52 10s. 0d., per annum in the 1850's but £60 0s. 0d., per annum in 1863. When good tenants gave notice to leave, rents were sometimes slightly reduced to persuade them to remain. Some tenants had leases of seven years but most appear to have been yearly tenants. The records are full of references to tenants being given notice to quit, usually in a year's time. However they did not always leave, a new arrangement having been made.

As the years progressed more and more of the land passed into the occupation of fewer tenants and it is difficult to determine exactly who had which pieces of land. In addition some Charity land was exchanged with other landlords. The row of Charity owned cottages at Copt Green which were occupied by four poor tenants were exchanged in 1858 for land elsewhere (situation unknown) owned by G. Miller Esq.

The poor cottage tenants paid between £2 0s. 0d., and £3 0s. 0d., per annum rent when they were in work and 4s. 0d., per annum when they were not. Even so many failed to pay and were frequently given notice to quit — but very rarely was anyone evicted. At Michaelmas 1867 John Barnett, Joseph Carpenter and Lydia Cox, all poor cottagers, were given notice to quit on Lady Day 1868. None left and the following year on Lady Day 1869 their arrears of rent were 'allowed' or discharged.

Although the Feoffees tried to keep the cottages in fair repair some were probably little more than hovels by to-day's standards. At Lady Day 1876 Sarah Reeves' cottage was empty but the Inspector of Nuisances would not permit it to be lived in again and it was therefore 'shut up'.

During the years 1856-1875 careful management gradually raised the Estate income from £182 3s. 0d., per half year at Lady Day 1856 to £206 19s. 6d., per half year at Lady Day 1875. It was not a large increase but one which enabled the Feoffees to continue assisting the poorer people of Lapworth as Thomas Prat, Roger Sly and others, in the distant past, had intended.

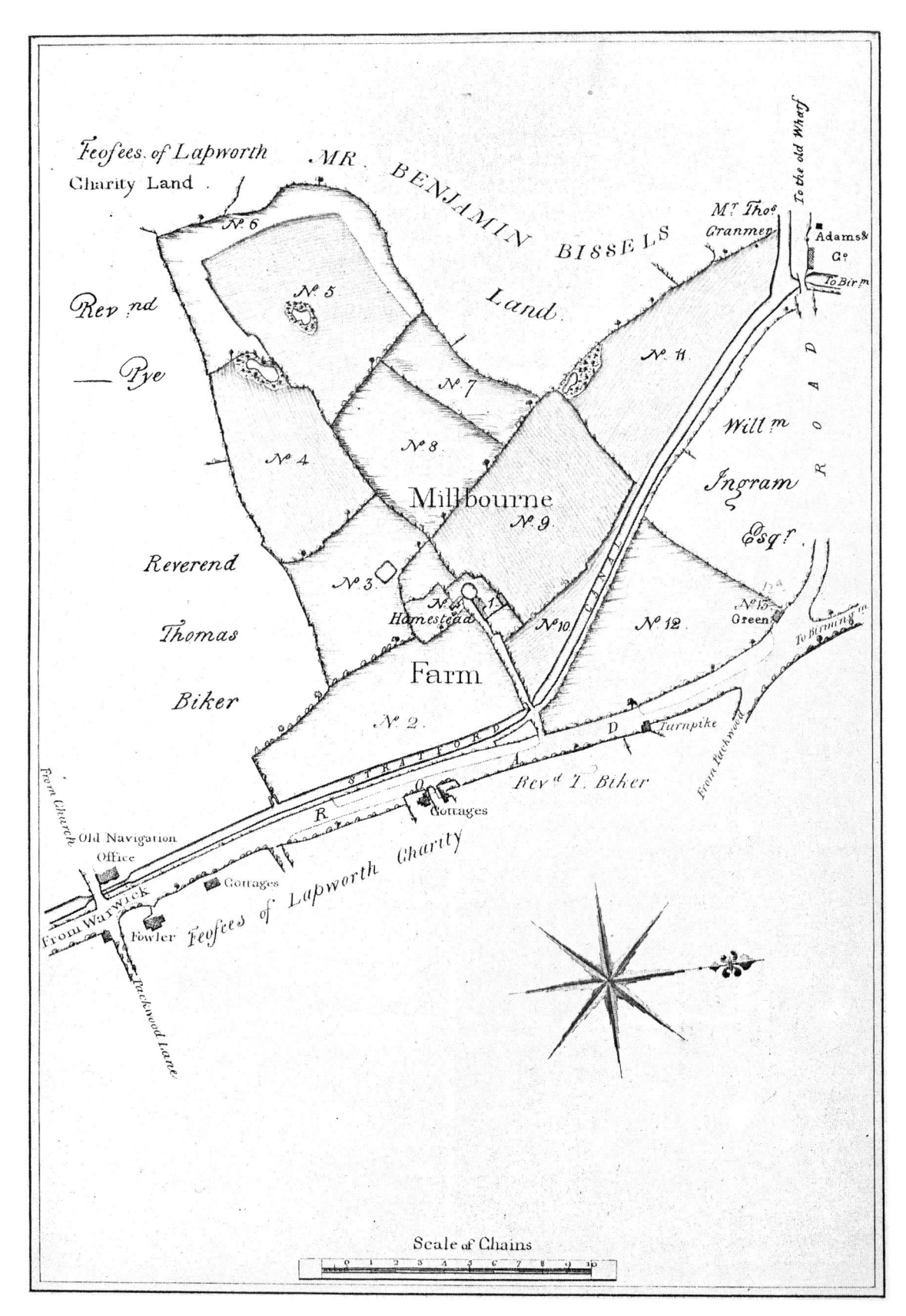

6
... 'UNWILLINGLY TO SCHOOL'*

Although attendance at school was not compulsory until the late 19th century, children, in many villages and towns, were offered the opportunity to learn to read and write prior to this time.

Grammar schools, giving a classical education of Latin, Greek and mathematics, and 'vernacular' schools, teaching reading, writing and accounting in English, sprang up throughout the country during the 16th and 17th centuries. A number prospered and still exist today,[1] some lasted only a few years, and others continued intermittently, operating as and when a master was available.

It is somewhat difficult to discover at exactly what date Lapworth first had a school. The name 'John Wight, Schoolmaster 1662' written on the flyleaf of the Parish Register suggests that a school existed in the village at this time, but whom he taught and where is not certain. It is possible that Wight was not the first schoolmaster in the parish, but no earlier indication than this of a school or a master has yet come to light.

Patrick Orpen, in his study of Warwickshire Schoolmasters of the 17th century,[2] considered that the school in Lapworth, of which Wight was the master in 1662, and which was run by others from 1674 - 1687 was a non-endowed grammar school. Such an establishment provided a classical education for boys whose family were prepared to pay the fees. The masters were usually graduates and ordained; sometimes curates waiting for preferment, sometimes the younger sons of gentlemen. Generally the social status of teachers was low and teaching was regarded as a 'despicable employment', 'too mean for a scholar to undertake or desire to stick to many years'.[3] Hence the fluctuating fortunes of schools which might, quite frequently, find that the master had moved on.

A classical education was of little use to poor children who simply wished to learn to read and write in English. Whether the grammar school continued in Lapworth after 1687 or not it was the poor children who concerned the rector of the day, Edward Welchman. In February 1699 he wrote to John Chamberlayne F.R.S.,[4] complaining that he had been trying to get a school for the poor of the parish for nine years, indeed ever since he arrived at Lapworth in 1690. One of the problems was that 'in this country the houses lie very wide, and children are not able to travel so far till they are five or six years old, and then their parents are, through poverty, forced to keep them at home to do something towards getting their bread'. But Welchman obviously persevered, and in February 1701 he wrote again to Chamberlayne 'I hope that now upon my Lord's (the Bishop of Worcester) generous offer of his assistance, it will not be so difficult to erect a school here, as it hath formerly been'. What the Bishop offered is not known and there is no direct evidence that a school was started. However, in 1704 Welchman wrote on the flyleaf of the Parish Register 'I planted the ashes in the churchyard before the school' and the following year '1705 - F Luckman made the arbour towards the school'. From these notes it would seem that a school was started, and that it was close to the church. It may therefore be concluded that it was at this time that a cottage which stood in the churchyard began to be used as the school premises. Welchman's school was not backed or financed by monies from the Charity lands at this time, and there is no record of a charity school at Lapworth in the last full detailed list of charity schools, village by village, made in 1724.[5]

The next hint of a school at Lapworth is in 1755 in a lease of Charity property[6] to Edmund Culcope, 'schoolmaster'. Later, in 1768, when Culcope made his will[7] he was again described as 'schoolmaster', however his name does not appear in the lists of either Oxford or Cambridge University and therefore he would seem not to have had a degree unless it was from a foreign University. The Culcope family had lived in Lapworth since at least the 1660's some members being substantial farmers. Edmund's will and the fact that he was able to lease

* W. Shakespeare *As You Like It*.

Broomfield House[8] and the attached land as his family home suggests that he was a man of means. He was often asked to witness the wills of local people,[9] his signature, large, round and very legible, being found on two-thirds of Lapworth wills made between 1722 and his death. He was also frequently one of the appraisers of probate inventories.

From this evidence it seems probable that he was not the master of the 'village' school, attended by the poorer children, but that he ran a school of his own at Broomfield where the sons of the better off farmers, possibly including some boarders, were given a useful and practical education with some Latin and Greek, but also history, geography and mathematics.

Although no reference to the 'village' school between 1705 and 1783 has been found it probably continued to exist, if intermittently. Certainly many Lapworth people were capable of signing their names, the standard of signature being quite good. Of those acting as witnesses to wills 74% were able to sign and of these 7% were women. The marriage registers show that a third of those who married between 1754 and 1790 could write their names; of interest is the fact that about as many women (43%) as men (56%) were able to sign.

Whatever had been happening in the intervening years by 1783 the 'village' school was operating, on a regular basis, in the cottage schoolroom at the edge of the churchyard. The cottage was one of a row of five which stood

The row of cottages in the churchyard — that nearest the road was used as the school until c.1828. They were demolished in 1892.

at the southern edge of the churchyard below the level of the graves. Four had their doors opening into the graveyard but the fifth, nearest the road, opened into a side lane. This was the one used as the school. The others were occupied by the master, the parish clerk and the sexton. An entry in the Disbursements of the Overseers of the Poor Accounts of 1783-4[10] — 'coals for the school' reveals the school's existence and that its coal and the master's salary were paid for out of the poor's funds. These were raised partly by a levy on the householders of the parish and partly by a receipt of the rents of the Charity lands. In time the school became part of the Charity Estate and was supported by it until quite recent times.

The master of the school from the 1790's (and possibly for a few years before) until about 1840 was John Mortiboys. He was born in Lapworth in 1761 the son of John Mortiboys of Rowington and Elisabeth née Culcope, a kinswoman and possibly a cousin of Edmund Culcope. In addition to his teaching activities for which he was paid £20 0s. 0d., per annum, he was the treasurer of the Charity Estate, a salary of £5 0s. 0d., per annum being paid to him for collecting the rents and keeping the books. He also made occasional journeys on parish business, such as visits to Birmingham to arrange apprenticeships for boys who, almost certainly, had been his pupils.

Under John Mortiboys' guiding hand the school flourished. At times there were more than 60 pupils packed into the small and increasingly dilapidated cottage schoolroom, for all the sons of resident parishioners were eligible for free tuition in reading, writing and ciphering. By 1815 the school was wholly supported by the Charity Estate funds and regarded as a charity school.

Some of the girls of the parish also had the opportunity to learn, for a school, exclusively for poor girls, existed in another cottage, now gone, close to Bear House Farm. The school is first mentioned in 1815 when Dame Brown was paid a salary of £5 0s. 0d., per annum[11] for teaching between 20 and 30 girls, reading, knitting and sewing. This school was also supported by the Charities, the girls being 'clothed every second year and provided with books from time to time'.[12]

By 1824 the school house in the churchyard was in a 'very ruinous condition',[13] and the idea of a new school was mooted. Mr. Thomas Harborne of Solihull, a carpenter and builder of high repute, was asked to draw up plans and on 27 July 1824 these were submitted to the Feoffees who approved them and ordered building to begin.

Despite the speed with which the matter was settled the project had been greatly deliberated, and it was generally agreed by the Feoffees, who included the rector, John Mortiboys and the leading farmers of the parish, that it would be good for the village and a sensible application of the funds.

The present school, new in c.1828, soon after it was built.

The plan of the new school was distinctive, imaginative and attractive. It combined under one roof the school house, the schoolmaster's house and the parish clerk's house. The apartments of the master and clerk, situated at opposite ends of the rectangular building, were each to consist of a parlour, kitchen and brewhouse downstairs, and three bedrooms above. The school was to occupy the centre of the building, and running the whole length of its front there was to be a piazza where the children could play in rainy weather. The whole edifice, of brick with a blue tile roof, was estimated to cost about £800 0s. 0d. Mr. Harborne was to be paid by instalments this being the most satisfactory arrangement for the Charity trustees.

The site chosen for the new school was a plot of land situated beyond the old school cottages and owned by the Charities. Measuring 1 rood 1 perch in size it was occupied by a house and garden let to Thomas Kendall, the parish clerk. The site was appropriated and work began.

When the Charity Commisioners visited Lapworth early in 1826 the building was not completed but Mr. Harborne had received a payment of £196 0s. 0d. By July 1826 the full, and enormous cost of the building £1306 13s. 11d., was made plain, for the balance then due to Harborne was £1110 13s. 11d. Paying it off in instalments of £200 0s. 0d., per annum, plus the interest accrued, took until 1833, the total cost including the wall, gate etc., being £1526 15s. 5d. Of course there were some design faults but the building has stood the test of time and after 160 years of regular and hard use the school is basically unaltered.

The new schoolroom was furnished with desks and forms, Woodward, the carpenter, being asked in April 1826 to provide as many 'as maybe wanted'; 'old material' was to be used in making them.

The first reference to the new school being in full use was in 1828 but it was probably occupied as soon as it was completed. Mr. Mortiboys, who was still the master, despite being 67 years old, found some difficulty in coping with the 'influx of young children'[14] who now wished to attend.

Despite having the new school building where all the children, both boys and girls, might have been expected to attend, the charity school for girls still continued under Mrs. Brown's guidance. The accounts of the school from Lady Day 1828 to Lady Day 1830[15] survive and show that there were, at this time, between 10 and 15 pupils attending, each paying 3d., per week for their tuition. The year was divided into four portions with 10 or 11 school weeks in each, but only a few of the girls attended consistently. Of the 18 girls listed in the accounts none attended every week, but two, Harriot Savage and Mary Staples both managed 85% attendance, and four others — Charlotte Woodcock (aged nine in 1828), Frances Townsend (aged four in 1828), Hannah Viners (aged six in 1828) and Ann Viners (started in 1829 aged four) — attended just over 75% of the time. Attendance was best between March and September and worst between Christmas and March. The weather might not have been the only reason for the difference — ill health, a lack of suitable clothing, a need to help at home and a shortage of money for the fees were probably contributing factors. As far as can be ascertained all the pupils, whose ages ranged from four years to 11 years, were the daughters of farm labourers.

How long Mrs. Brown's school continued is unknown and little is heard of the new school by the church until the 1840's.

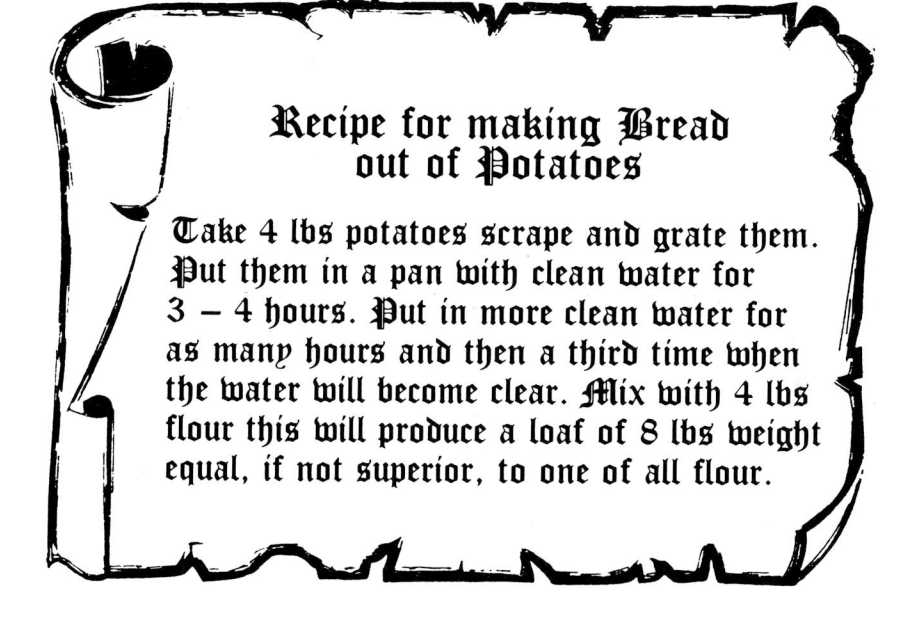

Recipe for making Bread out of Potatoes

Take 4 lbs potatoes scrape and grate them. Put them in a pan with clean water for 3 – 4 hours. Put in more clean water for as many hours and then a third time when the water will become clear. Mix with 4 lbs flour this will produce a loaf of 8 lbs weight equal, if not superior, to one of all flour.

Recipe for making Bread out of Potatoes taken from Aris's Gazette 26 October 1795

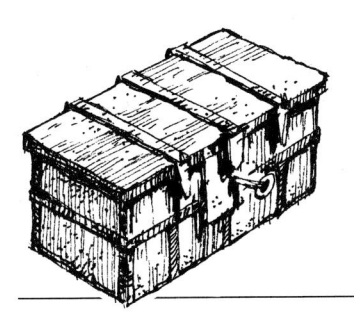

7
... 'TO BE PROVIDED BY THE PARISH'*

Throughout the centuries it has been necessary for some form of local administration to exist to keep order, care for the needs of the people and generally run things. In the medieval period this responsibility fell on the manor, the manorial lord and the manor court overseeing the people's lives. However during the 16th century, as manorial influence declined, the parish began to undertake these various tasks.

An arrangement already existed whereby two or more laymen of the parish, known as Churchwardens, looked after the upkeep of the parish church. This was generally extended until each parish had several lay officers who cared for law and order, the roads, and the poor. Each office was theoretically held for one year, the occupants being elected by all the parishioners at the Annual Easter Meeting. In some places, however, the positions were allocated round the householders of the parish so that each should take his share of the duties. Each office took up a considerable amount of time; records and accounts were supposed to be kept, these being examined and certified at the Easter Meeting. All the posts were unpaid (although expenses were met), and were carried out in addition to a full time job.

There were usually two Churchwardens, a Constable, and depending on the size of the parish, two or more Surveyors of the Highway and Overseers of the Poor. The money needed to maintain the church, to keep up the roads and to support the poor was, in theory, raised by levies from all the householders of the parish as a church rate, highway rate, and poor rate, but this was a troublesome and cumbersome, if correct, way of doing things and in practice many parishes evolved their own system.

At Lapworth although there were Churchwardens who looked after the needs of the church there appears never to have been a church rate levied or any proper official detailed Churchwardens' accounts kept. Instead the general expenses of the church — repairs, service books, bread and wine, bell ropes, cleaning etc., were all met out of the rents of the Charity lands.

At the end of the 17th century a system was in operation whereby the Feoffees of the Charities divided the Charity Estate into three fairly equal parts and these were allocated to the Churchwardens, the Overseers of the Poor, and the Surveyors of the Highway.[1] Each set of officers was left free to make the best of their respective portions, collecting the rents, keeping up the properties and paying their own disbursements as they saw fit. Some sort of rough accounts must have been kept by the Churchwardens but these have not survived. Similarly the accounts for the Highways have also disappeared. Possibly they were retained by one of the officers and never deposited in the parish chest.

It is only by accident that a small portion of the Overseers of the Poor accounts of the late 17th and early 18th century have survived for these were not placed in the chest either, but were found in a decayed state elsewhere.[2] They record payments to the poor for coal, wood, clothes and corn, for pauper burials, baptisms, and shot-gun marriages, and for setting poor children apprentice. Only one year of the accounts is complete.

The rental income from the poor's share of the Charity Estate, £21 6s. 0d., in 1688 and £22 17s. 0d., in 1701,[3] was not enough to meet the cost of the disbursements and a levy of the householders of the parish was necessary to make up the difference. In 1688 £18 4s. 4d., was levied and in 1701 the sum was £27 11s. 3d., the total cost of maintaining the poor of the parish at this period being between £40 0s. 0d., and £50 0s. 0d., per year.

*In a decent bason to be provided by the Parish. Rubric, Book of Common Prayer.

THE LATE 18TH CENTURY

By the end of the 18th century (the period for which a series of years of the parish accounts are extant) the system of running the parish finances had changed somewhat. The only accounts which survive, are those of the Overseer of the Poor.[4] By law these had to be inspected and agreed by the local magistrates, and it was perhaps for this reason that they were properly written up and kept safely. From them it is possible to discover that at this time the whole of the income of the Charity Estate was administered by the Overseer of the Poor. There was only one Overseer but as he had to be approved and sworn in by the magistrate, he was usually a reliable and honest man. Contrary to accepted practice the Lapworth Overseer was paid £10 0s. 0d., per year salary but this was possibly because he was also helping to administer the Charity finances.

The rents were collected half yearly producing an income of £127 11s. 6d., per annum in 1794-5, 1795-6 and £143 4s. 6d., in 1798-9. Out of this the Overseer of the Poor paid the expenses of the Charity Estate and for the upkeep and repair of the Charity property; for the maintenance of the church; and the schoolmaster's salary. The disbursements of the parish officers — the Constable, the Churchwardens and the Surveyor of the Highways — were also met. There are no details of their payments, just the totals expended, £3 0s. 0d., — £6 0s. 0d., per annum by the Churchwardens, £3 0s. 0d., — £7 0s. 0d., per annum by the Constable and £11 0s. 0d., — £22 0s. 0d., per annum by the Surveyors. Any residue went towards the support of the poor. By this period quite large sums were needed to maintain the number of people who were asking for assistance and several levies of the poor rate amongst the householders were necessary each year.

THE CHURCHWARDENS

The Churchwardens' duties were chiefly to ensure that the fabric of the church and the bells were properly maintained, that bread and wine was provided for communion, and that the appropriate furniture and service books were available. They were supposed to report to the Archdeacon any misbehaviour — swearing, adultery, drunkenness — amongst the parishioners and to keep an eye on the parson in case he too should misbehave or neglect his obligations. The cost of the Archdeacon's Visitation in 1798, including no doubt some hospitable refreshment, was £2 3s. 9½d. The names of the Lapworth Churchwardens are not revealed in the records.

THE SURVEYORS OF THE HIGHWAY

Although not a very large parish, Lapworth appointed two Surveyors each year. Mr. Bradbury of Lapworth Lodge Farm and Mr. Field of *The Boot* are named in 1794-5 and Mr. Bradbury, and Mr. Edwards of Arden Hill

Arden Hill Farm

Farm in 1795-6. Keeping the roads in repair was quite expensive although the Stratford Road and the Old Warwick Road were no longer the responsibility of the parish. Since they had been turnpiked in 1726 and 1767 their upkeep was in the hands of the Turnpike Trusts, although the parish almost certainly had to make a financial contribution.

The Surveyors' task was to estimate what materials were needed to keep the roads passable, to purchase them at the most reasonable cost and to arrange a labour force to do the work.

THE CONSTABLE

The Constable at Lapworth in the 1790's was Mr. Green. He seems to have retained the post for a number of years being assisted from time to time by Mr. Grafton, the tanner who lived at the Tan House. The Constable's duty was to maintain law and order within the parish, to report wrongdoers and to apprehend miscreants. Officially, to this end, he was supposed to supervise the ale houses, control the stocks, keep vagrants and undesirable people out of the parish, find lodgings for the poor and apprentice poor children.

It was also the Constable's job to keep the lists of freeholders, of those liable for the militia, and the Land Tax rolls up to date and to lodge them with the correct authority. This involved many journeys to Warwick, Stratford-upon-Avon, Henley-in-Arden etc., visits to the court, the Chief Constable and various magistrates.

THE MILITIA

Each county was obliged by law to raise a certain quota of men for the militia. To make up this number each parish also had a quota. The men were chosen by ballot and had to serve for three years. Those who did not wish to serve could provide a substitute or pay £10 0s. 0d., for one. Small farmers who could not leave their land had their liability discharged by the parish, better off landholders being expected to pay their own charges.

The Constable, in addition to keeping up the lists with the names and details (family size, obligations, dependents etc.) of all the men who were liable to serve, that is all men between 15 and 60 years of age, had to attend the ballot, inform those chosen and find a substitute if necessary. The family of any man who went as substitute had to be kept whilst he was away.

In peace time the men were only away occasionally for short periods of training. But in war time the militia could be embodied for indefinite periods and could move round the country guarding prisoner-of-war camps and garrisoning some coastal positions. From 1793 England was at war with France and the threat of invasion caused a great deal of militia activity from this time until Napoleon's defeat.

At Lapworth a substitute, name unknown, was serving throughout 1794-95 and 96 his wife receiving from the parish 19s. 6d., per quarter for her support. In June 1795 the parish paid for a substitute for the Navy plus expenses, the total being £16 5s. 8d. Whether this was another man, newly chosen, or the first man, not previously paid for, is not clear.

The militia was not the regular army and never fought overseas. It was really an early form of Home Guard intended to protect the country in case of invasion.

THE OVERSEERS OF THE POOR

The position of Overseer of the Poor was the most onerous of the parish offices and must have taken up many hours of the holder's time. The Overseers in the three years under review were 1794-5 Mr. Fetherston of Brome Hall, 1795-6, Mr. William Avery of Malthouse Farm, and 1798-9 Mr. John Smith (home unknown), all responsible farming men respected in the parish.

Since the Tudor period it had been the duty of each parish to support those inhabitants who were in need. Exactly who should be assisted with gifts of money or goods was clearly proscribed — all who were too ill, old or infirm to work were to be supported, as were children who were without parents or in need. All those who were fit enough to work must do so. In practice this meant that a number of women, a few old men, and one or two orphaned children were totally supported by the parish, sometimes for many years. Others were helped occasionally, usually at times of crisis when illness, death, birth or a spell of bad weather caused the normal working pattern of life to be upset. Unmarried mothers and their children were a great problem and a drain on the parish finances. The Overseers went to enormous trouble to try to discover the putative father and arrange a wedding or, if this was not possible, to extract money from him for the child's support. If all failed the child would have to be kept by the parish until it was old enough to be set apprentice.

The Overseers of the Poor accounts for the years Easter 1794 to Easter 1799 reveal the names of 90 people asking for help from the Lapworth Overseers. Just over half this number (50) were in receipt of regularly weekly sums of between 1s. 0d., and 5s. 0d., the majority, widows (16), children (3), unmarried mothers (3), women alone (10), older men (7), and elderly couples (3), being wholly supported by this allowance. Another eight, younger men, also received weekly pay presumably to supplement their wages.

The remaining 40 people received by-pay — small sums and goods given occasionally to those in temporary need.

REGULAR PAY

Widows

All the widows on regular pay received from the Overseers a sum varying between 1s. 0d., and 2s. 6d., per week depending on their circumstances. Those who were able, earned a little by doing small jobs for others — nursing the sick, sewing, or spinning. Widow Kendrick, who received only 1s. 0d., per week, worked at carding wool, (a process necessary before spinning) the parish paying 2s. 0d., for a new pair of 'cards' (carding combs) for her in January 1796. She also worked, in September 1795, with grass; the parish bought her a quantity costing 12s. 0d., which she probably treated, dried, and then plaited into lengths suitable for making hats, bonnets and other straw items.

For widows, paying the rent was a problem, and several of them had it paid by the parish. Widow Garner's rent was 10s. 0d., per year, but Widow Kendrick's was £1 7s. 0d., per annum and Widow Horton's £2 0s. 0d. From time to time most widows had a length of cloth given (usually two ells) to enable them to make themselves new clothes. The odd gift of an extra shilling also helped them.

Every household needed a fire all the year round to cook on, as well as for warmth in winter. In the 1790's coal cost between 10d., and 1s 0d., per cwt. Normally the poor managed to pay for most of their own fuel; firewood and sticks (kids) being gleaned in the woods and hedgerows by the women and children, and a little coal being bought. In the very severe winter of 1794-5 however, money for 'firing' was given to almost every poor household in November and again in February. The following winter was again very cold and 'firing' money was given to many people once more in November and February.

When a widow died it was almost invariably the parish which paid for the funeral. Widow Clover died in June 1798, her coffin cost 10s. 0d., and her shroud and burial expenses, which probably included bread, cheese and ale for the mourners, 19s. 3d.

Women on their own

The status of these 10 poor women, supported by regular pay, is difficult to determine. Some may have been elderly spinsters, others young widows, unmarried mothers or married women whose husbands were away in prison or in the army. The majority received between 1s. 0d., and 2s. 0d., per week from the Overseer with occasional extras such as cloth (at 1s. 9d., per ell) and shoes which cost about 3s 0d., per pair. Sarah Hancox, who had 2s. 0d., per week, had a child for which no extra allowance was made, although a linsey apron and handkerchief (2s. 6d.) were bought for it in December 1798 and its shoes were repaired (10d.). There is no indication anywhere in the records as to whether she was married or where her husband (if she had one) was.

Sarah Bird and Elizabeth Rider, who both received 2s. 6d., per week, are equally mysterious. Sarah received regular pay for 30 weeks as well as clothing in May 1794 (7s. 4d.) and February 1795 (6s. 3d.), and stockings (1s. 4d.) in December 1794. In February 1795 she was taken to Warwick, possibly to the court and later to Nuneaton, the journey costing 10s. 0d. Probably this was her home town for she disappears from the Lapworth records.

Mary Williams may have been elderly, ill, or had children to look after for she received the large sum of 4s. 0d., per week. She also had the occasional odd 1s. 0d., length of cloth, and firing money in 1794-5 and 1795-6. Alice Garner received 1s. 6d., per week with nothing extra of any kind. In May 1794 she ran away; where she went and why is an intriguing and unanswered question, but it caused Mr. Fetherston, the Overseer, great trouble and expense. He, personally spent three days going in search of her, as did Mr. Isaac Mortiboys. Each man charged the parish 15s. 0d., for their journeys, in addition the expenses of fetching her back came to £2 2s. 8d., a total cost of £3 12s. 8d.

Men

Of the 15 men receiving regular pay eight were allowed between 1s. 0d., and 2s. 0d., per week. As far as can be ascertained all were married and some were family men, William Leeson and Edward Woods having seven children each and Thomas Maids six.

Such a small weekly sum must have been intended to supplement the men's wages at a time when corn prices and consequently bread prices were beginning to rise. At this period village labourers earned about 1s. 0d., per day, their income being in the region of 6s. 0d., to 9s. 0d., weekly. If their wives and children did not or could not work this was all they had to live on. Their diet consisted mostly of bread (invariably baked at home) with cheese or a little bacon and occasionally a bit of meat. Tea had overtaken beer as the general drink although some beer and a little milk were consumed. Actual family budgets collected by Sir Frederick Eden in the 1790's[5] show that approximately half of any labourers income was spent on flour or bread; thus any rise in the price of corn was crucial. Men could not keep their families on their wages, however hard they tried, and had to turn to the Overseer for help.

Interestingly the extra money given to the Lapworth men was allowed before the crisis point was reached and was not increased throughout the period, although one had his rent of £1 6s. 0d., paid each year and two had firing money. Most of these men also had occasional help in the form of cloth, sheets or clothes.

Three of the eight men receiving 1s. 0d., - 2s. 0d., weekly had extra problems of illness in the family. John Barnbrook's wife was so ill in March 1795 that the doctor came to see her, which cost the parish 11s. 6d. Barnbrook's house, owned by the Charity Estate, had been extensively renovated, indeed almost rebuilt, during the year and perhaps this had proved too much for his wife's health. However, she recovered and they were able to repay the parish in 1799 by helping with Ann Prior when she was ill.

Thomas Maids' wife was also ill, but unfortunately she died leaving him with six children under 10 years of age. Whilst she was ill the parish helped with extra money, coal, cloth, and someone to nurse her. When she died they paid for the funeral (coffin 9s. 0d., expenses 13s. 6d.). How Maids, who was a thatcher, managed without her is not clear as he seems to have had only cloth (including 9 ells of shirt cloth — 16s.7d.), firing, a spade and small amounts of money to help him support his children.

William Leeson, a Lapworth man, his wife Catherine and six children appear to have only recently returned to Lapworth from Stoneleigh, where they had been living, when they needed assistance. In April 1798, Mrs. Leeson, who was pregnant fell ill and the parish paid Mrs. Greenhill, recently widowed, to nurse her. The child, a girl, was born in July.

John Brown, received 2s. 0d., per week regularly. He also received advice on four occasions from Mrs. Field, the landlady of the *Boot Inn,* the cost being 15s. 6d., — what did she tell him that was worth such a large sum?

Six other men, William Sanders, Thomas Kendall, William Luckman, Thomas Rogers, Samuel Cookes and Richard Jordan received larger weekly sums from the Overseer. Rogers was elderly; he had 2s. 6d., per week plus firing money and the occasional piece of cloth; he died in December 1797.

William Luckman, who was in his 40's, also had 2s. 6d., per week regularly and up to 4s. 0d., per week occasionally. This was probably because his daughter, Elizabeth, was ill. She died in January 1795 and was buried by the parish (cost 15s. 0d.). Luckman and his family had 2s. 6d., per week for a further year plus firing, but by 1798 were able to manage with 1s. 0d., per week for 12 weeks, and then without any help. Luckman's parents had been the tenants of Tudor Farm and Luckman himself had Spring Cottage Farm. When his mother died he took on her tenancy too, but by 1789 he had given up both farms and become a wage labourer.

Samuel Cookes had also been a farmer. From 1775 to 1793 he had land which was part of the Holte estate. In 1781 he took on an additional farm of 27 acres and this was extended by 1785 to 53 acres. He remained the tenant of the whole until 1793 when he gave up farming completely. Cookes had married Sarah in 1777, his first

Windmill Farm, also known as Tapster Farm, the home of Samuel Cookes

wife having died, but there appear to have been no children to help him either financially or with the farms. As a previously substantial ratepayer the parish supported him, allowing him the large sum of 5s. 0d., per week. They also paid Lydia Jordan for making him bed gowns and doing his washing on several occasions during 1798.

Richard Jordan first appears in the records in 1794 when he received 3s. 0d., per week regular pay for his child who may have been ill. The child seems to have survived and later the sum was increased to 4s. 0d., per week and given in Richard's name for the family. The following year he had firing money, lengths of cloth and a bed tick. By 1798 his regular pay had been reduced to 2s. 0d., per week but further lengths of cloth (6 ells of shirt cloth 11s. 6d., and 4 ells of hurden cloth 4s. 4d.) were given and his rent, in arrears two years, was paid. His wife, Lydia, earned a little money in this year by sewing and washing for Samuel Cookes.

Couples

There were three elderly couples who were supported regularly prior to the husband's death. Thomas Greenhill and his wife Elizabeth had 3s. 0d., per week plus firing money and occasional gifts of 1s. 0d. He died in March 1795, his burial was not paid for by the Overseer, but ale for his funeral was, and cost 3s. 0d. His widow was then allowed 1s. 6d., weekly and the occasional pair of shoes. She also did a little nursing, caring for Mrs. Leeson when she was ill.

Edward Yardley and his wife were kept for about nine months at 4s. 0d., per month before he died in January 1799. His funeral cost 37s. 0d., without any food or drink and seems to have taken place in Birmingham. The coffin cost 16s. 0d., which was quite expensive, and his shroud 5s. 0d.; sending someone to Birmingham 'to order the funeral' cost a further 5s. 0d. His friends at Lapworth, who were probably not able to go to Birmingham for the funeral, drank to his memory at the *Royal Oak,* the Overseer paying Mrs. Taylor, the landlady, 2s. 6d., for 'Edward Yardley's eating and drinking'. After his death his wife received only an occasional 1s. 0d., to help her.

Michael and Ann Gilbert had regular pay of 3s. 0d., and later 4s. 0d., per week plus firing money, they also had their rent paid, and a quantity of cloth including 8 ells of hurden (8s. 8d.) and 2 ells of shirt cloth (3s. 10d.). In October 1798 Michael died, his funeral costing £1 2s. 0d., 4s. 6d., of which was spent on bread, cheese and ale. Widow Gilbert was then given 1s. 0d., per week for her own support.

The Children

Mr. John Mortiboys was in Birmingham in 1798 arranging the apprenticeship of two Lapworth boys, Thomas Clees and William Chinn. Clees had a mother but Chinn appears to have been an orphan. He lived at Mr. Woodward's house (Mountford Farm) the parish paying 1s. 6d., per week for his keep. Like most boys William quickly wore out his clothes and £1 5s. 0d., was spent 'on clothing for him' in March 1795; the following year a pair of breeches and stockings for him cost 5s. 6d. Putting him out as an apprentice in Birmingham cost £2 12s. 6d.; he then disappears from the records.

Other children supported by the parish were William and Maria Haycock, twins born in 1790. Their father, William Haycock farmed Lapworth Farm, Spring Lane from 1781 to 1793 when he disappears from the records. What happened to their parents is unknown, but in 1798 the parish began supporting the children. Each was allowed 2s. 0d., per week but where or with whom they lived is not stated. Maria was kept for a whole year and also supplied with cloth (3s. 10d.), a newly made bed gown (and making 3s. 0d.), and a pair of shoes (4s. 0d.). William was supported for only 15 weeks before being apprenticed at eight years of age. He too was given cloth, 2½ ells of shirt cloth, out of which Elizabeth Green made two shirts and was paid 1s. 0d.; another shirt was made by someone else (10d., making, 2d., thread and buttons). His other clothes were mended (2s. 0d.) his indentures signed, and he was provided with a hat (2s. 6d.) and shoes (5s. 6d.). Then he was despatched to his new life leaving his twin sister in Lapworth.

Unmarried Mothers

Those who were most resented, for the financial burden they placed on the parish, were the unmarried mothers. Each case took up a great deal of the Overseer's time, for it was his duty to try and discover who the father was. The girl, who was regarded generally as wicked and a bad lot, was examined by the magistrates and warrants and summons had to be signed and paid for. All this involved much travelling to Warwick and Henley-in-Arden etc., for all concerned.

Three such women were being supported regularly in the 1790's. Elizabeth Lock's child, David, was born in February 1795; she must have been very ill for, most unusually, the doctor was sent for and she was lodged at the *Bell Inn,* the parish paying Samuel Butwell, the landlord £2 19s. 0d., for her board and lodging. Samuel Mander was thought to be the child's father and he was examined by a magistrate at Knowle (cost 10s. 4d.). No wedding resulted but possibly a financial settlement was made to pay for the child's maintenance, for Elizabeth received only 1s. 6d., per week regular pay, not enough to keep herself and the child.

Ann Prior's child Lucy was born in September 1798. For a month previously Ann had been receiving help and 'things' (6s. 8d.) from the Overseer as well as coal, a bed mat and cord, a pair of sheets, a bed tick, two blankets and mutton (2lb. — 9d.). On the 18th September, William Heritage was paid 6d., to fetch the doctor, probably from Knowle. The midwife also came and was paid 5s. 0d., for attending. Later a kettle, butter (¾lb. — 7½d.) more mutton (9¼lb.), extra fuel, ale and beer were provided to help her get her strength back. Ann Prior shared accommodation with Sarah Collit, another unmarried mother supported by the parish. Sarah's baby had been born in March 1798 and for a time Sarah looked after Ann, being given a pair of shoes for doing so. Perhaps looking after two babies and a sick girl was too much for Collit, and Sarah Barnbrook was sent to look after Ann Prior. Sarah Barnbrook nursed her through October, November and December, when the child was at last baptised. The Barnbrooks very much involved themselves with Ann, Sarah made her a frock, John went twice to Henley-in-Arden on her account and they looked after the baby for a short time. A petticoat, a frock, blue linen, calico, and flannel were provided for it at various times, but it did not thrive and died in September 1799 when just about one year old.

BY-PAY

The people who asked for the Overseer's help occasionally, numbered 40 and fell into much the same categories as those assisted regularly.

Most of the women on their own asked for help only with fuel, clothing or when illness or some crisis struck. In March 1796 Mary Brown received sums equalling 20s. 6d., in the short period of 16 days, an amount which in normal circumstances would have kept her for at least three months. There is no further reference to her in the poor records but the Parish Register shows that the following December she married John Heath of Claverdon.

Each parish was responsible for its own people. A man born in Lapworth could live and work elsewhere but if he were ill, in need or liable to be a financial drain on that parish, he would be either sent back to Lapworth or the Lapworth Overseer would be expected to send money for his support. Richard Clees appears to have been taken ill and died at Halesowen in January 1795. The Lapworth Overseer paid the bill for looking after him and for his burial, the total being the enormous sum of £8 17s. 6d. He also paid the expenses of Mr. Gosling (14s. 2d.), probably a Halesowen man. Clees' wife and son, Thomas, were subsequently supported by the parish, but a year after his father's death the boy was apprenticed, thus relieving the parish of the expense of keeping him. The schoolmaster made the arrangements visiting Birmingham twice. The parish paid £3 3s. 0d., consideration money; the indentures, signing them and the visits costing another 10s. 2d.

Six of the 28 men who asked for by-pay asked only for 'firing', due to the very cold weather. Most received 2s. 6d., or 2s. 9d., each November and a little less in February. Twelve other men had small sums occasionally and some had firing money. A further 10 men had more expensive items — four had cloth, clothes or their rent paid. Four were involved with summons, orders and visits to the magistrates, no reasons being revealed. George Smith, a small farmer who lived at what is now Bredon House, had his Land Tax of 17s. 4d., paid twice. He received no other financial help despite having 15 children. William Shaw and his family were obviously not Lapworth people and were considered to be a potential financial burden on the parish. After a visit to the magistrate at Henley-in-Arden, an order was issued and Shaw, with his family, was removed to their parish of origin.

ADMINISTRATION

In addition to the money given out to the poor the Overseers spent quite a lot on administration. Each time a levy was made round the householders there were lists to be checked and the levy had to be signed. This might cost anything between 6d., and 5s. 0d. Paper and a variety of notebooks were purchased each year, usually at 1s. 0d., per time.

Letters were received from time to time and before the advent of the Penny post these were paid for by the recipient. The cheapest letter received by the Overseer cost 8½d., the dearest 1s. 8d.

The many visits made, chiefly to Warwick, but also to Wootton Wawen, Henley-in-Arden, Birmingham, Alcester and Wellesbourne cost about 2s. 6d., per journey, plus expenses. The latter usually included some eating and drinking which might cost 1s. 6d. The journeys were usually to the court or to the homes of magistrates to collect warrants, summons, orders and to have them signed. Each one had to be paid for at about 2s. 0d., per signing. Occasionally a lawyer was consulted, the cheapest charging about 3s. 6d., per visit. When children were apprenticed their indentures had to be paid for (1s. 2d.), 'filled up' (4s. 0d.), and signed (2s. 0d.). The consideration money paid by the parish to the master was usually £3 3s. 0d., but might sometimes be £4 4s. 0d. This was on top of the cost of the visits, discussions and the ale consumed whilst making the arrangements.

Almost every meeting which was held on any subject was accompanied by the drinking of ale. A bottle at this period cost 3s. 0d., or 3s. 4d., and must have contained about two gallons. Usually one bottle, but sometimes two was provided at every meeting.

The cloth and shoes given to some of the poor were bought in bulk by the Overseer and then given out. As much as 35¾ ells of cloth were bought at one time at 1s. 9d., per ell, the usual amount given to one person being 2½ ells. Sheeting cost 1s. 2d., per ell and hurden between 1s. 0d., and 1s. 3d., per ell. Flannel was bought by the yard and cost about 1s. 0d. Shoes were bought from two local shoemakers Mr. Fowler and Mr. Sanders about twice a year. As people walked everywhere over rough, and often wet, unmetalled roads the shoes were stout, serviceable, but not a very exact fit and cost 3s. 0d., to 4s. 0d., per pair.

The cost of transporting coal for the poor was paid for by the parish and also the turnpike fee. However, very little coal was given away, perhaps having got it to Lapworth the Overseer sold it to the poor who paid for it with their firing money.

Four times a year the Overseer paid £7 4s. 0d., the charge of the County Rate. Each parish paid its share which was used for the maintenance of the major bridges in the county and for the prisons.

At Easter each year the accounts were audited, signed and approved by two magistrates and five or six ratepayers. This too had to be paid for and 'auditing the accounts' cost about 10s. 0d., per annum.

Hole House Farm

Lapworth 1801-onwards
8
'MEMORANDA PAROCHIALA'

1801-25

After the calamitous weather and poor harvests of the previous six or seven years 1801 was a golden year; there was a fine summer and an excellent and abundant harvest. Parson Woodforde started his harvest on 8 August; he finished on 31 August and recorded in his diary 'cut, dried and in Barn without any rain at all. Never known finer Weather during any Harvest'.[1] Even so the price of wheat did not fall, instead it reached an all time peak of 119s. 6d., per quarter.

Fortunately the following summer (1802) after a cold late spring, was also fine and the harvest good; as a result corn prices fell rapidly to 69s. 10d., per quarter. Five reasonable years followed, the harvests were moderate, wheat prices fluctuating between 59s. 0d., and 90s. 0d., per quarter. The latter was just about twice the average price pre-war. In 1808 the common land at Kingswood was enclosed and divided up between the manor tenants. The weather was cold and the summer wet, the first bad year in a run of five, the price of wheat reaching an astronomical 126s. 6d., per quarter in 1812. During these years there were again food riots in some towns including Birmingham. In 1813 and 1815 the summers were fine, the harvest good, wheat prices tumbling to 65s. 7d., per quarter.

In March 1801 the first ever official census of population was taken. At Lapworth, as elsewhere in the country, heads only were counted, no names or personal details being recorded; there were 575 people resident in the parish at the time,[2] including no doubt the navvies who were digging out the Stratford Canal. When the following year the result of the census was announced in the newspapers William Johns copied them into his note book — 'in Birmingham 69,384 inhabitants, in Coventry 15,988 inhabitants'; 'the grand total of persons' in England and Wales being '9,343,578 of which 1,410 were convicts'.

Throughout the spring and summer of 1801 invasion by the French was thought to be imminent and those living near the coast made great preparations to resist. However the crisis passed and in October peace was declared. In London there was much rejoicing and the mail coaches, travelling to the provinces were decorated with laurel leaves and banners proclaiming 'Peace with France'. In March 1802 the peace was confirmed at Amiens; in April William Pitt's hated Income Tax was abolished and on 1 June Thanksgiving services were held almost everywhere.

After years of having surveyors about the parish and two years of intense work by the navvies the three mile stretch of the Stratford Canal from Hockley Heath to Kingswood was completed in May 1802, making trade with Worcestershire, Birmingham and the Black Country much easier.

Unhappily the peace with France was short lived, in April 1803 war broke out again, fear of invasion was once more renewed and despite Nelson's victory at Trafalgar in 1805 it was 1815 before Napoleon was finally defeated.

In 1806 Rev. Pye decided to leave Lapworth and live in Cirencester where he had been appointed vicar. Possibly Lapworth was a little quiet for his wife and growing family. He kept his post as rector, returning frequently, but his parish duties were undertaken by a new curate the Rev. James Way, a native of Oxfordshire.

James Way served the parish for 10 years until his early death in November 1816 aged 41.[3] His infant son James, had died in June 1809 and his wife Elizabeth Garret Ross, who was born in Antigua, the following May. A white marble memorial tablet in the church[4] erected by their daughter and only surviving child reveals that they had three sons all of whom died when babies.

During his years in charge of the Registers. Rev. Way noted any deaths which were accidental. There were six in the parish between 1808 and 1811: two men were drowned in the canal in 1808, John Dolton of Tanworth died of intoxication in 1809 and the same year a boy, Joseph Woods, was killed by the bursting of a gun barrel. The following year William Mortiboys, a boy from Nuthurst and possibly about three years old was scalded to death. Another child, Robert Hassal, 'an infant' was burned to death in 1811. The necessity to cook and heat water over an open fire and to light the house by candles made such events an ever present threat.

The second decennial census was taken in May 1811, Mr. Green who was the Constable in the 1790's being paid £1 5s. 5d., for going round the parish counting the people. There were 517[5] a drop of 58 since 1801. In 1811 the practice of giving the age of death in the Parish Register was begun. The number of deaths amongst children under 10 years was always high (in the decade 1811-20 27% of the total) but in 1811 42% of those dying were children under 10 years of age, 21% being under one year and 16% under five years.

In 1812 the navvies were back in the parish working on the next section of the Stratford canal from Kingswood to Wootton Wawen.

Three years later in 1815, about the time the canal was being dug from Wootton Wawen to Stratford, the first moves were being made towards enclosing the common land in Rowington, including Bushwood Common. A small portion, about 22½ acres, lay within Lapworth parish and this was divided up and allocated in various ways. The rector of Lapworth the Rev. Pye, was allotted 3¼ acres of land in lieu of lost tithes and those Lapworth farmers who lived at the edge of the Common at Bushwood Grange, Bushwood Common Farm, High Chimneys and Meadow Hill Farm, were each given allotments in lieu of lost amenities, equalling about 10 acres between them. Some of these men also bought small areas of land — thin slips beside the roads and odd corners adjoining their farms. These, with other larger areas elsewhere were sold by the Enclosure Commissioner to defray the cost of obtaining and implementing the Enclosure Act,[6] which was not concluded until 1824.

At last, in June 1815, with a dramatic victory at Waterloo, the war with France was ended. The soldiers, some of whom had been away for years were carried home to England and demobilized. Many had their 'wives' and children with them, or following after; some of these alliances were formed abroad but a number of wives had accompanied their husbands to war not knowing otherwise if they would ever meet again. Some women were widowed more than once, marrying again if their husbands were killed. At the war's end there were many women and children travelling in Europe, usually in groups, towards the ports; all were carried home to England. On arrival the discharged soldiers and sailors, the women and children were given passes to their home villages and towns; this gave the right to travel through the country without being considered to be vagrants. There were no pensions or gratuities but the passes permitted them to obtain assistance from the officers of any parish they passed through.

From 8 May 1816 until August 1817, when the last man 'ill and in Distress' was given 1s. 0d., a continuous stream of travellers — men, women and children — passed through Lapworth, presumably following the Stratford Road, on their way home from the ports. Altogether 326 persons were helped, the total cost to the parish being £4 15s. 6d.,[7] a very reasonable sum. The travellers were more of a time consuming nuisance than an expense for they were given only a few pence each — usually 2d., or 3d., — but it varied, one person alone might receive 6d., yet a man, his wife and four children might get only 1s. 0d. The first travellers to pass through Lapworth were men alone or in a group for they could progress fairly quickly to their destination. In July came the first woman alone and the first married couple; then the first woman alone with two children. In August married couples with children passed through, and more women alone with children. Although men travelled together there is no record of women together, even when they had children to care for. The largest numbers arrived in November and December 1816 and February 1817. In April 1817 there was only one man and after that a few stragglers. When the figures are broken down there were 92 men alone or in groups, 11 women alone, 24 couples, 17 couples with 43 children, 27 women with 62 children, two men with three children and 'four persons'.

In the decade 1816-25 there were five hot and sunny summers and five poor ones. That of 1816, following a severe winter, was particularly wet. Despite the five favourable years only three harvests were described as good (1818 and 1820) or abundant (1822), the rest being below average or poor. Although Peace had brought an immediate fall in prices, including food, there were still shortages in poor harvest years and renewed riots. For Peace also brought unemployment, a fall in profits and wages as the war boom ended and markets shrank. What William Cobbet called 'the false and bloated prosperity'[8] of the war years was over and a post-war depression replaced it.

On the death of James Way a new curate, the Rev. George Childe, was appointed to care for the parish.[9] Little is known of him but during his time at Lapworth he and his wife, Mary Ann, had three children; Harry, and the twins Robert and Georgina; Georgina lived only a year dying in May 1820. The family left Lapworth in

1826 but Mrs. Childe was buried at St. Mary's when she died in 1834 aged 46.

In 1820, after a reign of 59 years, George III died. The parish purchased a black cloth to hang over the pulpit in the church for, what seems an exorbitant price, £21 11s. 6d. A year previously they had engaged Isaac Brown to paint the Royal Arms on a board which was to hang in the church. The cost, which also included gilding the clock face, was £32 6s. 7. This board still exists and now hangs in the north aisle.

On 28 May 1821 the census was again taken, there being 622 people in the parish[10] an increase of 20%.

An enlargement of the churchyard, by closing and taking in the lane which previously ran round the east side of the church, was carried out in 1825. The cost of the work was £21 12s. 0d., and the expenses with regard to the consecration were £26 12s. 0d., plus other incidental charges which included giving the bell ringers and the singers £1 0s. 0d., for their part in the service.

1826-1850

In 1826 the Charity Commissioners visited Lapworth; they found the new school partially completed and considered that the local farmers were over the worst of the post-war depression.[11] In the same year a new curate, the Rev. Donald Cameron, arrived in the parish at the invitation of Mr. Pye. During their years in Lapworth, Cameron and his wife Frances had two children, Donald and Letitia. They left in 1838, the Rev. J. Wilding taking on the curacy; he stayed about a year until the next rector, Rev. George Tyndall, was inducted, Mr. Pye having died in March 1838.[12]

Cameron, like James Way, noted accidental deaths in the Parish Register and the Rev. Tyndall continued the habit. In the 20 years 1827-46 there were 15 such deaths in the parish. The cause of six of them is not stated, but of the rest, one death was caused by a stage coach accident; two children, aged six and four years, were burnt to death in separate incidents, and there were six individual cases of death by drowning in the canal. Amongst the latter were an elderly man, an old woman and four boys aged 12-15 years.

In the five years 1826-31 there were three good summers but only one excellent harvest, in 1827; 1826 was so hot and dry that there was drought; 1828 and 29 were wet with poor harvests and 1830 was changeable.

1830 saw the death of that most flamboyant of Princes and lampooned of Kings, George IV. The kingdom he left to his brother, William IV, was again torn by riots. This time an 'agricultural rebellion' in which farm workers, particularly in the southern and eastern counties, rose in revolt against their low wages, hunger, and living conditions generally, and against the introduction of threshing machines in particular. The widespread adoption of these machines took away the worker's traditional winter work of threshing by beating out the grain with a flail.[13] During the riots ricks were burned and the machines wrecked by men demanding a wage of 12s. 0d., a week; since the rapid fall of prices at the end of the war the average pay of farm workers generally was 9s. 0d., per week.[14]

In May 1831 a new census was taken, the population of the parish being 656 persons,[15] a rise of 5% since 1821. Thomas Johns recorded in his notebook that there were 355 males and 301 females in the village. In October of that year a 'new disease' Asiatic Cholera arrived in England from the east. The virus, which particularly struck those living in low, marshy and unclean places, spread throughout England in 1832. There was national consternation and fear for the disease struck suddenly; death was not inevitable but might occur after about 12 hours.[16] Fortunately Warwickshire was not badly affected, the county had 133 cholera deaths, the most being in Nuneaton (56), Coleshill (32) and Birmingham (21). The worst outbreak was at Bilston in Staffordshire where 742 people died in seven weeks.[17] There were some cases in 1833 but generally the disease was thought to have left England and moved south to the other parts of Europe.

The weather during the 1830's was, on the whole, good with five fine warm summers. There were three plentiful harvests plus two good and three moderate ones, wheat prices falling to 39s. 4d., per quarter in 1835 after two excellent years and rising to 70s. 8d., per quarter in 1839 after two poor harvests. There were two outstanding winters in the decade, that of 1835-6 when it snowed a great deal, drifts of 50 ft. disrupting communications and 1837-8 when severe frosts lasting two months killed the evergreens and the temperature reached $-14°F$ in London — the lowest recorded in the city during the 19th century.

In 1837 the young Princess Victoria, who is reputed to have stayed one night at *Hockley House* when it was an inn, became Queen. The following year the Tithe Commissioner and his assistants arrived in Lapworth to survey all the land and start work on formulating a new scheme of tithe payments to the rector.

1838 was another year of illness for the children of the parish, 50% of the deaths being amongst the under fives; five babies of less than 10 months dying between 15 April and 29 July. Expert opinion has suggested that it was a childhood ailment, probably whooping cough which killed them. The records show that 1844 was also a bad year for the children of the parish, 45% of people dying being under 10 years, but the deaths were spread through the year with no indication of an epidemic. The age of death figures reveal that a surprisingly large number of people lived to be over 80 years of age; 10% of those dying in the 40 years 1811-50 being over 80 years and a further 2% being over 90 years.

On 7 June 1841 another census was taken. For the first time names, ages to the nearest five years, and some occupations were recorded. There were 729 people in Lapworth, 370 males, 330 females and 29 not specified, they occupied 141 houses another 10 houses being empty.[18]

The summers during the 1840's were generally good — there were seven which were fine and sunny (1844 being a drought year) and seven very good harvests. In several years there were very hot spells leading to storms, and the resulting humid atmosphere encouraged potato blight. In Ireland the blight ruined the crop and led to famine there in 1846.[19] Foot and mouth disease in cattle was also prevalent but on the whole the 1830's and the 1840's to 1848 were reasonable years for farmers. In 1846 the Corn Laws were repealed after considerable campaigning against them and from 1848 Britain was open to all imports from abroad. The effect was a fall in grain prices and a short depression lasting until 1852, especially amongst wheat growers, but it was 30 years before the full impact was felt.

The newest form of transport was the railway which was spreading its lines across the land. The Birmingham and Oxford Junction Railway proposed a route between the two towns which passed through Lapworth and Rowington. By August 1848, when the Great Western Railway absorbed the Birmingham and Oxford, the route was laid out and work had probably begun.

In February 1848 the Rev. Tyndall died and was succeeded by the Rev. Charles A. St.J. Mildmay who had the useful habit of writing notes on parish events in the register. In his notes he refers to cholera which had returned to England in the autumn of 1848 and was again sweeping through the country. There were 293 cholera deaths in Warwickshire, 202 of them being in Coventry. Bilston again suffered very badly; 1365 people in the area (including also Wolverhampton, Tipton and Sedgley) dying.[20] A collection was taken in Lapworth to help the Bilston people £11 0s. 6d., being raised. By November 1849 the cholera was thought to have once more left England and a national day of General Thanksgiving was held. Lapworth church was crowded at both the morning and the evening services 'especially with men'.[21]

Within the parish in 1849 typhus was the problem, a number of people dying of it. In the autumn measles was prevalent but fortunately not serious. The following year a petition to the Queen was taken round the parish; it was against 'Papal aggression'. The nation, already disturbed at the rise in numbers and influence of the Roman Catholics, was incensed when the Pope set up Bishops in England. The rector notes that the petition was 'almost unanimously signed by the whole body of the parishioners'[22]

Kingswood Stores and Post Office, pre-1912

9

'HORSES TO BE UNHITCHED'*

Just when the golden age of coaching was about to begin, a new form of transport, for goods rather than people, was gaining popularity with Midland entrepreneurs — the canal. Birmingham, the largest commercial town in the area, was growing rapidly and with increasing prosperity, but its inland position and distance from navigable rivers was a disadvantage, thus a company was formed and the Birmingham Canal Act obtained in 1768.

The success and usefulness of the Birmingham Canal Company stimulated other companies to obtain Acts, and further canals followed; it was a period of canal mania. By the end of the century a network of waterways covered the area making it possible to send Birmingham goods, by canal, to many parts of the country. Significantly by 1770 coal could be brought from the South Staffordshire coalfields and sold in Birmingham at 7s. 0d., per ton, a little more than half the price before the canal was built.

During the great period of expansion, when schemes for new canals and branches were continually being proposed, the Birmingham Canal Company opposed any scheme to divert traffic from travelling the greatest possible distance over its canals and earning the maximum toll. It bought up any rival company which suggested such a thing, or forced it to pay heavy compensation in tolls. Yet nothing was done to improve its own routes which were now outdated, narrow, shallow, tortuous, and inadequate for the weight of traffic using them.

One suggestion, made by the Dudley Canal Company, was to link Stratford-upon-Avon with Birmingham and the Black Country. They envisaged mutual advantages for farmers and industrialists; coal from the Dudley area, firebricks, and salt would travel south, and agricultural produce, grain, and limestone would be carried back. An Act was passed in 1793 authorising the construction of such a canal, and a survey, the first of many, was made by John Snape. He proposed a route from a junction with the Worcester and Birmingham Canal (then unfinished) at Kings Norton through to Stratford-upon-Avon via Hockley Heath. From Hockley Heath the proposed canal would follow the Old Warwick Road for a short way, then turn southwards, passing near to the church, and run parallel with Tapster Lane joining the valley of a little tributary of the Alne at Preston Bagot. This plan was never put into operation and indeed there were several abortive schemes before a final line was agreed.[1]

At the same time the Birmingham Canal Company, furious at finding its canals by-passed by the scheme, promoted the Warwick and Birmingham Canal to provide a more direct route for water traffic from Birmingham to London. An Act authorising the building of this waterway was passed, also in 1793, and the canal, which just touches Lapworth parish at Kingswood, was completed in 1799.

Meanwhile capital of £120,000[2] was raised for the Stratford-upon-Avon Canal from landowners and farmers along the route, outside interested parties and Stratford businessmen, who were keen to see their town drawn into the canal system. The local shareholders hoped to profit by building wharves, re-selling coal and having outlets for their agricultural products. Work, under the direction of engineer Josiah Clowes,[3] began in 1793 at the northern end, and by May 1796 the canal had reached Hockley Heath. Although no major engineering work had been done on the stretch, the money was exhausted.

A further Act was passed in 1799 authorising another £50,000 to be raised and the route of the canal was again changed to make it pass through the village of Lapworth and join the Warwick-Birmingham Canal by a link at Kingswood. Fresh surveys were made and a new engineer, Samuel Parker, continued the work in 1800. The two miles, six furlongs, three chains and 90 links of the canal,[4] including locks, joining Hockley Heath with the Warwick-Birmingham Canal at Kingswood was completed by May 1802.

One of the unwritten rules of the canal was that horses were unhitched at the locks.

Having got this far the Stratford-upon-Avon Canal Company showed a marked disinclination to go further. There were many discussions, arguments and new ideas, none of which were acted upon and the people of Stratford began to wonder if they would ever have a canal; but for William James it might indeed have remained a dream. James, who became known as the 'Father of the Railway',[5] had a vision of Stratford being an important transport centre, a junction for canal, river (he had interests in the Upper Avon Navigation), and rail. He planned that it was to be the northern terminus of his proposed railway to Paddington with branches to Coventry and Cheltenham.

Of course more money was needed to complete the canal and in 1809, under a new Act, 2,000 new shares were offered at £30 0s. 0., each.[6] Two gentlemen took up 100 and 105 shares each, the rest being acquired in much smaller numbers. The Earl of Abergavenny and James West of Alscott Park, near Stratford, had 30 shares each and Robert Mander of Irelands Farm, Lapworth had 10 shares. There was no rush to buy and only 1452 shares had been taken up by February 1810.

This reluctance to speculate could have been due to the shares being subject to a call. The Stratford-upon-Avon Canal shares, offered in 1793 at £100 0s. 0d., each,[7] had by 1802 had £150 0s. 0d., called on them, the shareholders having to find the extra money. A great many of the shareholders were yeoman farmers and minor gentry having a flutter, with five or 10 shares, in the latest fashionable craze, and they could not afford to lose or pay out more. Some who did not sell out quickly enough got their fingers burnt. One way out, used by a few, was to refuse delivery of the letter from the Canal Company asking for more money. At that time the postage was paid by the addressee on receipt, if he refused to pay the letter was not delivered.[8]

The southern section of the Stratford-upon-Avon Canal is 13 miles long and has 36 locks between Kingswood and the Avon. Work began in 1812 and was completed to Wootton Wawen in 1813. Another £30,000 had to be raised in 1814 plus £35,000 more in 1815, but finally the canal was opened all the way through to Stratford in June 1816.

This later section had many features not found in the northern part notably the cast iron acqueduct at Wootton Wawen, the unusual barrel roofed lock houses and the over bridges with a gap for the tow lines. The barrel roofed houses of which there are three within Lapworth were designed by the engineer Josiah Clowes.[9] They were intended to combine a degree of 'durability with economy' using the techniques of the canal builder. Erecting brick walls was easy, for bricklayers were part of the canal building team, but the roof posed a problem. It was solved by building four brick walls enclosing a space 14 ft. by 35 ft. and laying iron bars along the top of the brickwork. These were joined at the corners to make a flat rectangle which was strengthened by cross bars. The brickwork was then continued upwards, curving over to form a roof as when constructing a tunnel or bridge. From above, the roofs looked like tunnels and the houses added an unusual and attractive feature to the landscape.

The split bridges were a new answer to the old problem of crossing the canal, without casting off the tow line, when the towpath changed sides. The split bridges were built of iron, in two sections, so that the tow line could pass through the slot between them; both time and energy were saved by their use.

Earlswood Lakes,[10] which supply the whole of the Stratford-upon-Avon Canal with water, were authorised in 1815. The Warwick and Birmingham Canal won the title to a lock full of water from the Stratford Canal for every boat passing through Kingswood junction, and the falling lock on the connecting branch was built for this reason. The stop lock at the Kings Norton junction is, unusually, fitted with guillotine gates because the fall might be in either direction depending on the level of the two canals.

Competition between the Birmingham-Warwick Canal and the Stratford-upon-Avon Canal was very intense especially in the coal carrying business. At one time the Stratford Canal lowered its rates to 7¾d., per ton and coal was sold in Stratford for 10d., per hundredweight. Despite the dilution of business, trade on the Stratford Canal flourished for about 40 years. At the height of canal prosperity a Stratford trader, Richard Greaves, noted that 50,000 tons of coal arrived at Stratford, 16,000 tons of limestone being sent to Birmingham; 181,700 tons of merchandise giving receipts of over £13,000 in 1838.

In 1838 the first railway route between Birmingham and London opened and by the 1840's plans were afoot to spread the network. The railway companies, anxious to supercede the canals as freight carriers as soon as possible, bought out the canal shareholders, if they could, intending to run the canals down and transfer the trade to the railways.

Despite the lively trade which the Stratford-upon-Avon Canal had enjoyed since its opening the shareholders had never had a very good deal. In 1825[11] the Company's £75 0s. 0d., shares were quoted at £16 10s. 0d., and about 1830 they were paying a dividend of only 1½%. In 1846[12] the Oxford, Worcester & Wolverhampton Railway Company offered £173,322 for the Stratford-upon-Avon Canal Company and the shareholders were happy to sell.

The Warwick Canal by contrast remained independent. It had been cheaper to build and was always less trouble and more successful than the Stratford Canal. In the 1830's when the Stratford Canal Company shares were quoted at 41s 0.,[13] each the Warwick and Birmingham Canal Company shares were quoted at 270s. 0d., each.

HOCKLEY HEATH

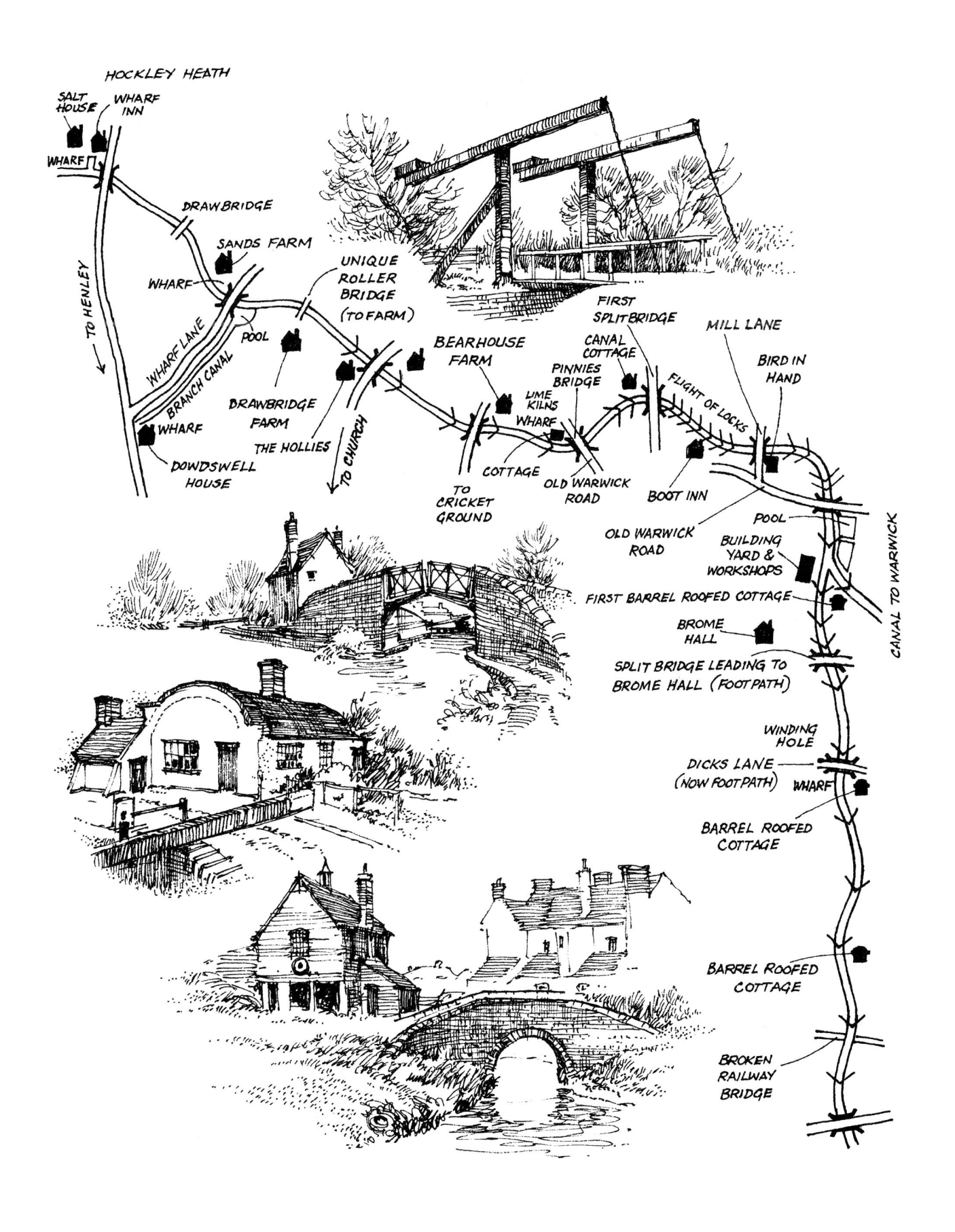

SALT HOUSE
WHARF INN
WHARF
TO HENLEY
DRAWBRIDGE
SANDS FARM
WHARF
WHARF LANE
BRANCH CANAL
POOL
UNIQUE ROLLER BRIDGE (TO FARM)
DRAWBRIDGE FARM
THE HOLLIES
WHARF
DOWDSWELL HOUSE
BEARHOUSE FARM
TO CHURCH
TO CRICKET GROUND
COTTAGE
LIME KILNS
WHARF
PINNIES BRIDGE
CANAL COTTAGE
FIRST SPLIT BRIDGE
MILL LANE
BIRD IN HAND
OLD WARWICK ROAD
BOOT INN
FLIGHT OF LOCKS
OLD WARWICK ROAD
POOL
BUILDING YARD & WORKSHOPS
FIRST BARREL ROOFED COTTAGE
BROME HALL
SPLIT BRIDGE LEADING TO BROME HALL (FOOTPATH)
CANAL TO WARWICK
WINDING HOLE
DICKS LANE (NOW FOOTPATH)
WHARF
BARREL ROOFED COTTAGE
BARREL ROOFED COTTAGE
BROKEN RAILWAY BRIDGE

SCALE : 1 MILE

SALT HOUSE, HOCKLEY HEATH

SPLIT BRIDGE AND WORKSHOPS, LAPWORTH

ROLLING LIFT BRIDGE

DETAIL OF MECHANISM

LOCK 8, LAPWORTH

The canals acquired by the railway companies became an embarrassment to them. They were obliged by statute to maintain them and many were kept navigable which in private hands would have been let go. Under railway ownership the Stratford Canal continued to operate as before but as the century progressed, some retrenchment in staff was made.

THE CANAL MEN

The coming of the canal brought new occupations to Lapworth, various lock-keepers, canal carpenters and bricklayers, toll-collectors, clerks, boatmen and the canal agent all finding work along the canal and making their homes nearby. Unfortunately it is not until the census of 1841[14] that records exist giving the names and actual occupations of the canal employees. By this date the heyday of the canal was almost past, the threat of the railway looming large on the horizon.

In 1841 the canal agent or manager was John Kershaw. He lived in a Georgian house (now called Bridge House) beside the canal where, until the waterway was completed to Stratford, the 'Navigation Office', toll clerk, etc., had also been situated. It was Kershaw's job to oversee the whole length of the Stratford-upon-Avon Canal, ensuring that it was properly maintained by the engineer and lengthsmen (maintenance men). He was also expected to promote the business side by employing efficient and honest toll-collectors, lock-keepers and clerks.

Next in status to the agent was the toll-collector who checked the boat cargo, gauged the boats and collected the toll. The details of each boat using the canal, the tonnage carried at the depths marked on the boat's hull, were recorded in an official book which was issued to all toll offices. To gauge a boat the toll-collector simply checked the boat's freeboard, or area above the water line, against the book, worked out the toll which depended on the commodity, perhaps 1½d., per ton per mile for coal[15] and 2d., per ton per mile for other goods, and collected the money. Such men were picked for their honesty and were usually well paid, £70 0s. 0d., per annum plus a house being about average in 1840.[16] Charles Allen, described as a 'writing clerk' was probably the toll-collector for the Lapworth stretch of the canal. He lived in a quite large house overlooking the Kingswood junction pool and was possibly the son of Jacob Allen, one of the lock-keepers.

There were five lock-keepers at Lapworth in 1841 — Richard Smith, James Robinson, William Howse, Jacob Allen and Richard Rogers, — all except Rogers being over 45 years of age. There were seven buildings called lock-houses between Hockley Heath and Lowsonford but only four were then occupied by lock-keepers, and it is possible that some sort of rationalization to cut down on staff was already taking place. Richard Soley, the canal carpenter, occupied the lock-house in the middle of Kingswood Basin and Edward Bayliss, the canal carpenter, the lock-house behind the *Boot Inn*. The long flight of locks nearby was managed by lock-keeper James Robinson, who lived in a small cottage at the top of the flight.

Lock-keepers, usually one to every flight of locks, did not work the locks, (the boatmen did that) but they might help, in the interest of speed, when the canal was very busy. The lock-keepers's job was to ensure that the boatmen did not damage the lock-gates or structure, to enforce the bye-laws, to make sure the tow-horses were unhitched at the locks, that they were properly shod and not breaking up the tow-path; and to make certain that the water, always in short supply, was not wasted. He had also to try and stop quarrelling about who should be first to use the locks. The lock-keepers were forbidden to trade with the boatmen and were consequently well paid, 20s. 0d., per week, plus a house and garden, being the average wage in the 1840's.

Altogether there were 10 canal employees and their families living and working in Lapworth in the 1840's and 1850's. In later decades this was reduced to seven or eight employees, one or two of the craftsmen apparently doubling as lock-keepers. In 1871 and 1881[17] the five lock-keepers of 1841 had been reduced to two, one living in the cottage at the top of the long flight of locks behind the *Boot Inn* and the other beside Walter's locks (No. 28) shortly before Lowsonford.

Originally the boatmen and their families lived ashore in canal side cottages but after the coming of the railway, pressures to keep the boats continually working forced many families to live wholly aboard. Of the 10 boats tied up at Lapworth on census night 1861[18] five were the permanent homes of the families aboard them.

To provide the boatmen with beer and a place to relax there were numerous canal side inns. These also sold necessities for the boats, such as rope, and groceries and food for the boatmen's families. Only one pub or beerhouse appears to have opened in Lapworth to serve the canal people and that was the *Bird in Hand*. It stood beside the canal bridge at the bottom of Mill Lane and in 1841 was simply a grocer's shop. By 1861 it had become the *Bird in Hand* beerhouse although still providing provisions of all kinds.

The purpose of the canal was, of course, the transportation of goods and here and there along its route were wharves where commodities needed, or for sale by, the local community could be set down or picked up.

THE WHARVES

There were five wharves within Lapworth, two in Wharf Lane and one at Pinners Bridge, at Dicks Lane and at Lowsonford. It is not possible to know exactly what goods, or their quantity, were handled at each wharf but coal must have been a major item off-loaded, whilst lime, grain and perhaps cattle were on-loaded for sale in the markets of Stratford, Birmingham and the Black Country.

The first wharf in Wharf Lane was beside the canal bridge; it is now the site of a marina. The second wharf was specifically for coal and was at the end of a branch canal, 250 yards long, which started beside Wharf Lane bridge and ran parallel to Wharf Lane. It crossed Spring Lane by a drawbridge and ended at the rear of Dowdeswell House, which was then the house and business premises of successive coal dealers. The branch canal was closed and filled in c.1870's when it presumably became cheaper and more convenient to move coal by the railway.

The wharf at Pinner's Bridge also dealt chiefly in coal, the occupant of the adjacent house usually being a coal dealer. John Hannes who lived there in 1861 also dealt in lime, a small lime-kiln being set into the canal bank a little way from the wharf. Here limestone would be burnt to convert into lime; it was then suitable for use as a fertiliser, or in the making of mortar for building purposes.

Dicks Lane Wharf was a major trading post, although nothing is now left but the pool. Here coal was landed and agricultural produce and lime loaded. Nearby was another lime-kiln and there was road access to Rowington and to Lapworth and Bushwood. The last wharf was at Lowsonford but just within the Lapworth parish boundary.

Gospel Oak Farm

10
A LIVING FROM THE LAND

1800-30

At the beginning of the 19th century the farming at Lapworth continued to be mixed — dairying, fattening, and growing various crops — the resulting cattle, sheep, cheese, grain and hay almost certainly going to Birmingham and the Black Country to feed a rapidly expanding population in the industrial area. From 1799, when the Warwick and Birmingham canal (which brushed the edge of the parish at Kingswood) was finished, Lapworth products could be sent easily to either market; and the completion of the Stratford-upon-Avon canal as far as Kingswood in 1802, brought Dudley market, thought by some to be superior to Birmingham, within trading reach.

Warwickshire was still considered to be 'almost throughout a dairy county',[1] and the evidence of William Johns' notebook confirms that at Lapworth quantities of cheese continued to be made. Johns also reveals what a profitable crop hay could be, finding a ready market in Birmingham. All transport was horse drawn, even the canal boats used horse-power and the demand for fodder must have been prodigious; a working horse required 12 stones of hay and 12 gallons of oats to eat each week.

In 1801 less than a quarter (18.43%) of the parish's 2810 acres was under crops. The Acreage Returns,[2] promoted by the Government to try and determine, parish by parish, the national acreage under the principal crops, record that at Lapworth there was sown: wheat 272 acres; oats 105 acres; barley 59 acres; peas 31 acres; beans 27 acres; turnips 17 acres; and potatoes 7 acres; a total of 518 acres. The figures, collected by the local clergy, are not wholly reliable but they confirm that Lapworth farmers had not moved into large scale corn production as was happening in some places. The report's reference to turnips is the first record of them being grown in the parish. They were probably the yellow fleshed Swedish turnips (swedes) which had been introduced into England comparatively recently. They did better on the damp clay land than the previously grown hard white turnips. The small amount cultivated suggests that they were not yet widely popular in the parish, the traditional peas and beans being preferred as winter feed. The potatoes were probably intended for the animals also although, with the shortage of wheat, some humans might have been prepared to eat them.

The first few years of the century (1801-8) saw much improved weather conditions, consequently there was an increased yield of corn and a welcome fall in prices. Supplies, however, were still not wholly adequate and the cost of food was high compared with pre-war levels. Farmers in many areas met the demand by growing wheat on every available acre; open fields and commons were enclosed and even marginal land, which at other times would not have been considered worth the effort and expense, was cultivated. The rewards were high, farmers and landowners (for rent rises soon followed the profits) doing well financially. There is no evidence that farmers in Lapworth rushed into wheat production but some may have extended their acreage. Thomas Johns, who took over the family farm on his father's death, appears to have changed to a more varied kind of farming, including more cattle and crops. He broke up some old pasture and prepared it for arable cultivation. His father would not have approved of such action stipulating, when he leased land in 1802, that it was not to be ploughed.

It may have been with the intention of growing more grain that the tenants of Kingswood manor decided to enclose Kingswood Common in 1808. Each tenant's allotment of new enclosure was approximately half the size of his old enclosure. This was an excellent bonus for the larger tenants, but mitigated against the smaller men who found themselves with only a few perches of ground in lieu of common rights and grazing.

Gradually, more and more Warwickshire farmers moved out of cheese production, Adam Murray writing in 1812 comments that cheese 'was taking leave of the county', that farmers were 'giving up their dairies' because they could make more profit 'by feeding cattle and sheep as meat than from butter and cheese'.[3] One contributing reason could have been that the larger, heavier, 'improved' cattle, usually of a Longhorn type, which were so profitable for meat, failed to produce quantities of suitable milk. Presumably the Lapworth farmers also moved out of cheese in favour of more grazing, fattening and wheat but there are no extant records to confirm or refute this.

What is known however is that local farmers were making such good profits by 1814 that the Lapworth Charity Feoffees decided to raise the rents of their property. These had been incresed in the 1790's but now they were put up again. Mr. Ingram had his rent raised by 89%, Mrs. Fowler and Mr. Hobday by about 150%, Mr. Bradbury by almost 200% and Isaac Mortiboys by 215%, but the majority were between 107% and 125%.[4]

At the end of the war in 1815 prices fell and there was a general recession. Manufacturers were hit as the demand for guns, bayonets, uniforms, buttons etc., ceased; the gun trade in Birmingham took many years to recover. Corn again came from the continent, wheat prices were lower bringing a welcome reduction in the cost of bread but affecting those large farmers who had put most of their acreage under corn. In 1818 60% of the agricultural labourers in the south and east of England were said to be unemployed.

It is unlikely that the farmers of Lapworth passed through this crisis period completely untouched by events, they were bound to be affected by what occurred to trade in Birmingham, but the paucity of evidence makes it difficult to determine exactly how they fared. Those who held Charity property were allowed 'a temporary abatement of £10 per cent' upon their rents by the Estate 'the value of agricultural produce having declined'. When the Charity Commissioners visited the parish in 1826 'they thought that this rebate should be ended and the proper rents received',[5] suggesting that they considered the worst of the recession was over. There is no indication in the Land Tax Returns (by a wholesale change of tenants) that Lapworth farmers were forced out of their farms by insolvency or bankruptcy. Of the 46 farms recorded in the Lapworth Land Tax Returns[6] (not including Kingswood) only three — Malthouse Farm (c54 acres), Lapworth (Moat) Farm (c57 acres), and Spring Cottage Farm (c15 acres), — had four different tenants in the 12 years 1818-30, but why these changes occurred is not known.

1839-43

THE TITHE APPORTIONMENT

The Tithe Apportionment[7] recorded all the landowners and tenants in the parish with the names and acreages of their fields. Analysis of this detailed information shows that in the years 1839-43, when the tithe schedule was being drawn up, agreed, and finalised, the 2810 acres of land in the parish were owned by 64 different persons. Of these, 53 owned 50 acres or less (24 had 5 acres or under and 13 had 5-20 acres each) the bulk of the land being owned by 11 people. The largest owners were W.H. Cooper, the lord of the manor (737 acres), Earl Cornwallis (327 acres) and Hannah Ingram (201 acres).

THE TENANTS

The schedule listed 142 tenants; of these, 60 tenants had an acre of land or less each, 20 having a half to one acre and 40 tenants having half an acre or less. In almost every case this land represented a garden plot attached to their house or cottage; even the poorest of cottagers had a few perches on which to grow vegetables.

There were 24 tenants with between one and five acres of land each and a further 15 tenants with between five and 10 acres each. Of these 39 tenants, six were people of independent means with a small acreage of land close to their house. Thirteen tenants were craftsmen, publicans, wharfingers or agricultural workers, with a field or large allotment and there were small 'farmers' who must have also worked at something else. Seventeen tenants were non-resident in Lapworth, there being no house or cottage to their holding of land, and no record of them living elsewhere in the parish.

The names and holdings of the remaining 43 tenants who each had 10 acres of land or more, are set out in table form overleaf:

LAPWORTH FARMS 1839-43

Farm Name	Tenant	A	R	P	
Lapworth Park Farm	George Hodges	260	3	34	
Lapworth Lodge Farm	Thomas King	201	0	33	These 10 tenants each had more than 100 acres of land in cultivation. They were the leading men of the parish and full-time farmers. They employed a number of farm labourers, some of whom lived-in. Of the 1455 acres they held, 960 acres were in arable cultivation and 461 acres under grass.
Irelands Farm	John Mander	174	1	32	
High Chimneys Farm	Joseph Osborne	153	3	02	
Brome Hall Farm & Gospel Oak Farm	Martha Hildick	122	0	05	
Hole House Farm	Ann Hicken	122	0	03	
Mountford Farm	William Ball	113	0	22	
Arden Hill Farm	George Hands	105	1	34	
Land farmed from Bushwood Hall	George Gibbs	101	1	34	
Malthouse Farm (L) & Lapworth Farm	Thomas Canning	100	2	20	

* * * * * * * * * * * * * * * * *

Farm Name	Tenant	A	R	P	
Blockbury House	David Buffery	89	2	11	The nine tenants in this group each had between 50 and 100 acres of land, the majority having more under arable crops than under grass. The exceptions had split farms with land in various parts of the parish. One was John Bradbury, a seed merchant who may have cultivated grass for his business.
Hazelwood Farm	John Bradbury	77	1	22	
Sands Farm	John Bellamy	63	1	08	
Bear House Farm	Henry Lancaster	62	1	04	
Bushwood Common Farm	Thomas Tibbitts	58	1	01	
Lapworth (Moat) Farm	Isaac Greaves	57	3	03	
Malthouse Farm (K)	Joseph Parsons	55	1	30	
Common Farm (K)	Thomas Bradbury	55	0	12	
Windmill (Tapster) Farm	John Brookes	52	2	19	

* * * * * * * * * * * * * * * * *

Farm Name	Tenant	A	R	P	
Catesby Farm	Thomas Parsons	43	1	23	Many of the tenants in this group, with between 30 and 50 acres of land, had other occupations. Smith was also a grocer, Rainbow a maltster, Billings an innkeeper, Baldwin a coal dealer. Those who were only farmers had mixed farms.
Chestnut Cottage Farm	Job Hands	39	2	15	
Kingswood Farm	John Watton	37	0	38	
Boot Inn	Jonathan Billings	36	0	30	
Land near Packwood	John Fetherstone	35	1	31	
Brook House Farm	Thomas Rainbow	34	1	20	
Drawbridge Farm	Thoms Baldwin	34	1	14	
Bushwood Grange	Martha Hicken	32	0	12	
House later Bird-in-Hand Inn	Thomas Smith	30	3	25	

* * * * * * * * * * * * * * * * *

Farm Name	Tenant	A	R	P	
Broomfield House Farm	Thomas Cheshire	27	2	08	The tenants in this group, with between 20 and 30 acres of land each, had it all under grass or they had a second occupation; Benbroke was a carrier and Cheshire and Bayliss 'gentlemen' farmers.
Lapworth House Farm	Edward Bayliss	25	1	04	
Tudor Farm	William Hawkins	25	0	07	
Farm (now Cedar Lawn)	Joseph Benbroke	23	3	18	
Yew Tree Farm	Thomas Gibbs	23	3	16	
No House	James Bradbury	21	2	07	

* * * * * * * * * * * * * * * * *

Farm Name	Tenant	A	R	P	
Mill House Farm (K)	Hannah House	19	0	28	The tenants in this group, with between 10 and 20 acres of land each were really smallholders, but all except the rector called themselves 'farmer'. Five farms were mixed, one was wholly arable and three were under grass. Possibly these tenants supplemented their incomes by helping out elsewhere.
The Rectory	Rev. Tyndall	16	0	37	
Spring Cottage Farm	Ephriam Taft	15	0	28	
Yew Tree Cottage (K)	Richard Heath	17	2	12	
Tan House Farm	Michael Farley	14	2	09	
Tapster Brook Farm	John Pritchett	14	0	10	
Bredon House	Richard Smith	13	0	09	
Chain House	Peter Wooldridge	11	2	30	
Meadow Hill Farm	William Taylor	10	1	05	

* * * * * * * * * * * * * * * * *

The tithe survey recorded the culture of the land only as arable, grass, woodland and water. Of the total acreage 1484 acres were in arable cultivation, 1204 in grass and 33 acres were taken by woodland and pools. Thus by 1840 just over half of the parish land (52.8%) was under arable crops, a considerable increase since 1801.

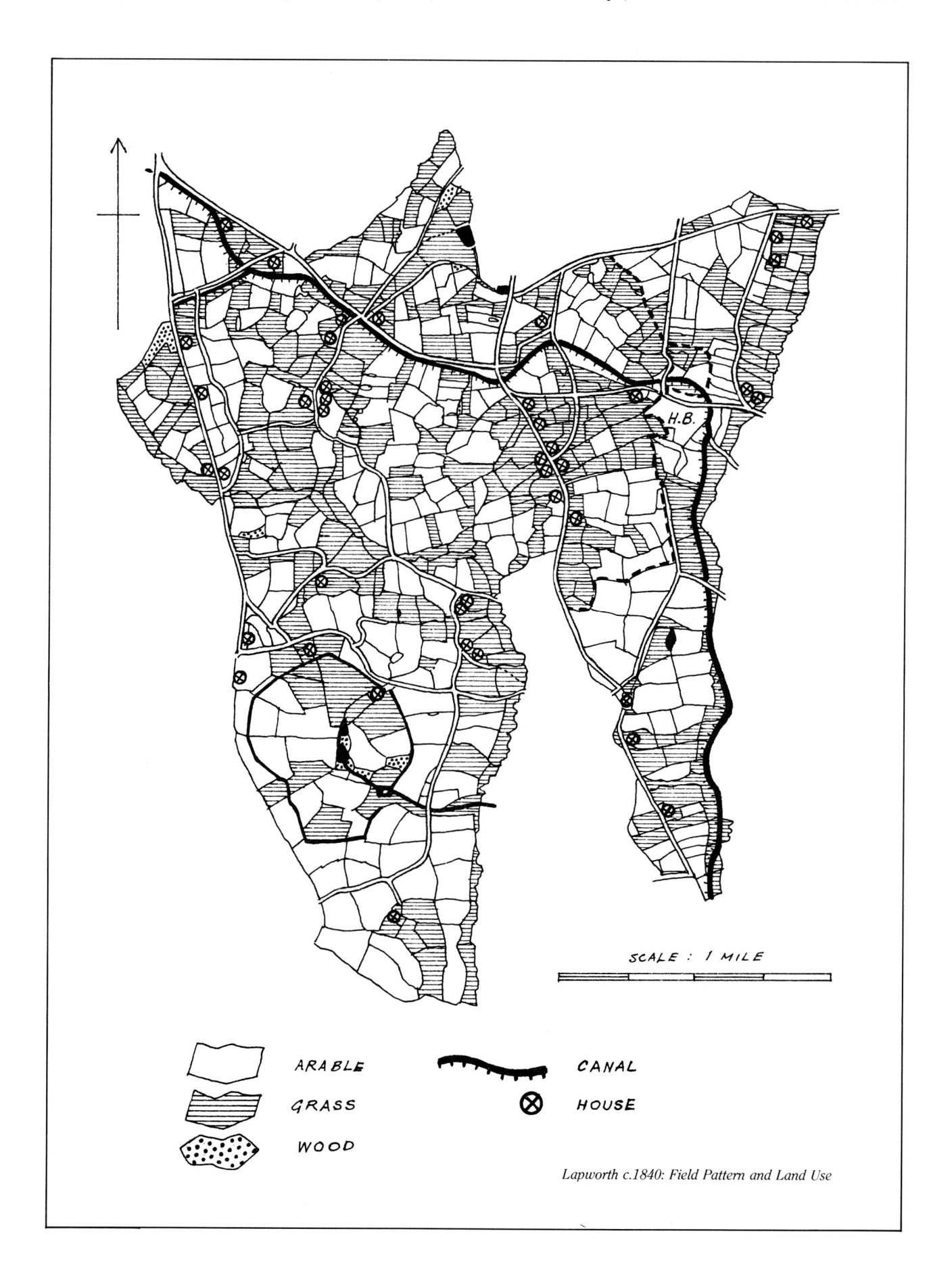

Lapworth c.1840: Field Pattern and Land Use

1843-81

During the 1840's a period of progressive farming began. New ideas, stemming from the recent establishment of agricultural associations and journals, led go-ahead farmers to drain their land, fertilize it with such items as imported guano and potash, and to sow improved strains of seeds. They refurbished their buildings, invested in a variety of machines, and carefully controlled their stock breeding. The result of this 'high farming' was a golden age of raised production and increased prosperity.

Not all farmers however were capable of this scientific approach, many lacked the capital and knowledge and were too set in their ways to change, besides which their farms were too small for the necessary investment to be worth while. At Lapworth some of the latest ideas may have been adopted by the larger farmers but there is no sign of new buildings, for example, amongst the smaller ones and it is unlikely that they made many, if any, changes.

Decade by decade the census returns show no change in farm size and no sign of amalgamation, there was however quite a turn over of tenants particularly between 1851 and 1861 when 42.5% of farms had new occupants. There were also many new tenants in 1871.[8]

The figures produced by the Department of Agriculture for 1867[9] show that at Lapworth, at that date, 59% of the land was under mowing grass, 15% being clover and other temporary grasses, and the rest (44%) permanent grass. Of the remainder of the land 21.5% was under arable crops and 12.25% under beans, peas, turnips and vetches grown for stock feeding. There were 158 dairy cattle, 180 other cattle, 382 pigs and 1059 sheep. These figures show that some 20% of land had been taken out of arable cultivation since 1840 and put under grass. From the extensive acreage described as mowing grass it would seem that local farmers were producing large quantities of hay; and in addition mutton, pork, beef, milk and some wheat and barley. All these products could be easily transported, to wherever they would make the highest price, by the railway.

Milk and hay were just about the only two products not subject to foreign competition, which since 1846 and the Repeal of the Corn Laws had been gradually growing. From the 1870's the imports increased — wheat from the American Prairies, wool from Australia; American, Dutch and French cheese and, with the advent of refrigerated ships, foreign meat also. Bad weather during the 1870's did not help matters and agriculture entered a depression; in 1881[10] 72.3% of Lapworth farms had different tenants from those recorded in 1871.

Old established families — the Manders of Irelands Farm; the Parsons of Malthouse Farm, Kingswood; the Hickens of Bushwood Grange; the Kings of Lapworth Lodge Farm and the Hodges of Lapworth Park Farm — amongst others had all left the parish by 1881. Nine farms were being worked by bailiffs, presumably put in by the owners in place of the previous tenants.

1892

A rate book of 1892[11] listing both the owners and the tenants with their acreages of land but few farm names, shows that by this date further changes had taken place in the land ownership and occupation of Lapworth farms. The most important change was the break up and sale of the manorial demesne. J.E. Watts, the lord of the manor, and the owner of the manorial lands had mortgaged them some time previously. In 1892 the mortgagees sold the estate piecemeal; the title of lord of the manor and just over 7 acres of land were bought by Mr. J. Weiss; J.E. Watts retained Yew Tree Farm (which was let) plus 3½ acres of dingle and pits, land possibly suitable for sporting purposes. William Udall purchased Lapworth Lodge Farm and part of Lapworth Park Farm, in all 360 acres let to William King; Udall owned and occupied a further 11 acres of woodland, previously part of Lapworth Park Farm. Another 15 acres of this same farm was sold to William Vernon. Irelands Farm was bought and occupied by the Couchman family, solicitors in Henley.

Much other land in Lapworth had also changed hands by this date and the largest owners were G.O. Arton, Henry Billings who was born at *The Boot* and lived at Catesby House, and William Garrard of Kingswood Grange. All were apparently business men and typical of the new people who were increasingly moving into the parish.

11

THE CHURCH

THE BUILDING

The church of St. Mary the Virgin is a short, wide building with a separate tower and spire. There has been a church on this site for at least 800 years the earliest almost certainly being built by the lord of the manor, possibly one of the Marshall family. About 1190, when Nicholas was the rector, it is thought to have consisted of a small rectangular stone building,[1] its extent being determined from the 12th century work which remains in the nave. This originally had no aisles;[2] a north aisle was added in the early 13th century and a south aisle about 50 years later. During the 13th century the chancel was rebuilt and an adjoining north chapel constructed.

In 1373 Richard de Montfort, together with others of Lapworth, founded a chantry dedicated to the Blessed Virgin, St. Thomas the Martyr and All Saints, for the repose of the souls of the founders, their families and numerous neighbours. Masses were sung daily in a specially built chapel situated at the west end of the church above an open porch. There was no access into the chapel from the church, entrance being via a pair of narrow stone staircases in the porch. The chapel was lit by three windows and had a holy water stoup in the south wall, in the east wall a window looked into the church.

The tower erected in the late 14th century stands to the north of the church; until 1872 it was totally detached but is now connected to the church by a vestibule. The octagonal spire which tops the tower was added later, but at what date has not been determined.

About 1460 the whole church was remodelled; the clerestory was added, the aisle walls rebuilt, the chancel arch widened and the present fine timbered roof inserted. The north chapel (now called St. Catherine's Chapel) was also rebuilt in the 15th century by the Catesbys who held the manor at the time, this chapel apparently being the responsibility of the lord of the manor. In the chapel, a chantry for the repose of the soul of William Catesby, was endowed by the family and dedicated to St. Catherine.

In 1547 when all chantries were suppressed by Henry VIII, both the chapels at Lapworth would have been stripped of any jewels and valuable ornaments, and the property which supported the chantries claimed by the Crown.

The church later had internal alterations made to suit the religious demands of the Reformation and of subsequent fashions, but none of the details were recorded. The 19th century was a major period for church restoration and three were undertaken at Lapworth in 1807, 1860 and 1872. During this century extensive repairs have been carried out and several fine examples of modern craftsmanship have been added as commemorative gifts to enhance the beauty of the church.

THE ADVOWSON

For over 700 years the advowson, or the gift of the living, of St. Mary's has been in the hands of the scholars of Merton College, Oxford.[3] They first received it post 1270 from John de Glen who had been given it by William de Harecurt, the then lord of the manor. In 1275 the scholars granted it to the King (Edward I) who bestowed it on the Provost and canons of Mont Cenis in Piedmont. However, in 1277 the King revoked the gift and restored the advowson to Merton who still retain it. It is their prerogative to appoint the rectors of the parish, and over the centuries many graduates of the college have occupied this office.

Illustration depicts an early 12th Century Window, found in 1872.

THE RECTORS

As far as can be ascertained there have been 49 rectors of Lapworth over the centuries. Until recent years each was supported by a quantity of farmland known as the glebe, and by the tithes.

In 1714[4] the glebe consisted of a large rectory house (described as being of six bays), two barns and a stable (also of six bays), two gardens, two orchards, and 29¾ acres of land scattered throughout the parish. Each rector either farmed the land himself or as was more usual, leased it out for a money rent. The house was his total responsibility and might be extended, demolished or let as he chose.

The tithes consisted of a tenth part of each parishioner's produce — corn, hay, calves, lambs, milk, eggs, fruit etc., which he was obliged to give annually in kind to the rector. In later periods the tithes were often commuted to a money payment which was negotiated between each farmer and the rector. In 1805 Thomas Johns[5] 'made an agreement with the Rev. Mr. Pye for the tithe', Johns paying the rector £2 11s. 6d. In later years when Mr. Pye, although still rector, had left Lapworth Johns helped collect the tithes on his behalf.

After the Tithe Commutation Act of 1836 the complicated tangle into which tithe payment had fallen nationally was regulated. As a result the rectors of Lapworth received a rent charge of £362 0s. 0d., per annum from the parish lands plus the income from letting (or working) the glebe.

Except for a short period of 13 years every rector of Lapworth between 1736 and 1839 was an absentee, each preferring to live in a market town where he had another benefice. Dull, rural Lapworth was left in the care of curates, whilst the rectors, and particularly their wives and families, enjoyed a lively social life, better company and a higher level of conversation elsewhere. Edward Welchman moved to Solihull; Charles Bean lived at Warwick where he was the vicar of St. Mary's. A politically active Whig he was close to the Earl of Warwick for whom he was, in effect political agent.[6] Joseph Kilner preferred Cirencester as did Anthony Pye who deserted Lapworth in 1806 to be the vicar there.[7]

From 1839 the Lapworth rectors lived wholly in the parish. The Rev. George Tyndall, who followed Mr. Pye, did not even have a curate, taking all the services and duties himself except for the occasional holiday. He died at Lapworth in 1848 'of an affection of the lungs'[8] at the age of 50.

He was succeeded by the Rev. Charles Arundell St. John Mildmay, a young unmarried gentleman of means. He was generous to the church, conscientious, and concerned about the poorer people in the parish. He married about 1853 and by 1861 had five children. Between 1856 and 1859 he had periods of bad health and had to go abroad; during his absences curates were in charge of the parish. Rev. Mildmay had a number of such assistants, few of them staying very long. His first curate was the Hon. and Rev. Aubrey Spring Rice, a contemporary and friend who also lived at the rectory. A later curate, Rev. J. Townsend, lived at Hockley House, Hockley Heath, which until a few years previously had been a coaching inn. His last curate was Charles Burd (1859-63) who was later the vicar of Shirley.

The next rector was J.R.T. Eaton, another bachelor, who married whilst at Lapworth. During his rectorship the major restoration of the church took place. In 1878 he left Lapworth for Alvechurch in Worcestershire and was succeeded by Rev. Kenrick Prescot who stayed until 1896. All the rectors took an interest in the school but Rev. Prescot was particularly keen. He or one of his curates called regularly and Mrs. Prescot, with other ladies in the village, visited to look at the the girls' progress in needlework.

THE RECTORY HOUSE

The rectory which Edward Welchman occupied was old and timber-framed. During his years as rector he did a great deal to it, jotting notes of his improvements in the Parish Register.

'1690 — I new floored the parlour and built the chimney on the chamber over the . . .
1693 — I rebuilt the big barn
1695 — I repaired the middle part of the house.
1695 — I rebuilt the bigger barn and the stables. Andrew Archer Esquier gave me the stone wherewith I groundsilled the lesser barn.
1702 — I set a new roof on the east end of the house.
1703 — I made the cellar and staircase and gate . . .
1706 — I built a round end to the upper barn and the chamber over the big kitchen.
1715 — I new tiled the west end of the house'

After Welchman and his family left Lapworth in 1736 the house was occupied by successive curates or possibly let with the farm land. By 1793, when Mr. Pye became rector, it was probably in a poor state of repair and he quickly decided to replace it.

The new house designed by Thomas Johnson of Warwick, the architect of the old gaol and St. Nicholas' church at Warwick,[9] was large, square and of three stories. The entrance front faced away from the road and looked over the garden and fields, whilst at the rear a wall with a central gate hid the kitchen area and courtyard from public view.

When Mr. Pye moved to Cirencester the rectory was presumably occupied by his three curates — Rev. James Way (1803-16), Rev. George Childe (1817-26) and Rev. Donald Cameron (1826-38) who cared for the parish in his absence.

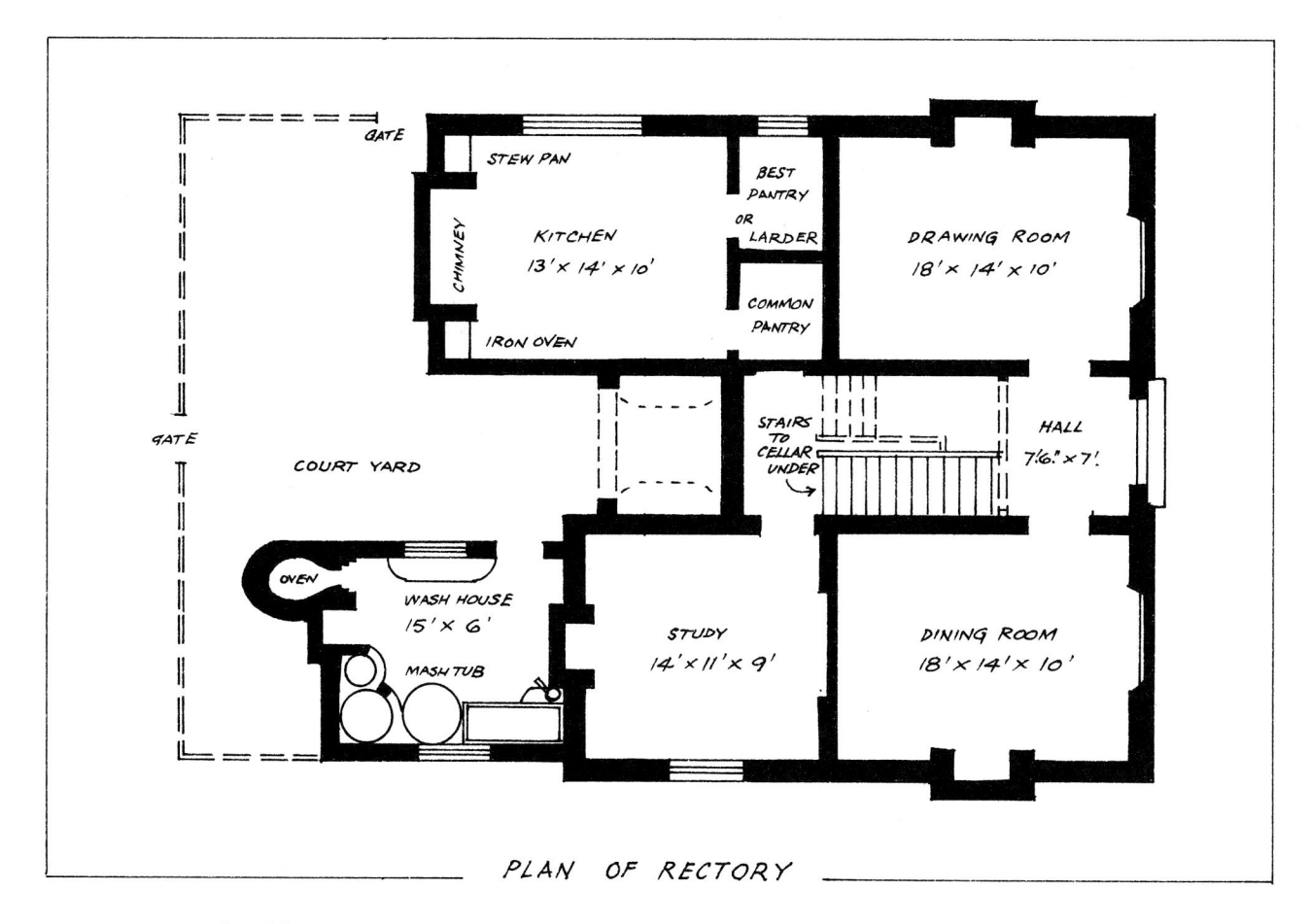

Copied from the Architects plan of 1794, when the main entrance door was on the west front of the house.

The next rector Rev. George Tyndall was resident in the parish and he considerably enlarged and improved the house.[10] He also built new stables and a coachhouse, spending altogether about £1,000 0s. 0d. His successor, Mr. Mildmay, thought the brick walls of the rectory were rather thin and he therefore had them cemented and the house 'thoroughly drained'. Three years later in 1851 he 'altered the entrance to the Parsonage', moving the front door and entrance hall to the side of the house and consequently changing the arrangement of the rooms. He also made 'the bank and small walk to the Church on the N.E. side'.

There are no further references to changes and the house stood until the late 1950's or early 60's when it was replaced by a modern and more convenient rectory.

The west front of the Rectory after the entrance had been moved to the south side and a bay window added to the Drawing Room, left.

TITHES

Although there is no record of any dispute at Lapworth between the rector and his parishioners over the tithes this was not the case everywhere. In many places the clergy, the landowners and the tenants were in continual conflict over who should pay and why. During the early 19th century it was apparent that something must be done nationally to rectify the situation. Various Acts of Parliament attempted, unsatisfactorily, to do this and it was 1836 before the Tithe Commutation Act finally resolved the matter.

Under the Act a commissioner visited every parish and with the help of field assistants made a survey and very detailed map of all the land and buildings. An attached schedule recorded the name, size, owner, tenant and culture of every field. From this information the amount of tithe payable on each acre was worked out. It was based on the movement of local prices of wheat, barley and oats over seven years.

The Tithe Commissioner probably arrived at Lapworth in 1838, for by February 1839 an agreement had been reached between all the parties, although it was September 1843 before every particular was finalised. The whole parish was estimated at 2,810 acres of which 2,778 acres were subject to tithe.[11]

All previous arrangements made by the rector with regard to the tithes were now void; from this time the tithe, or rent charge as it was henceforth to be known, was fixed and did not change; it was to be paid by the landowner not the tenant.

In future the rector was to receive £362 0s. 0d., per annum rent charge plus a modus (a payment made by long custom) of 2d., per acre per annum in lieu of the tithe of hay and clover; 1d., per annum for every milk cow grazed, in lieu of the tithe of milk; and 4d., per annum for every calf produced in the parish. These payments were due annually at Michaelmas. Lapworth Park Farm and Lapworth Lodge Farm were excluded from the modus as set out above. Instead each farm paid the fixed sum of £1 6s. 8d. These were the only payments to the rector from the old Park land (estimated at 450 acres) for the commissioner determined that they were 'Tithe Free'.

The glebe land as detailed in the tithe schedule was very little different from that in the Terrier of 1714. Although some of the field names had changed it is possible to equate the two with considerable success. In 1843 the glebe equalled 29 acres 0 roods 25 perches, plus 22 acres of new land given to the Lapworth rector in lieu of tithes lost through the enclosure of Bushwood Common, making a total of just over 50 acres. The new allotment was free of rent charge but the 29 acres of original glebe, if leased or let out to tenants, was subject to a rent charge of £12 0s. 0d., per annum.

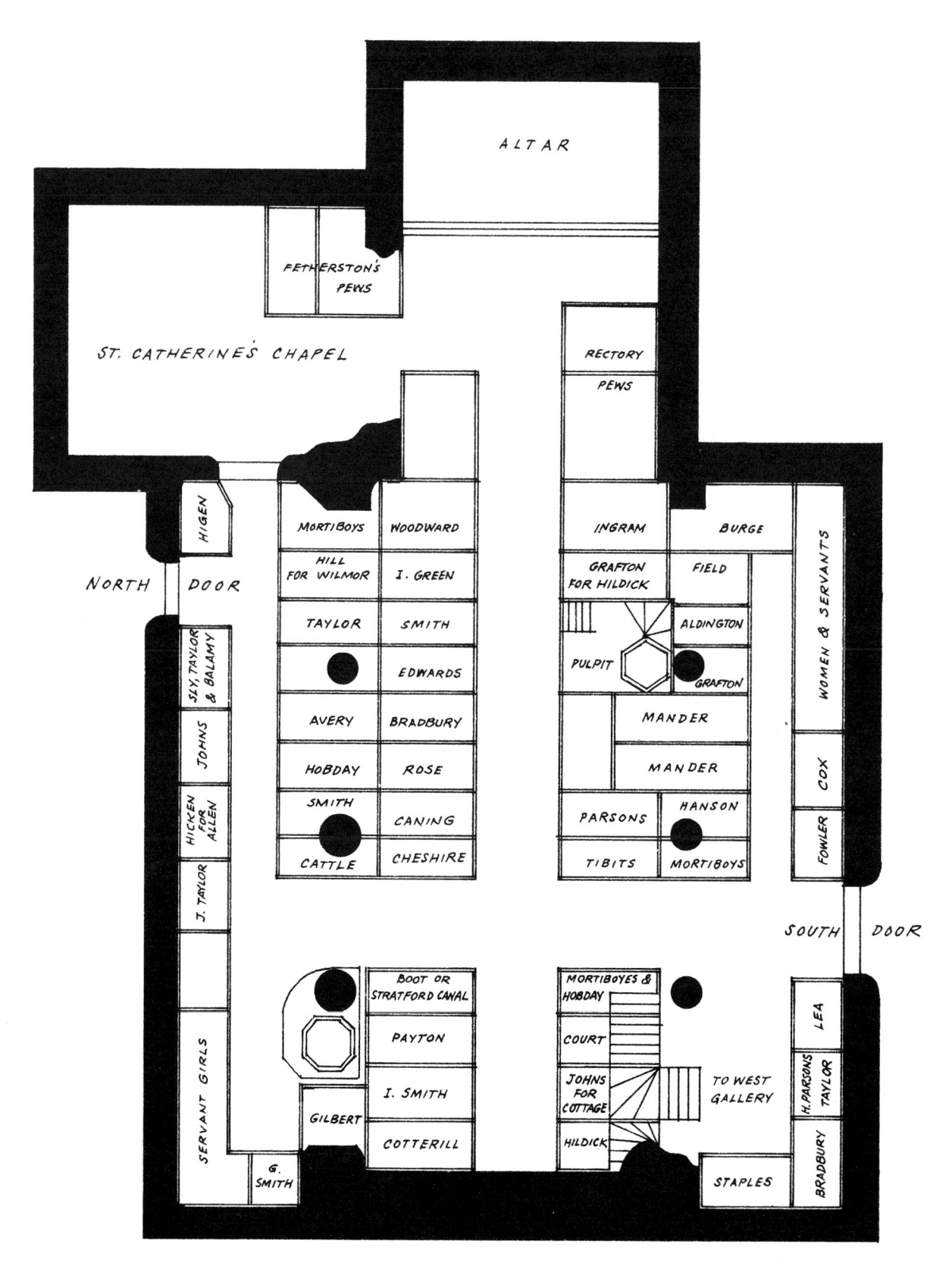

Plan of the interior of the Church c.1807.

THE 19th CENTURY RESTORATIONS

In October 1806 the Feoffees of the Charities[12] decided that 'money gained from the sale of timber last year be applied to the repair of the church'. The sale of further timber was envisaged and these proceeds too were to be used for the church. The result was a 'restoration' which in reality was quite the opposite.

There was already a plain gallery at the west end of the nave and the major part of the work, which started in 1807, consisted of fitting high box pews into the body of the church. There were 52 pews, 37 placed in regular rows down the nave and part of the aisles, with 15 around the edge of the walls. The pews which were described in 1840 as 'not in good taste'[13] were allotted to individual houses, not families, and where people sat depended on which house they lived in. Two long pews were for the servants; that in the south aisle for 'women and servants', and that for 'servant girls' at the rear of the north aisle. Three other very large pews were set just inside the chancel; two together on the south side were the rectory pews, who sat in the third is not stated. Perhaps it was for the lord of the manor, should he choose to attend a service. Two other large pews were set just inside St. Catherine's chapel, these were occupied by the Fetherstone family. The pulpit, octagonal in shape and raised up several steps, occupied a commanding position in the nave.

In order to make room for the pews a doorway in the north aisle was blocked up and the par-close rood screen, which was 15th century and had painted armorial bearings of the Catesby, Brome and Arden families, was removed.[14] The screen was broken up and formed into altar rails, an altar reredos, and panelling for the walls within the altar rails. The stone work of the east window was much decayed; because of the cost of restoration the window was bricked up, but leaving a straight, narrow slit of light down the centre. On each side of the slit were placed boards bearing the Creed and the Commandments. The final touch of the restoration was the removal of the timbered porch which stood at the south door.

No further major repairs were carried out at the church until 1860, but in 1855 an organ, built by Nicholas of Worcester, was installed.[15] It was placed in St. Catherine's chapel (with the consent of Mr. Miller, the lord of the manor) and was probably the first ever in the church. The Misses Kershaw, who had been collecting money for a harmonium, seem to have suggested having an instrument to Mr. Mildmay the rector. When he opened a subscription fund they gave the £40 0s. 0d., they had collected, but only £2 0s. 0d., was raised in the parish; the total cost of the organ was £120 0s. 0d.

1860 — THE CHANCEL

In 1860 Mr. Mildmay undertook the restoration of the chancel for which he, the rector, was traditionally responsible. The work was completed in September 1860 and cost about £750 0s. 0d.,[16] the rector meeting a large part of the expense himself.

Under the direction of Mr. G.E. Street much of what had been done in 1807 was removed. The chancel was in such a bad state of repair that the south wall had to be taken down entirely and rebuilt. A new roof was put on and the east window unblocked and renewed. Stained glass (executed by Clayton & Bell) was placed in the two south windows, one being a memorial to Alfred Lapworth, the other was given by John Fetherstone.[17] The woodwork made from the rood screen was removed and an alabaster reredos of The Last Supper, by Earps of Lambeth, placed behind the altar. Tiles filled the wall space on either side and similar tiles were placed on the floor. The chancel was furnished with choir stalls, carved reading desks, a stone pulpit and an oak lectern. The nave and chancel were separated by low pillars of Irish stone with a plain baluster of Bath stone. During the work the memorial slab of Owen Bonnell was lost; probably buried, with others previously on the chancel floor, below the present floor level.

The chancel rail of Irish stone removed from the church to a garden in the parish.

When the chancel was completed thoughts were turned to the rest of the church. A licence to carry out changes was obtained in 1861 the cost of the work being estimated at £700 0s. 0d., but it was 1872 before it could be undertaken.

1872 — THE CHURCH

The restoration of 1872[18] appears to have been very thorough and to have left the church fabric in a good state of repair: something which it had needed since 1807. The box pews and the west gallery were removed from the nave as was the lath and plaster ceiling. Under this was discovered the fine late 15th century oak roof which is seen today. Layers of plaster were scraped off the walls exposing the grey stone work and revealing, in the north wall, a small early 12th century window with a rounded arch; a remnant of the original church. At the east end of the south aisle a piscina and its credence table were found, adjuncts of St. James' altar which stood there in earlier centuries. Blocked windows were also revealed in this aisle and two, just above ground level at the west end, were opened and glazed.

The chantry chapel at the west end of the church and the porch beneath it received considerable attention. One arch of the porch had been previously blocked, this was opened up and the staircase repaired. The chantry chapel had been connected to the church for many years, probably from the time the gallery was erected. It had been used as a vestry, entrance to it being through a west window. The chapel was again separated from the church by renewing and reglazing the window, then restored. The vestry was transferred to the base of the tower.

The restoration was completed by placing open seating in the nave, erecting an organ in St. Catherine's chapel, and putting stained glass in the east window of the chancel (gift of the rector), and in two windows in the south and north aisles (the gift of Mrs. Tyndall and the Kershaw family). The total cost of the work, £1600 0s. 0d., was more than twice the sum estimated. Merton College, the rector, the Feoffees and the people all contributed and managed to raise the money. The church was re-opened by the Bishop of Worcester, Dr. Philpot, on 16 October 1872.

In May 1883 the stone work at the top of the spire was found to be in a dangerous condition. Mr. Chatwin, the architect, was consulted and he recommended Joseph Blackburn of Nottingham to do the necessary work. The top 16ft. of the spire was to be taken down and rebuilt, imperfect stone replaced, and the whole spire repointed. A new roof for the top of the tower and a new weathervane brought the estimated cost to £220 0s. 0d. As usual a subscription fund was started, the rector giving £50 0s. 0d., Mr. & Mrs. Garrard of Kingswood Grange £40 0s. 0d., and Merton College £5 0s. 0d. Only a few parishioners contributed, but this was not surprising in view of the depressed state of agriculture and the large number of new people in the village. The work was completed in January 1884; it took just over a year to raise the necessary money — £245 9s. 6d., but all was settled by Easter 1885.[19]

THE CLOCK

Lapworth church clock is of a type found only in the Midlands.[20] It was originally installed in the 16th century; it then had no dial but a striking mechanism of the 'kick start' type. Such a mechanism was made only by professional clockmakers, not by blacksmiths who made many clocks at this period. The frame of the clock is unusual, being vertical, and of wood rather than of iron, which was the fashion when it was made. The clock is still wound by hand two or three times a week.

Gowan Bank, Kingswood

12
... 'HOW MANY POOR I SEE'*

1816-8

The treatment and maintenance of the poor during the 1790's was described in some detail in Chapter 7. During those years the Overseers of the Poor of Lapworth gave assistance to 90 cases of poor individuals and families in the parish, the cost being between £300 0s. 0d., and £350 0s. 0d., per annum: 1794-5 £304 8s. 0½d., 1795-6 £334 9s. 1½d., 1796-8 No Accounts, 1798-9 £311 9s. 6d.

Approximately 20 years later the number of people asking for help was much the same, the Overseers of the Poor in their accounts for the years 1816-7 and 1817-8[1] assisting 101 cases, again both individuals and families. This was a rise of only 12% since the previous period, but the cost had risen enormously to £585 13s. 0d., in the former year and £720 1s. 1½d., in the latter year, an increase of 88% and 131% respectively since 1798-9.

The Charity Estate no longer gave their income (or even part of it) to the Overseers, the large sums expended being raised wholly by levies on the householders of the parish, each paying in proportion to his holding of land. The accounts show that seven levies were taken in 1816-7, but there are no details as to how many ratepayers there were or how much each paid. An estimate, however, can be made — the population of the parish was just over 500 people, made up of about 150 householders. With 101 individuals and families asking for help it would seem that the burden of supporting the poor fell on about 50 householders. Those ratepayers who were themselves at the bottom of the financial scale often found that they could not pay their levies and, indeed, needed assistance themselves. In March 1816 Thomas Higgins, aged 70, a tailor with three acres of land, asked the Overseer for help and was given 4s. 0d., per week. Due to his financial problems he could no longer pay his poor levy and was excused his arrears of 14s. 6d.

By 1816 there were two men each year acting as Overseers of the Poor instead of one in the 1790's; Robert Cranmer of Brook House Farm and Joseph King of Catesby Farm held the posts in 1816-7 and Richard Heath of Yew Tree Cottage, Kingswood and Samuel Cranmer also of Brook House Farm in 1817-8. The people who were helped with money and goods were much the same as in the 1790's — those needing temporary help (52), those requiring continual support (49) including the ever growing group of men whose wages would not stretch far enough to support their families.

During the long years of the Napoleonic war when so many people enjoyed good profits and a high standard of living, agricultural wages, although they did rise, failed to keep pace with the price of almost every necessity. John Wedge of Bickenhill writing in 1815 about the condition of Warwickshire farm workers commented 'The weekly wages of an agricultural labourer are, at an average, not more than 12s. . . . The family of such labourer generally consists of himself, his wife, and from two to six children; when, out of this 12s. per week, he has provided fuel, clothing and also shoes, candles, soap, salt and beer (if any beer he can obtain), all of which are heavily taxed; and likewise set apart from 6d. to 1s. per week house rent, it will be perceived that, in very few instances, so much as 3d. a day for each one of his family can be spared for food'.[2] If the agricultural weekly wages at Lapworth were about average, and there is no reason to suppose they were higher, similar tight budgets would have pertained in many cottages in the village and it is easy to see why a few shillings extra from the Overseer, and help with rent and clothes made life more bearable.

*'Whene'er I take my walks abroad, how many poor I see!' Isaac Watts.

In the years under review 22 Lapworth working men and their families received regular assistance from the Overseer; 12 men had between 1s. 0d., and 6s. 0d., every week and 10 had sums varying from 1s. 0d., to 10s. 0d., per time very frequently but not every week. The latter payments were made especially to men with several children, the Overseers apparently preferring to give, say 8s. 0d., every two or three weeks for a short period when circumstances required, rather than be committed to 3s. 0d., or 4s. 0d., per week throughout the year. Although these varied sums were given at irregular intervals, they were given so often that they were clearly not crisis payments but a continual expectation. William Wardell had a wife and six children, he had coal, his rent paid (£2 2s. 0d.) and varying sums throughout the year — 17s. 0d., per month in January and February 1817; 8s. 0d., in March; 12s. 0d., in April; 16s. 0d., in May; 10s. 0d., in June; 4s. 0d., in July; then nothing more until November when he received 3s. 0d.; 6s. 0d., in December and 10s. 0d., in January 1818. The cost of helping these men was £127 1s. 5d., in 1816-17 and £177 0s. 9d., in the following year, being 34% and 40% of the regular-pay disbursements.

Catesby Farm

As a rule Overseers were rather mean to widows and the elderly but in Lapworth, at this time, they were (probably unintentionally) quite even handed, no one group of the regular poor getting a much larger or unfair proportion of the funds than the other. It cost between £60 0s. 0d., and £70 0s. 0d., per year to keep the nine widows who were supported by the parish, each having between 2s. 0d., and 3s. 0d., per week plus the occasional shift (2s. 0d.), bedgown (3s. 0d.), petticoat (3s. 0d.) or sheet (4s. 0d.). Three of the women — Mrs. Clees, Mrs. Brookes and Mrs. Yardley — had been widows and kept by the parish for over 18 years, all being mentioned in the records of 1798-9.

Six elderly men, some with wives, Thomas Higgins, George Fisher, Benjamin Denstone, Joseph Masters, Edward Woods and Richard Hawkins, were kept for a similar sum. George Fisher had 2s. 0d., per week in July 1816, a sum he probably considered insufficient for in August he went with the Overseer to Henley-in-Arden to visit the magistrate, the journey costing 2s. 6d., and the examination 1s. 6d. As a result his weekly allowance was raised to 3s. 0d. Denstone and Woods had both been supported by the parish since the 1790's. In 1805 Denstone had married Widow Kendrick, who was also poor and kept by the parish; the Overseers must have been delighted at their union for it saved the parish a considerable amount of expense all round. In 1816 the Denstones lived on 3s. 6d., per week.

Richard Hawkins and Edward Woods died in 1816 and Joseph Masters the following year, the two latter being buried by the parish. Prior to his death Masters had been ill enough to have the doctor, the visit costing 18s. 6d., and his funeral £2 10s. 0d. Woods was buried on 12 October, his funeral charges being £1 11s. 0d., (burial fees 6s. 6d., expenses £1 4s. 6d.). By 28 October the Overseers had moved Widow Woods to a different, and no doubt, smaller cottage. She was given 8s. 0d., and 2s. 6d., per week to keep herself. She was soon busy helping others — she cured 'Jos Greenhill of the itch', probably scabies, for which she was paid 1s. 6d.

Richard Hawkins and his wife Ann had eight children (1790-1806) and the youngest was probably still living at home when his father died. Widow Hawkins received 4s. 0d., per week to support her and help with her rent. She also received money for child-bed linen (6s. 0d.); this was for her daughter Ann (born 1791) who already had two illegitimate children (1809 and 1812) and who seems to have had a third in 1816 or 1817. Ann Hawkins was a problem, she appears to have been living and possibly working in Rowington. The Lapworth Overseers were paying her 6s. 0d., per week — presumably for her two Lapworth born daughters, who may have lived with Mrs. Hawkins, their grandmother. The Rowington Overseers had enough problems with their own poor and they would not have been willing to support Ann and the new baby. There were several meetings at *The Boot* and visits to the magistrates about her, for it was imperative that the Overseers discovered who was the child's father and arrange a marriage before any further mishaps occurred. It was eventually determined that Joseph Palmer of Warwick was the child's father. In November 1817 the parish embarked upon a campaign to secure a marriage; the Overseer and Mr. King (the Constable) went after Palmer (7s. 0d.) the expenses for the horses and themselves being 13s. 0d. There were several further journeys to Warwick, Henley-in-Arden and Rowington (cost £1 6s. 8d.) and two summons (4s. 0d.), meetings and expenses (£1 8s. 5d.). Perhaps a marriage licence was thought too extravagant for eventually the banns were put up in Rowington and Warwick (3s. 6d.), the journey to Warwick costing 5s. 0d. During December Palmer was examined by the magistrates and a certificate given (5s. 0d.). The Overseer and Mr. King rode to Warwick, journey, horses and toll costing 15s. 11d., and the Overseer went another time with his horse and cart (10s. 0d.). As the wedding day, 23 December,[3] approached John Wood was entrusted with the care of Palmer (5s. 0d.) in case he ran away. Finally they all journeyed to Rowington for the marriage. Lapworth paid the wedding fees (7s. 6d.) and gave the bridesmaid 1s. 0d., they paid for the ring (10s. 6d.) and charged 5s. 0d., for attending the nuptials. After the wedding they gave Palmer 3s. 0d., and on 29 December went to Warwick with him (5s. 0d.), the toll gate and expenses being 1s. 0d. The parish continued to support Ann's two other children at a cost of 6s. 0d., per week.

At this time it was not the Overseers' policy to support unmarried mothers for very long. They helped when necessary but after the child was born, if a marriage could not be secured and the mother was well enough, generally she appears to have been expected to support herself. The children of course had to be supported, the average payment being 3s. 0d., per week. An illegitimate child called Bustin, no other name is recorded, was kept by the parish at 3s. 0d., every week from May 1816. Each year his father, the mysterious Bustin, paid a lump sum to the Overseers to cover the child's expenses, but no details are given. Other illegitimate children — Mary Beesley the daughter of Sophia (born 1810); Ann Smith's child; Thomas the son of Elizabeth Wilson (born 1812); Alice the daughter of Sarah Maids (born 1811); Thomas the son of Ann Hutton (born 1814), — were all supported as were Palmer's child and Ward's boy who may have been orphans. The total cost to the parish of these children was £63 1s. 6d., in 1816-7 and £55 7s. 2d., in 1817-8.

From the 1770's as the population increased there was, throughout the country, a general decline in moral standards and an increase in the number of illegitimate children born. During the 1790's the births of seven base children were recorded in the Parish Register; in the decade 1800-9 five were recorded, but in the following period 1810-9 there were 19 such births, a considerable increase. A few girls married almost immediately but others did not and one or two, like Ann Hawkins, had more than one illegitimate child — Elizabeth Wilson had three, Sarah Maids two, and in later decades Elizabeth Wade, Caroline Bunn and Mary Pardoe two each. Sarah Maids' sister, Hannah, also had an illegitimate child and it is the case that some families did tend to have a more relaxed idea of morals than others.[4] In the 1820's there were 10 base births, in the 1830's 12 and in the 1840's 15. Fortunately for the parish funds not all the charges for these girls and their offspring fell upon the parish, the Overseers spending more time and effort than in previous periods to gain some financial settlement or a marriage where possible.

They spent about £30 0s. 0d., on achieving a marriage between Pheobe Mills and Jonathan Sidaway, although he was almost certainly not the child's father. After the wedding they continued to support the child but they had at least got Pheobe, who was a nuisance and expensive, off their hands. A Lapworth girl, Pheobe was living in Old Swinford when she first appears in the records in 1816. The Lapworth Overseers were supporting her, sending her money from time to time, £5 3s. 0d., being paid in April 1816. She wrote to the Overseers twice in September 1816, the postage being paid by the parish (10½d., and 2d.). Soon afterwards she arrived in Lapworth and a visit was made to the magistrate, the horse and cart (6s. 9d.), examination and expenses costing together 17s. 3d. She was given 2s. 0d., and a pair of shoes (4s. 6d.), two shifts (9s. 2d.), and 8s. 0d., to 'carry her home'. In December, and January 1817 she wrote twice again to the Overseers (postage 1s. 11d.). In March 1817 money was taken to her at Old Swinford (£10 1s. 6d.), Mr. Keen who took it charged

6s. 0d.; whilst there he treated her to bread and cheese (10d.). On 25 October 1817 Pheobe was again taken to Henley-in-Arden to get a licence which, with bread, cheese and ale and the turnpike, cost 7s. 1d., On 29 October someone went to Stourbridge on her account to 'swear her child' (£1 5s. 0d.). On 4 November Jonathan Sidaway, went with Mr. King and the Overseer to Henley-in-Arden to the magistrates (4s. 6d.), he then stayed with Mr. Grafton at the Tan House who gave him board and lodging (8s. 0d.). On 10 November Pheobe Mills received seven weeks pay for the child (£1 1s. 0d.) and on the same day she and Sidaway were married, the parish paying for the ring (10s. 6d.) and the fees etc., (9s. 6d.). They were given £1 4s. 0d., to 'carry them home' to Old Swinford and Jonathan received 'a pound for his work'; was this agreeing to marry Pheobe? In December Lapworth sent the child 12s. 0d., and in February 1818 a further £9 10s. 0d.

The 50 people who had only occasional help cost the parish £93 2s. 5½d., in 1816-7 and £63 19s. 3d., in 1817-8 20% and 13% of each year's disbursements. The majority had help costing £1 0s. 0d., or less, but a few involved the Overseers in much troublesome expense.

At this time they were particularly quick to act if a person who was not Lapworth born, or who did not have legal settlement in the parish, asked for assistance. They were hustled off to the magistrates, and removed at the earliest possible moment before they cost the ratepayers too much money. Thomas Woods, and John Pardy and his wife were removed to Rowington, Isaac Smith to Preston Bagot, and William Barnbrook and Daniel Hancox to their settlement parishes. John Philips and his wife were sent to Kent where they officially belonged, the cost including board at the *Royal Oak* (£6 0s. 10d.) and the journey to Kent (£2 5s. 6d.) totalling £9 11s. 4d.

The traffic in people was not all one way, other parishes also removed those without legal settlement. In the autumn of 1816 Joseph Greenhill and his family were sent to Lapworth, his birthplace, from Eydon in Northamptonshire, where they had been living and obviously had become a charge on that parish. Greenhill travelled back and forth twice in September and October 1816, Widow Wood treating and curing his 'itch' whilst he was in Lapworth. In December Mr. King fetched Greenhill's wife and goods from Eydon, it taking four days and costing £2 8s. 0d., and a further £3 18s. 5d., expenses. The bill, presented by the Eydon Overseer, for supporting the Greenhills, came to £14 9s. 4½d. Back in Lapworth they were supported by the parish at a rate of about £1 0s. 0d., per month until June 1817. During these months Mrs. Greenhill appears to have been ill, they were cared for by Isabel Chinn, who was paid about 3s. 0d., per week from January to June for her help. During part of this time young Greenhill was boarded at *The Boot* (£1 4s. 0d.), where Joseph Greenhill was given 'eating, ale, corn and chaff' (19s. 0d.); he also received new clothes — two shirts (5s. 6d., each), a pair of breeches (11s. 6d.), a pair of stockings (2s. 3d.). In March work was done on a house for them, Samuel Gazy, the carpenter, making a new door and stairs and doing other work for £2 10s. 6d. The parish then bought Greenhill a spade (4s. 9d.) and he was ready to start work. This he seems to have done and subsequently caused the parish very little expense.

In the two years 1816-8 £339 9s. 4d., was spent on administration; expenses were necessarily high with so many trips being made to Henley-in-Arden, Warwick and other places further way, and numerous warrants, orders etc., being needed. In addition there were the regularly recurring expenses such as the County Rate, (now approximately £10 0s. 0d., per quarter), the frequent meetings at which bread and cheese as well as ale was often provided, adding between 10d., and 5s. 6d., to each set of expenses.

The bell ringers were also given ale instead of money for ringing on 5 November and at Christmas, the cost being 10s. 6d., each time. Ale was provided too for the workers who were working on the 'Vestry Room' at the church; this may have been when the west chantry chapel was made into a vestry, but this is not certain. The cost of the work was £36 12s. 2d., a stonemason and the carpenters Samuel Parsons and Samuel Gazy being involved.

One unusual expense was £3 0s. 0d., paid in September 1816 to Mrs. Carpenter to enable her to 'free her husband from prison', where he had been since at least May. No hint was given as to what he had done and why he was there.

When the accounts for 1817-8 were examined Mr. Pye, the absentee rector who had returned to the parish for the meeting, objected to certain expenses paid at the *Royal Oak* and *The Boot* totalling £33 11s. 2½d. Part of this amount had been incurred when John Buttwell was kept in the parish prior to his marriage with Hannah Turner, but what the balance was spent on is unknown. The matter was taken before the Petty Sessions where Mr. Heath, the Overseer, explained the charges to the magistrates. What he said to them is not recorded but they were 'satisfied with the account given by him'.[5]

THE POOR COTTAGES

Considering together the various records which are available for the period 1790's to 1881 — the Overseers of the Poor accounts, the Charity records, the census returns and the Parish Registers[6] — it is possible to formulate a picture of those on the lowest rung of the Lapworth social ladder.

In the Tithe Apportionment of 1839[7] 46 buildings were described as cottages, some being single houses and others two or three dwellings joined together. The cottages were dotted about the parish, some close to farmsteads where their occupants worked, others were situated on odd pieces of land at the road side or at road junctions. A little can be learned about the occupants of most of the cottages from the census returns, but it is the families who lived in the cottages belonging to the Charity Estate whose lives are the most rewarding to look into.

These people had lives which were simple, hard and frugal; to the modern onlooker they appear to have consisted chiefly of birth, work and death. It is to be hoped that there was some happiness too. Of the 40 known tenants who occupied the 18 Charity Estate cottages in the years 1814-1875 it is possible to look in detail at the lives of 29 of them. All but two of the men earned their living as agricultural workers; many had difficulty making ends meet and, of the 18 tenants listed in the Estate survey of 1814,[8] eight received assistance from the Overseers in the 1790's and 11 (four of them being the same people) support in the years 1816-8.

Outbuildings of Malthouse Farm, Kingswood

Only two of the male tenants 'retired', that is stopped working, and probably only then because they could no longer physically continue; the remainder worked until they died. Edward Sprag who repaired the roads in the 1840's was still working at 82 years of age; William Fantham, Joseph Hobday, William Craddock, James Ward, Elias Carpenter, John Reeve and Thomas Nash were all working at 70 years plus, and William Heritage, Thomas Ward, Thomas Maids, Thomas Reynolds, William Horton, John Constable, Thomas Underhill, Thomas Dee and John Barnet at over 60 years of age. Not all men could stand such years of toil and six male tenants died in their 40's or 50's.

The women who were left to struggle on alone had a life of penury, although some, like Sarah Brookes, filled their days helping others; when she died in 1837 she was 90 years of age; those who had the opportunity married again. Elizabeth Townsend who was widowed in 1837, married John Crump, her lodger, in 1841; they lived for some time in her cottage but the Feoffees objected, for he was not poor and owned a house on the opposite side of the road, into which they then moved.

Widowers also had a problem; 19th century housekeeping — fetching water, heating it, washing clothes, cleaning, keeping the fires burning, cooking, baking, knitting, sewing, patching, darning and budgeting frugally for a family — was a full time job and could not be fitted in with working long hours on the land. Elderly men alone could perhaps manage with the help of married daughters and friendly neighbours but men with several children needed a servant or a wife. Eleven men were left as widowers and four married again. Mary Ann the wife of Edward Townsend (the son of Elizabeth Townsend) died in 1849 aged 36 years leaving him with five children aged two to 12 years. He had moved into the family cottage when his mother and Mr. Crump left. In 1851 he and the children were being cared for by a servant but by 1861 he had married Sarah Edgecox, his next door neighbour. She was the widow of John Edgecox, the tailor; she had eight children but only two lived with her, their stepfather and his youngest son.

Altogether the 29 families had 163 known children between them; there may have been others who were not recorded, for by this period not all parents took every child for baptism. William Reeve who lived in one of the Pound Cottages had 13 children, Thomas Reynolds his neighbour had 10, as did Thomas Townsend (by two wives, Elizabeth being his second). Joseph Carpenter had nine children and Sarah Brookes and Edgecox, the tailor, eight children each. Four families each had seven children, four each had six, five each had five and four had four children each. At least 12 families had one or more children die, infancy and the early teens to early 20's apparently being the most vulnerable periods for the offspring of these poor families.

All the children had the opportunity of going to school, but until attendance was compulsory much depended on the parents' attitude. However some of the girls certainly attended Mrs. Brown's school.[9]

As soon as the children were old enough they went out to work, the girls into service and the boys chiefly into agricultural work. Sarah Reynolds was a servant at *The Boot* and Maria Horton at Malthouse Farm, Kingswood. Henry and Charles Reeve both worked for George Gibbs at Bushwood Hall, Henry (18) as cowman and Charles (14) as stable boy. Their older brother John, when aged 13 had worked for Thomas King at Lapworth Lodge Farm. James Carpenter (16) was a carter boy at Blockbury House and Thomas Ward (16) a farm worker at High Chimneys. A few young men became craftsmen, William Underhill a blacksmith, John Edgecox junior a cordwainer and William Reynolds a platelayer on the railway. Dressmaking was the only trade for girls — Sarah Edgecox carried on her business from the house she shared with her brother John, and Mary Barnet from her father's cottage where she also kept house for him. Many young people left Lapworth inevitably being drawn to Birmingham. Subsequently some grandchildren from areas such as Sparkbrook, Birmingham and West Bromwich seem to have been sent to live with grandparents in the healthier air of Lapworth.

Poor cottagers shelling peas (after W. H. Pyne, 1845)

Under the new Poor Law arrangements after 1834 out-relief to poor able bodied families was stopped and the alternative to poverty in the village was the workhouse. The Charity Feoffees gave help as and where they could with the limited funds available. In 1835 they offered lump sums of not more than £8 0s. 0d., per annum to those working men with families who asked for nothing, but did need help. The same year they started a clothing club and asked for voluntary contributions from the wealthy; Lord Cornwallis a Lapworth landowner, gave annually to the funds. As always they arranged apprenticeships — John Barnet's son being apprenticed to Mr. Allen, the shoemaker, of Rowington in 1844 at a cost of £4 0s. 0d.

Agricultural workers suffered a low period in the 1840's, and there was considerable distress amongst the labouring poor. In order to earn extra money Thomas Underhill and his wife Sarah lived apart for a time, she being the living-in servant at Thomas Rainbow's whilst he stayed at home in their cottage. Many villagers were helped in small ways by the Feoffees; in 1845 William Horton who was ill was given 12s. 0d., to keep his family for two weeks, John Edgecox 'was in distress' and received 3s 0d., William Craddock could not pay his rent, William Reeve was given a bag of potatoes. A list of the poor made in 1845 named 59 people, including all the cottage tenants.[10] Most of them received between 3 cwt. and 6 cwt. of coal but George Commander had 3s. 0d., in money instead: Viners, Craddock and Underhill had nothing, possibly they had already been helped in other ways.

Circumstances did not improve and coal, money, shoes, sheets, and clothes for the children continued to be given. William Reeve's and Edward Townsend's large families had the most gifts of shoes, trousers, shirts and round frocks.

During these years there was considerable ill-health in the country as a whole and cholera and typhus fever were sweeping through the towns, killing many. In 1849 Mr. Mildmay, the rector, recorded that typhus 'was very bad in the parish'.[11] This virus infection caused by bad living conditions — poor food, lack of fuel and clean clothing — was carried by body lice.[12] It was very contagious, the patients having a fever, a measles-type rash, coated tongue and a crust round the mouth; they became very weak and often delirious. George Commander, Mary Ann Townsend and John Townsend may have died of typhus, Mrs. Elizabeth Mander, her daughter Sophia, and her husband, of Catesby Farm, certainly did, according to the rector. In the autumn of 1849 measles was the problem 'affecting both young and old' but there were 'no serious cases'. Two years later whooping cough in the parish caused the death of Catherine the schoolmaster's infant daughter who was the rector's godchild.

Since 1841 many people had abandoned the country life and moved to the towns where there was a great demand for workers. The loss of people from the village was not wholly realised until 1851 when the census showed a drop of 96 in the population. The rector recording '6 tenements being at this time disinhabited'. On conditions in the parish he later wrote:- 'The year 1852 [was] marked by the death of nine out of twelve men [buried] in the year being below 40 years of age'. In 1853 'more illness in this parish than has been known for many years during the whole winter: tho there was no epidemic beyond influenza to account for it'. 'A very bad harvest this year, unfavourable weather both for hay and corn, acres of both entirely lost'. His notes for the winter of 1854-5 are a vivid comment on the plight of the poor 'very severe weather recurring in February and prices being unusually high a soup kitchen supplying the poor with soup at 1d. a swail[?], rice sold at 1d. a lb was begun. The poor were also supplied with pea seed and potatoe seed for their allotment lands. Wages were from 10s. to 11s. per week and flour 13/6d. a strike, meat 7½d. and 8d. a lb'.

The rents charged for the Charity Estate cottages in 1814 are to be found on page 53. Apart from Thomas Underhill and William Bate being asked in 1825 to pay £2 0s. 0d., per annum each or quit their cottages nothing further is recorded of the rents until 1856. By 1826 the number of cottages for the poor had been increased to 21 Thomas Dee's cottage having been made into two dwellings and a house in Wharf Lane turned into two cottages.

The rent rolls of 1856 onwards[13] lists all the tenants but it is not always possible to know which property they occupied. By this date there had been some re-arrangement in the cottage premises and instead of 21 cottages there were only 15 or perhaps 16. The three cottages at Kingswood Brook were reduced to two and occupied by Widow Astley who paid 4s. 0d., per annum rent and Joseph Hobday who paid £2 0s. 0d., per annum; both were at times in arrears. Widow Astley's cottage remained empty after she left in 1867 but Hobday took her garden for an extra 7s. 6d., per annum. By 1877 he too had gone and his cottage was also left vacant.

The four cottages at Copt Green were by 1856 reduced to two and occupied by Widow Fantham and Widow Young; both paid 4s. 0d., per annum rent the usual charge for widows and those without work; occasionally they were in arrears. In 1858 the cottages passed out of the Estate's possession; by 1861 Mrs. Fantham had moved to the row of cottages beside the church which had once housed the school. Although very old, unhealthy and in poor condition they were used for single, elderly people and in 1861 were described as the 'alms-houses'.

The five cottages at The Pound were by 1841 made into four; they were occupied by Edward Sprag, George Commander, John Constable and James Ward who had succeeded his father as tenant; later Sprag and Ward were moved to the 'alms-houses'. The tenants at The Pound in 1856 were John Constable who paid £2 0s. 0d., per annum rent, William Horton, William Reeve and Thomas Reynolds who each paid 4s. 0d., per annum rent, although in work; all were sometime in arrears. When Constable died his widow was moved out, and her cottage given to Joseph Carpenter senior. Carpenter's cottage, in the Old Warwick Road, being, in turn, given to his son. In 1877 Horton also went to the 'alms-houses'.

The three cottages in the Old Warwick Road (now the site of Yew Tree House) were made into two by 1841 and occupied by William Craddock and John Viners. Viners soon left and John Barnet moved in paying 4s. 0d., per annum rent whilst Craddock paid £2 12s. 0d., per annum. Both men fell into arrears; Barnet was given notice to quit but did not leave and at his death his daughter took on the tenancy at 5s. 0d., per quarter. Craddock's rent was 4s. 0d., per annum from 1869.

The two cottages opposite Drawbridge Farm (now the site of Danesbury) remained in two and were occupied in 1856 by Edward Townsend and Joseph Carpenter senior, both paid 4s. 0d., per annum rent but this was increased in 1861 to £2 12s. 0d., per annum. Carpenter moved to The Pound in 1872 his son taking over his cottage. The adjacent cottages (now the site of Winston House) were occupied in 1841 by Thomas Underhill and John Edgecox. Underhill was still there in 1861 (at £2 0s. 0d., per annum rent) but it is not clear whether Edgecox's cottage was occupied again after he died.

The two cottages in Wharf Lane (now Bumblebees) were occupied by Widow Lydia Cox (from 1841-71) and James Staples; when Staples left, her son, William, became her neighbour. She paid 4s. 0d., per year throughout but the others paid £2 0s. 0d., and later £2 12s. 0d., per annum.

The Charity Cottages in Wharf Lane. Now one house called Bumblebees.

The 'alms-house' cottages continued to be used for the elderly although by 1881 only three were occupied. A few people lived there for 10 years but Jane Briscoe, the shoemaker's widow, was there for more than 20 years. The cottages became so decayed that c1890 Solihull Sanitary Authority condemned them and ordered them to be pulled down; Mrs. Sarah Jeffs the last tenant there went to live with her daughter Mrs. Neal. Immediately there was uproar in the village. Mr. William King of Lapworth Park Farm objected and did all he could to preserve the cottages, even collecting money for their repair. A heated discussion was carried on in the pages of the 'Ferrers Magazine' between December 1890 and March 1891. It was claimed that the poor loved living there and only left when they were turned out or sent to the workhouse, 'rather than go one old man hanged himself and a lady died of grief'. The rector replied, refuting the allegations and giving the facts. Of the last tenants Mary Newton and Thomas Smith had died in 1879; Elizabeth Smith, a cripple, and the only person to go to the workhouse in 13 years, had done so at her own request and died there in 1886. Mrs. Jeffs (aged 83) was still alive, as was Jane Briscoe (aged 90) and Maria Smith, her husband having died in hospital in 1887.

Mr. King canvassed the 146 electors in the parish — 117 replied, and 114 were in favour of restoration. But it was no good, the cottages were too 'dilapidated, insanitary, and depressing to live in' and the land was needed for a churchyard extension. They were demolished in 1892. During the work a brick was found bearing the date 1692; the parish asked to keep it and place it in the churchyard wall as a momento; Solihull S.A. refused — the brick was needed as proof that the cottages had been pulled down — it might be viewed on application![14] Where can it be now?

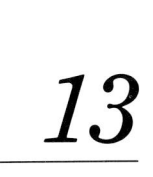

13
TRADES AND OCCUPATIONS

The main occupation in Lapworth was always agriculture and those trades which were allied to it — blacksmiths, wheelwrights etc. Other trades did exist, but in the 18th century it is only through probate records and deeds that some of them are revealed. From such references it is known that carpenters, masons, cordwainers (shoemakers), brickmakers, tanners and a hatcheller (flax dresser) worked in the parish, two or three generations of a family frequently following the same trade. Each of these craftsmen also had some land and a few animals, their craft not being profitable enough to support them entirely.

Some trades like brickmaking were seasonal, the clay, dug out in the autumn, being left during the winter for the frost to break up. The following spring the weathered clay was prepared, then churned up by hand or in a pug mill before being rolled, kneaded, and shaped into bricks. This was done by throwing clay, by hand, into a mould; two to three thousand bricks could be made by one man in a day. The bricks were then placed on long open racks for at least two weeks and dried; this could only be done in spring and summer. When dry they were burnt in clamps; layers of green (raw) bricks being arranged on a layer of burnt bricks and fuel, to form a stack. More burnt bricks were placed over the top and sides; the stack was set alight at both ends and allowed to burn itself out, a process taking several weeks.[1] Setting and firing the clamp required considerable skill. Four fields in Lapworth called Brick Kiln indicate brick making sites; that close to Lapworth Lodge Farm was owned by Mr. Bradbury whose brother was a brickmaker in Rowington. The Baker family, father and son,[2] occupied another site in Lapworth but where is unknown.

Brickmakers

The tanyard worked by the Overton family gave its name to Tan House Farm where they lived. When William Overton died in 1722[3] skins and hides — '18 Dry hides, 91 Wett Hides, 11 hides and 2 Skins, 97 Calf Skins and Bark' — valued at £141 15s. 8d., were in the yard and sheds. The bark, usually that of oak trees, was used in the tanning process. Later the business passed into the hands of John Grafton who was there until 1818.

Although many farmers brewed ale and beer at home, inns were visited regularly and were popular places for local meetings. The *Boot Inn* is probably the oldest pub in Lapworth, although the *Bell Inn* is mentioned in the late 18th century. The *Navigation Inn* at Kingswood (in Rowington parish) is a very old inn, reputedly medieval.[4] It originally served the needs of travellers along the road to Warwick, long before the canal, with which it is now associated, was considered. The *Royal Oak* appears to have been established about 1785, probably to serve the increased coaching traffic then using the Stratford Road. The site, prior to the building of the pub, was a brick yard owned by Robert Mander of Irelands Farm.

THE 19th CENTURY

From 1813 the Parish Registers give the occupation of the fathers of children being baptised, and from these records it is possible to learn something of the variety of trades in Lapworth during the period to 1849. 'Farmer' and agricultural 'Labourer' are the most frequent occupations given, but many others occur regularly.

Brickmaking was still carried on in the parish, three families, the Williams and the two Egelston brothers, being recorded until the late 1820's. The canal made the transport of machine made bricks, uniform in size and colour, possible and easy; in time this drove out the local brickmakers for there are none in the parish later in the century.

John Green, who had his smithy at the *Bell Inn,* is the only blacksmith mentioned until the 1840's when three smiths were recorded. There were a number of wheelwrights in the village, including one or two who did not remain for long, but during the 1830's when coach traffic was at its peak there were three in business at the same time — James Hunt, Thomas Quinney and Thomas Richmond — and in the 1840's Richmond, Thomas Bate and Henry Hill, perhaps a son of Henry Hill the farmer.

Wheelwrights

From the 1820's there was always one carrier in Lapworth and during the 1830's there were three. These men, Richard Smith, Francis Fetherstone and Joseph Barnbrook, carried goods and people cheaply but slowly, about the countryside, particularly along the by-ways. They undertook shopping, carried messages, and were a life line for people in rural areas who could rarely get to the local market town themselves. The passage of the canal through the parish made the carriage of very heavy goods easier. Coal was much cheaper after the advent of the canal and there was always at least one coal merchant in the parish during the period under review.

Several of the men whose children were baptised worked for the Canal Company as lock-keepers, clerks and boatmen. At least one of the seven carpenters named worked on the canal, the lock gates and much else made of timber needing constant attention.

Until the 1830's there appears to have been only one shoemaker in the parish, then Robert Briscoe and David Hammond each set up in business and by the 1840's there was enough trade for two more men to open workshops. All ordinary people wore locally made shoes in which they walked great distances whilst going about their daily business, they needed to be strong and waterproof and were more like boots than modern shoes.

Clothes too were usually locally made either at home or by a tailor. There were three tailors in the village in the 1820's to 1840's — Thomas Cox, John Edgecox and Joseph Richmond — and two more at Hockley Heath. Even in towns clothes were not available off-the-peg as mass manufacturing had not yet begun and clothes were quite expensive.

Rake making and wood turning were common trades at Hockley Heath.[5] Rakes of all sizes were an essential part of farming, particularly at haymaking and harvest time and all agricultural hand tools and implements had wooden handles made of turned wood. The Wadell or Wardle family lived and had their wood workshops at the boundary of Lapworth parish, close to where Hull's garage now stands. Other woodworkers were John Pountney and John Lancaster, both coopers in the parish. Possibly their barrels were shipped out by canal for there were no large brewers in Lapworth. There were however three maltsters, Richard Cotterill, Thomas Turvey, and Thomas Rainbow who farmed and had his malthouse at Brookhouse Farm. There were two other malthouses in the parish at Malthouse Farm, Lapworth and Malthouse Farm, Kingswood. Malt was made out of barley, an early variety with a double row of beards being the best type for malting.[6] The grain was steeped in water to absorb moisture, then spread out on a malting floor to germinate and grow; at a precise point this was stopped by placing the green malt in a kiln in which it was dried and heated. Comparatively small quantities of malt were made at one time, for it was apparently important not to mix and process together barleys grown on different soils, or even different fields.[7] Whether the maltsters of Lapworth malted only locally grown grain, including their own, or whether they brought it in from a distance is not known, nor where it was ultimately used for brewing. At this time the local innkeepers were still brewing their own beer, for the monopoly of the breweries had not yet begun, but they would not have used large quantities of malt; it was possible to make 274 gallons of beer with 15 bushels of malt[8] (malt costing 8s. 0d., per bushel in 1821), the process (but on a larger scale) being similar to tea making.

1851-1881

1851

The census of 1851[9] was the first to record the occupation of all the employed people in the parish. Agriculture was still the work which most men went into, there being 35 farmers (30 male and 5 female) at this time. There were also 15 'assistant farmers', usually their sons and young relatives who were learning the art of husbandry. Just over 100 farm labourers toiled with them, little in the way of machinery yet being available.

Very few women worked outside the home; married women spent their days cleaning, cooking and washing with few tools or aids. The majority had to carry all the household's water from the well or pump and then heat every drop needed for washing the dishes, the clothes, and the family. This and all cooking was carried out with a coal fire and simple oven. The larger farmhouses and some gentlemen's homes had female servants: they were also to be found on smaller farms where there was no wife or where a mother had died leaving small children.

Unmarried young women were sent into domestic service, often at the age of 12 or 13. Few, it would seem, had the opportunity to be more than general scullions for in 1851 few houses had more than one female servant. On the larger farms there were usually two or three unmarried farm labourers living-in plus the family, which might include an unmarried daughter who would also work in the house, but the work must have been very hard for teenage girls. At the rectory there were three female servants and at Bridge House two, but this was the exception. In the whole parish there were 32 female servants, the average age being 21 years.

An alternative to service was dressmaking, (there were three dressmakers) laundry work (there were two laundry women) or marriage. Farmer's daughters did not go into service and they had to wait until a suitable man made an offer for their hand. In 1851 there were 14 unmarried farmers' daughters or similar, aged between 21 and 43, in Lapworth. There were plenty of suitable unmarried men — seven farmers aged between 30 and 55 and 12 farmers' sons aged 21 to 47 years — but they were very slow to take the plunge. Probably they could not afford to; only one of the seven farms had more than 60 acres of land, probably an insufficient acreage if worked by old fashioned methods, at a time when others, with larger acreages or better land, were pushing ahead with new ideas, draining their fields, and cornering the market.

At this time the tradesmen were little different from those recorded earlier in the century — carpenters (4), smiths (3), tailors (2), wheelwrights (3), cordwainers (5), rakemakers (2), and maltsters (1). There was also a flour dealer, a corn dealer, a bricklayer and a stonemason — the last two probably working for the Canal Company. Six other men who worked on the canal lived in Lapworth; less than in 1841, for the business of the canal was beginning to be hit by the railways which were now rapidly expanding. Sometime before 1841 a beerhouse had opened at Kingswood in the small house, *Cherry Trees,* which stood beside the cross roads. Francis Fetherstone, who had previously been a carrier, settled there with his wife and three children. On the opposite corner (in what is now the Punch Bowl) was a butcher's shop run by William Healstone. By 1851 the shop had gone and the house was occupied by James Hammond, a labourer. Here by 1861 the Hammonds had opened a beerhouse; *Cherry Trees* had closed and the licence been transferred to what became the *Punch Bowl Inn.*

1871

A railway station had been built at Lapworth by 1855 and this started a change in village society which continues to the present day, for the train brought the parish within easy reach of Birmingham, and made commuting possible.

The attraction of living in the countryside brought more people to Lapworth and the census of 1871[10] reveals quite an influx of newcomers. Some took existing houses but at least two large new houses — Kingswood Grange and The Terretts — close to the station and suitable in size and appointments for merchants and others with families and servants, had been built since 1861.

All these newcomers required servants and employed between them a butler, four cooks, two housemaids, a housekeeper, a gamekeeper, a groom/gardener, two grooms, two gardeners, a coachman/gardener and three nurses, but these specialist abilities and the high standard of training demanded, were not available in Lapworth amongst the indigenous population. All but one of these jobs, that of groom, were occupied by people from elsewhere in Warwickshire, from Salop, Cheshire, Rutland, Worcestershire and Somerset. Not all these servants lived-in — the gamekeeper, the groom/gardener, and the coachman/gardener lived in separate households with their wives and children. They, like their employers, brought new ideas, standards, fashions and way of life into the parish, broadening the outlook and affecting, if only slightly, all who met them.

The Terretts was occupied by Mr. Shirley Palmer, a surgeon and his family, and Kingswood Grange by Mr. William Garrard, a manufacturer and his wife and baby. Other newcomers were Richard Smith, a commercial traveller in leather, Mrs. Harding and her (absent) husband, the Melson family, Mrs. Fenton and her clergyman son who had a tiny school with two boarding pupils. There were two households where the master and mistress were away from home on census night, their imposing servants (one had a butler) being left in charge.

Other newcomers were the railway employees, the station master William Hoston, his clerk William Lee, and three labourers — Samuel Quinn, George Moseley and Fred Alcock. Hoston had been at Lapworth only about a year having previously lived at Packwood and Solihull.

Two men, Philip Taylor, a clock jeweller, and John Martin, a metal worker, both Birmingham born, lived at the *Boot Inn* as lodgers and, no doubt, travelled to their work daily by train.

Mill Lane, Kingswood, with the Bird in Hand Inn on the right

Just along the canal from *The Boot* was the *Bird in Hand* beerhouse which stood where the flats with the same name are to-day. Situated below the level of the road, the building was occupied in 1841 by Thomas Smith, a grocer, who probably served both the village and the canal people, being conveniently close to a bridge and the locks. It was not until 1871 that his son, also Thomas, opened the house as an inn serving the boatmen of the canal with food and beer. The heyday of the canal was over and the fewer boatmen had to work longer trips than they once had. They therefore ceased to live ashore, instead their homes, wives and children were all on the boat. Canal side pubs became more common and popular, a place to get away from the boat and relax for a while.

1881

The census of 1881,[11] the latest available for study, shows the effect that the agricultural depression of the 1870's had on the farmers of Lapworth. There were a number of changes of tenancy and nine farms were being worked by farm bailiffs. None of these men were local, two of them coming from Scotland and one from Dorset.

Amongst the other farmers, several of them were also newcomers and there was a change in domestic life style. All except one of them were married, many being young enough to have children at school. Amongst the older offspring some had chosen jobs away from farming, particularly in the service of the railway. Even the girls were spreading their wings, one farmer's daughter being a pupil teacher and another a milliner.

The number of newcomers and commuters had increased, particularly in Kingswood and close to the station. At The Terretts Mr. Shirley Palmer had his daughter, son-in-law, who was a banker in Birmingham, and their children living with him, and Dingley Dell was occupied by two retired hat makers. In Station Lane lived a woollen merchant, a coach builder, and a retired publican, and a jeweller. The latter, Samuel Sutton, lived at Kingswood House which his father had opened as an inn; hoping, no doubt, to refresh those who were thirsty after travelling on the train. In Old Warwick Road lived the local Inland Revenue Officer and, possibly at Fairview, a spectacle maker who employed six men and three girls at his business in Birmingham.

There were about a dozen households with a better class of, or 'trained' servants — a butler, cooks, housemaids, grooms, coachmen, gardeners — and at Kingswood Grange, a French governess. A number of the men, gardeners, grooms, coachmen, lived out with their wives and children and it is often only possible to guess for which household they worked. The increased number of gardeners (six) indicates that there were more people unwilling to toil themselves, and perhaps, that gardens were becoming a pleasurable adjunct to a house rather than a vegetable plot. The presence of two gamekeepers in the parish suggest that sport — fishing and shooting — may have been one of Lapworth's attractions for the wealthier new residents.

The craftsmen and tradesmen changed little in the decade 1871-81 and there were still carpenters, bootmakers, bricklayers, wheelwrights, a carrier, a maltster and a blacksmith. There were now also seven dressmakers, a milliner, two shopkeepers, a baker, a draper, a mason and two sawyers, some of whom must have been attracted to the village by the needs and demands of the changing population. There was no miller and it would seem that with the depressed state of agriculture the windmill had ceased to work.

The canal continued to employ a variety of craftsmen as well as the manager, clerk and lockkeepers, whilst on the railway the numbers continued to grow, eight G.W.R., men including two platelayers, a porter, a clerk, and the station master living in Lapworth.

Sands Farm

14
'CHILDREN WHO ATTEND REGULARLY DO WELL'*

1841-69

By 1841 Mrs. Brown's school had closed, Mr. Mortiboys had retired and Charles Marston had taken his place as master of the school. The salary, on which he supported a wife and four children, was still £20 0s. 0d., per annum the same as in the 1790's. Marston left Lapworth in 1845 William Cattell and his wife, Mary Ann, taking up the joint appointment of master and mistress at the single salary of £50 0s. 0d., per annum, with the house and garden free of rent and taxes. Out of their salary the coals for the school room had to be purchased; between November 1845 and October 1846 eight tons were used the cost being £7 12s. 9d. They were also expected to take the children to church and to Sunday school, and Mr. Cattell had to act as treasurer to the Charity Estate.

Boys and girls were still taught separately, the boys learning the three R's and the girls reading, sewing and knitting as they had 30 years previously. Parish children were taught free of charge, those from other parishes could attend but had to pay — 1d., per week for one child, 1½d., for two children and 2d., per week for more than two children: payment was in advance of tuition.[1] Boys were expected to leave at 10 years of age but girls could stay on until they were 12 years old.

In 1848 a new scheme for running the Charities was put into operation. Under this the total cost of running the school was not to exceed £90 0s. 0d., per annum including all salaries, stationery, repairs, property insurance, indeed all expenses whatever connected with the school, schoolhouse and master's house. In fact the total sum usually set out was only £80 0s. 0d., per annum. All the children were to be instructed in reading, spelling, and religious knowledge, the boys were also to learn writing and arithmetic, the girls might take these subjects too, but at the master's discretion! Charity money was to be available for putting out ex-pupils as apprentices and servants.[2]

During their years at Lapworth the Cattells had two daughters Sarah Ann and Catherine. The latter died, when still a baby, in the whooping cough epidemic of 1851 and her father died in 1860 aged only 46 years. Mrs. Cattell moved away, but 30 years later she and Sarah Ann, also a teacher, were back in the parish living on the Stratford Road and possibly teaching at Hockley Heath School.[3]

The Cattells were succeeded by Isaac and Sarah Yeomans who had five children and had previously been at a school in Warwick. They stayed at Lapworth for eight years and were followed by Mr. and Mrs. George Chamberlain who remained only a few months.

1869-89

The next headmaster was Edwin Sly a native of Rowington; he was only 24 years old when he was appointed in February 1869, his sister Harriet, aged 22 years, being the schoolmistress.[4] Sly was a kind, conscientious and humane man. During his headship many changes took place in education, the chief of which were 1) the 1870 Education Act which made attendance at school compulsory until the age of 13; 2) the Agricultural Childrens Act of 1873 which made it necessary for pupils to have a certificate from the school giving leave of absence when they were needed to help with vital agricultural work; and 3) payment for schooling. The results of these events are recorded in fascinating detail in the Lapworth School Log Book[5] which starts in January 1873. In it Sly, and later his successor Alfred Horace Davey, recorded in their copperplate handwriting, snippets of the daily life of the school — attendance, illness, the weather, the Inspectors' reports — which give an interesting insight into the regime of a Victorian school.

Extract from the Government Inspector's report 1883.

TERMS AND HOLIDAYS

The school year was, as now, divided into three terms but there was no academic year as such and the attendance register started each 1 November and finished each 31 October. The Easter term began every year between the 6 and 12 of January, always on a Monday. There was one week of holiday at Easter and another week at Whitsuntide. Later in the year a longer break of four to five weeks was taken; called the harvest holiday, it enabled the older children to work in the fields. In several years the holiday was adjusted to suit the time of the harvest, in 1879, for example, the harvest was very backward and the break did not begin until 29 August, for the master knew that the children would not attend school if they were needed at home. The Christmas break lasted about a fortnight starting only a day or two before Christmas day.

There were usually three or four half holidays during the year — for the school treat, after the school had attended church on Ash Wednesday and Ascension Day, and after the examinations. When it was polling day a whole day's holiday was given. The school treat, provided by the rector or his wife, consisted of presenting prizes to those children 'who had been satisfactory during the past year'. The children were then allowed to play in a field till evening 'when they were dismissed'. In January 1876 a very special treat, and one which they probably long remembered, was provided by Mr. Sanders of Blockbury House. 'The pupils gathered . . . about 4p.m. and partook of tea'. A Christmas tree 'was lighted up about 5p.m. and the presents afterwards distributed', they 'received two each, besides oranges, sweetmeats etc. After . . . Mr. Simonds exhibited his diorama to the bigger boys and girls and all seemed delighted'. In subsequent years tea and a magic lantern show were arranged, but there are no further references to Christmas trees.

In 1876 the school treat was slightly different, in addition to the usual events tea was provided by the rector, and afterwards an inscribed inkstand was presented to Edwin Sly to mark his departure from the parish and the school; his sister was presented with a bible. Half holidays had to be given each year for Hockley Mop and for Hockley Heath Club and the Royal Oak Club feasts. Both were saving clubs that provided enjoyable annual outings for members; whole families attended, emptying the school, for such events were not to be missed.

Ever conscious of the demon drink the rector in 1880 gave the children a tea connected with the Temperance Association, and a Band of Hope was started, several children agreeing to join. The children had very little excitement in their lives and these teas and meetings were red letter days to which they looked forward with great anticipation. In all excluding weekends, the school had an average of 49 days holiday per year.

LESSONS

Until 1874 the whole school (about 60 children) was taught in one room, but then a single storey extension was built. This was rather dark at first but later the windows were altered to make it brighter and improve the ventilation. The two rooms (38ft. 10ins by 13ft. 9½ins and 26ft. by 15ft.) were heated by coal fires and filled with desks fitted together in rows. The boys and girls were taught in five Standards plus the Infants, the lessons — reading, writing, dictation, geography, arithmetic and scripture — were almost certainly learned by rote and were probably rather boring. There were no games, the only light relief being singing, and needlework for the girls. The children wrote on slates until Standard II and then on paper.

Each year a Government Inspector came to test the children and look at the school; the Diocese also sent an Inspector who examined the pupils in religious knowledge in great detail. Both Edwin Sly and his successor Alfred Davey were considered to be good teachers who kept a disciplined and efficient school. In 1874, at the Inspector's suggestion, a pupil teacher was engaged to help with the lessons. This was Thomas Cranmer, a senior pupil who had been absent from school for 15 months but recently returned — he was paid £1 16s. 0d., per nine weeks. Cranmer left after three years training, his place being taken by James Hicken; he was not altogether satisfactory and left in 1879. Margaret Ball, a pupil who helped one day when Hicken was ill, succeeded him. She was keen, conscientious and good with the children. When in January 1886, after much hard work and study she left Lapworth to take up a scholarship at Whitelands Training College, Chelsea, a great achievement, she was presented with a purse containing £7 10s. 0d., as a token of appreciation.

The annual Government examination was open only to children who had attended on more than 250 half days. In 1875, out of a register list of about 80 pupils, only eight Infants and 26 over-seven's were tested; by 1883 more children qualified to enter and 88 were examined. From 1879 the children prepared several different songs each year for the Inspector who chose two or three as test pieces. A favourite, on the list almost every year, was *'Hurrah, Hurrah for England'* an indication of the patriotism which was instilled in the children. They also learned great chunks of poetry by heart for the exam — at least 75 lines of such epics at *'The Eve of Waterloo'* from *'Childe Harold's Pilgrimage'*, and *'Triumphs of the English Language'* — not all together suitable choices for simple village children.

On the whole the teaching was good 'and those children who attend regularly do well but those who are often away make it impossible to call [their progress] good'.

ATTENDANCE

Lapworth children usually started school between the age of four and five years. They turned up to be admitted at all times of the year and on any day of the week. As they grew older, having learned to read and write, many of the parents thought attending school unimportant, especially if the children were needed at home. The parents did not bother about the regulation absence certificates and kept the children away between January and April to go bird scaring, bean dropping (planting), gardening, dandelion and cowslip picking. In the summer it was haymaking and currant picking and in autumn harvesting, gleaning, gardening and acorn collecting which kept the children away from their lessons.

These were all short absences but some children were away for long periods — John White returned to school in June 1873 having been at work for a year, Elizabeth Linney was away for three months and many others too were away for weeks and months, no reason being given. Such breaks were against the law, but no action was taken until January 1876 when the local magistrates decided to enforce the law and prosecute parents 'who neglect to send their children to school'. At once attendance improved, long absent children appeared and those who wished to work applied for certificates. These were granted if the children had already attended on 150 half days since their last birthday.

Attendance having improved the school managers decided that from 25 March 1876 the children should 'pay pence' for their tuition — 'For the children of farmers 4d. per week; for the children of tradesmen, shopkeepers and artisans 2d. per week; for the children of labourers 1d. per week. No further charge will be made for labourers who have already two children in the school'. The scheme actually began on 3 April, a week's grace having been allowed. Many parents refused to pay and several children were withdrawn. Another week passed, then those children who failed to bring their pence were sent home. By 1 May most of the children had returned to school with their pence but the Woodward family resisted for seven weeks.

Mr. Davey was particularly concerned about the children being away so often (through illness as well as work) and the effect it had on their learning ability; his log book is full of comments about them 'slipping back' and forgetting what they had learned. In June 1879 in desperation he wrote a sharp letter to Mr. Clifford the School Attendance Officer at Solihull complaining of Clifford's inactivity over the absent pupils; he also complained to the new curate, Rev. Charles Partridge, and gave him a list of the absentees. Partridge at once visited all the parents, as did the Attendance Officer. From this time Davey was in constant touch with Mr. Clifford sending fortnightly lists of those away and matters did improve.

A few families still resisted paying the pence and put off doing so for as long as possible. Mrs. Courtnell, whose husband was a canal man and who herself worked at *The Boot*, particularly resented paying for her three children. They were continually being sent home for non-payment; in 1880 they were away from school for four months because of her intransigence. For a period at the end of 1881 Mrs. Courtnell removed her children and sent them to the Catholic School at Bedlams End (Chadwick End) but after three months she sent them again to Lapworth. The three Griffin boys were also frequently absent and did not pay their pence. Mrs. Griffin claimed that she had sent the money for three weeks but George, her eldest son, had spent it. Finally in March 1883 the Courtnells and Henry Jennings, the Griffin boys' step-father, were summoned before the magistrates at Solihull and attendance orders were made. Elizabeth, the last Courtnell at school, left in December 1883 but the Griffins remained; during most of 1884 they paid no pence at all, then in November Mr. Davey took firm action, and the arrears, of 5s. 2d., were immediately paid. George Griffin left, but his brothers continued an intermittent attendance, never for long enough however to qualify to enter any of the exams.

THE WEATHER

There were many days when the weather was so bad that the pupils were unable to get to school or arrived extremely wet. Both Sly and Davey noted the weather in the Log Book in explanation of the attendance figures.

As all the children walked to school, some from Kingswood, Copt Green and the bottom of Lapworth Street, deep snow or heavy rain were major deterrents. Although most children would have had stout shoes or boots, it is doubtful if many would have had wellington type boots and the mackintosh coat was not yet a common garment.

Extracts from the Log illustrate local conditions:-

'1873 8th Feb: Very small attendance this week because of severe weather, heavy snowstorms preventing the children from getting to school. Only 6 present on Tuesday.

5th Nov: Attendance very good this week, very fine weather.

1874 16th Oct: Poor attendance during this week, very wet weather, also due to the children's elder brothers and sisters being at home for Michaelmas.

30th Oct: Fair attendance of boys this week but few girls owing to poor weather.

27th Nov: Very scanty attendance since Wednesday owing to heavy falls of snow and severe frosty weather.

16th Dec: Only 5 children today due to heavy falls of snow and severe frost.

1875 21st July: Owing to a great quantity of rain falling during the night the roads and fields in many places impassable. Small school only 13 present. Walter Reeve from Kingswood had been compelled to wade through water up to his knees. I was obliged to change his boots, stockings, and trousers.

20th Oct: Great deal of rain during the night and roads in many places covered and impassable. Only 6 pupils today.

1880 19th Nov: Attendance this week has been very small owing to the severity of the weather. Several children have been unable to get to school the water covering the roads.

26th Nov: Very wet this morning, many so wet as to oblige them to dry their clothes before starting work.

1881 19th Jan: There has been a great fall of snow during the night and it still continues to fall making it almost impossible for children to travel upon the roads. Only 1 child, Annie Richmond who lives next door to the school, was present this morning. I sent her home and closed the school.

20th Jan: The snow is lying in very deep drifts in the road, only 3 children came. Did not keep school for these few.

21st Jan: 5 children came today. I again closed the school.

28th Jan: Attendance during the week very small because of the severity of the weather.

4th Feb: Attendance still low due to the weather. Many children are suffering with chilblains and unable to wear their boots.

1882 16th Mar: Very wet today. Water came through the roof of the school rooms, so much so, it was necessary to place tubs to catch it and also to sweep it out of the front door.

1886 28th June: Weather fine and haymaking pretty general and therefore short attendance today.

1887 24th Jan: 65 present today. Weather still unsettled and roads are in a very bad state in many places — covered with a thick coating of ice and very dangerous.

1883 3rd July: Very wet, low attendance.

6th July: Wet again, only 32 this morning.

16th July: Weather very wet, attendance very unsatisfactory.

20th July: Weather wet, low attendance.

1888 13th Nov: Very wet only 41 present, of these several got their clothes very wet and had to dry them before the fire.

1889 11th Mar: Only 9 present today, let them out early. So few owing to snow several inches deep.

12th Mar: 27 today. No new snow but it is 6 inches deep.

15th Mar: Attendance very low this week, average 42.6 out of 78.

22nd Mar: Attendance better, 75 out of 78 the weather being settled and fine.

1889 7th May: Just as the children were about to be dismissed this afternoon a violent storm came on. I kept most of the children back until it was over. Several parents came for their children and took them away just as it was about to begin.

24th May: Several children, especially the small ones, away with sickness. I believe it is caused by the heat. '

COUGHS, COLDS AND OTHER DISEASES

The majority of Lapworth School children in the 1870's and 1880's lived in damp houses, slept in cold bedrooms, had a plain and meagre diet, poor washing facilities and probably inadequate clothing, it is not surprising therefore that they were often away from school with coughs, colds and sore throats. They also caught the usual childhood ailments of measles and whooping cough. At that time there was no vaccination against such diseases or effective drugs to aid recovery if a child was very ill. Early in October 1874 several children developed whooping cough, some returned to school within 10 days but Margaret Ball was away for several weeks not returning until February 1875. A further epidemic occurred in 1883; it began at the end of April, many children having very heavy colds and persistent coughs which disturbed the lessons. Arthur Pinner's cough was so bad that he was sent home with a note asking that he stay away until he was better; whooping cough was suspected. The pupils continued to cough in lessons until the middle of May when whooping cough was confirmed. Arthur Pinner returned in mid June, still coughing, and was sent home again. Another outbreak in 1888 lasted all through April and May, a few children being ill for several weeks.

Measles was another ailment which, from time to time, caused considerable absence from school. In June 1880 Edward Wiggett caught measles but, despite the other children being warned by Mr. Davey to keep away from him, it rapidly spread through the school. On 16 July the school was closed to prevent the infection spreading, but when lessons were re-commenced on 2 August only 17 pupils attended, many still being ill. There was another, but less widespread, outbreak in the summer of 1883 during the whooping cough epidemic, the two ailments apparently being closely associated. A further epidemic occurred late in 1889; half the school was already away with colds and sore throats when on 6 December the parish Medical Officer closed the school as a measles epidemic was believed to be imminent. After five weeks the school re-opened, but those who attended were very weak from their bout of measles and unable to do a full day's work. For some days they were sent home early and it was March before attendance improved.

It is doubtful if any of the children saw a doctor unless there was an emergency; a caring headmaster was therefore a useful watchdog of the scholars health. Many parents appear not to have understood that some ailments, even serious ones, were catching. They sent their children to school when others in the family had typhus fever (in 1874) or scarlet fever (in 1875, 1879, 1881) only to have them sent home again. Diphtheria was a child killer and in 1881 when Jacob Courtnell was suspected of having it, a note was sent to all the parents; fortunately it was a false alarm. Smallpox, however, did frighten all parents and when it was diagnosed at Hockley Heath and in the parish in 1878, many parents kept their children at home.

Ringworm and head lice were occasionally a problem. The affected children were sent home until they were clear again, but one family persisted in attending in an 'unclean state'. The rector therefore procured some 'staves acre ointment' for them to rub into their hair; they refused to use it at school, their mother demanding that the treatment must take place at home.

A sad case was William Clarke who died very suddenly in 1882 after eating large quantities of crab apples, unripe blackberries and hazel nuts.

Several children were obviously not strong. Most of these pupils' parents were anxious that they should not be punished if they could not do their lessons. Ada Bryan could not sleep and would not eat on school days; Mary Smith was thought to have 'inflammation of the brain'; Ellen Needle had 'general weakness'; and Florence Johnson was frequently away, even when she was at school she was considered to be 'far from well'.

No food was available at school and those who did not go home for lunch brought dinner bags or baskets. In September 1883 several girls had food stolen from their bags; attempts to discover the culprit failed, but after several days of further thefts a certain girl was seen eating on the way home. When accused she confessed and was punished by standing on a stool for the whole day. A few days later she stole again — an apple pudding — and was again punished in the same way, a note being sent to her parents who 'promised to punish her and wished me to do the same'. More food was taken by her and she again spent the day on the stool, further punishment being given after school. Mr. Davey felt sympathy for her, however, as she suffered 'very badly from scorbutic affliction'.

aabbccddeeffgghhijk

Little is heard of Mrs. Davey in the Log but she was in charge of needlework. She must have been an excellent teacher for her pupils produced very fine and delicate work, some of which still exists in the village. The ladies from the larger houses — Mrs. Falcon, Mrs. and the Misses Hudson of Bridge House (then called The Hollies), Mrs. Prescot, Miss Dugard of Lapworth House, Mrs. Whitworth of Broomfield House and others — called frequently to 'examine the needlework', often bringing their friends with them. It is said that some of these visitors brought their mending and patching for the girls to do, but this may be village gossip.

On their way home from school the children, the boys in particular, messed about and often mis-behaved. This upset Mr. Davey very much, as he was continually telling them to go straight home, but they scrumped apples, teased horses, swung of the school railings, trespassed, and bullied smaller children. However after a whole day of sitting still, with no opportunity to 'let off steam', it is to his credit that, on the whole, they behaved so well.

Kingswood Grange

15

'MEMORIALS OF A WARWICKSHIRE PARISH'

Robert Hudson, church warden, Feoffee of the Charity Estate, and canal manager, sat in his study at The Hollies surrounded by books and papers. He had finished writing his business letters and was looking forward to an interesting evening with his work on the history of Lapworth. He rang for the fire to be made up then returned to his work. It was proceeding very satisfactorily, he had completed the major portion of his manuscript — from the earliest of the parish records until the middle of the present century — his next task was to consider more recent times. He thought of the many years he had spent in sorting through the yellow parchments which he had found in the old chests in the church, and the happy hours of deciphering them and discovering their contents. The people of the past — the Marshalls, the de Bishopsdons, the Catesbys, the Bromes — were very real to him.

With the fire built up and extra lamps around him Robert Hudson opened the box of papers which he had brought home that afternoon. He had enjoyed a capital day: Mr. Prescot had asked him to visit the rectory to discuss parish business and then to stay for luncheon. About midday the Rev. Charles Burd, the vicar of Shirley, had called and been invited to join them. Mr. Burd had been the curate at St. Mary's when Hudson, a native of Yorkshire, had first come to reside in the parish and manage the canal in 1861. They had not met since the day the Bishop of Worcester had re-opened the church after the restoration of 1872. Burd had been in Lapworth today to inspect the cottages in the churchyard, soon to be demolished. He was a public spirited man, engaged on many committees connected with health and education within the Solihull Sanitary Authority area, and he knew Prescot well.

During lunch Charles Burd had remarked how changed he found Lapworth, the Bell Inn smithy gone, the Post Office removed from the corner of Grove Lane to near the Bird in Hand Inn, and little traffic along the canal. Travelling down Lapworth Street in his gig, Burd never saw a face he knew until he reached the Osbornes at High Chimneys. He had not known until he called on them that the Mander family, with whom he had lodged during his time in Lapworth, had left the parish. Mr. Burd's first call had been in Kingswood, which he had hardly recognised. He had taken his daughter, Marion, to spend the day with the Misses Holden who lived at Gowan Bank, a large new house close to the station. So many other new buildings had been erected since his last visit to the parish, Fair View, Devon House, Oak Villa, even a pair of semi-detached villas, and close to them in Station lane, the Kingswood Mission Room.

Prior to Mr. Burd's arrival, Kenrick Prescot had shown Hudson a box of papers which he had assembled together, and which he thought might be of interest for the next part of his history. The opportunity to examine them at the rectory had not occurred and he had therefore brought them home.

He could see at a glance that the box contained a notebook, letters, bills and many loose sheets of paper, he read the first few sheets:

'31st July 1855. A Confirmation was held in the church by the Bishop of Worcester: the first known here. There were in all about 200 Catechumens.'

'1851 The Sunday School was commenced about 1830 under the Rev. Donald Cameron, Resident Curate. We now have three unpaid male and three unpaid female teachers: average attendance 100. Day school, average attendance for the last five years 110: in this year 108; Males 52, females 56. Average expenses of the school £55.'

'Kingswood Mission room established 1886-9 by Rev. Kenrick Prescot and trustees, on land having a frontage of 15 yards onto the road from Kingswood to Lapworth. It is to be used for services and other meetings but not political meetings.'

'*'By Gone Lapworth*'

Mr. Robert Hudson will give two addresses in the Schoolroom, Lapworth, on
Wednesday 14th November   'Before the Reformation'
Thursday 15th November   'Queen Elizabeth to Queen Victoria'
Admission Free.   Rev. K. Prescot will preside.
Door open 7 pm   Start 7.30pm '

'*Lapworth and Kingswood Cricket and Quoit Club, The Recreation Ground, Kingswood. 5th August 1891   the estimated cost of levelling the ground is £6. Mr. Tonks suggests that the herbage be left at 5s per annum and this is agreeable to the trustees.*'

'*1851   The church is computed to hold 300 beside the school. The average congregation is*

Morning Service	220	Evening Service	150
Scholars	95	Scholars	95
	315		245	'

A Letter dated September 1890 to The Chairman of the Licencing Committee, Henley — '*The parishioners of Lapworth knowing that the licence of the Bell Inn in Lapworth Street is due for renewal wish for it to be closed as a public house. It is no longer needed by residents or travellers; the traffic on the canal which formally supported the inn is now small and that along the Warwick-Birmingham Road since the coming of the G.W.R. is unimportant. The Bell Inn house is very small, only suitable for a cottage and cannot be rebuilt to accommodate parties from Birmingham there being little ground. The inn has been a nuisance to the neighbourhood.*'

'*1853   Miss Ingram died at the advanced age of 90 leaving £20 to be distributed amongst the poor, she wished to be buried in the church and as she was the last of the family I therefore consented, but charged £10 fee to prevent the occurance of such request.*'

'*A meeting of the ratepayers has been arranged for 1st October 1889, it is to be held at the school. The Rev. Prescot has protested at the school being used in the day time and in term time because it disturbs the children.*'

'*1852   Mr. George Gibbs of Bushwood Hall died most suddenly without a moments pain at Solihull as he was stepping into his gig to come home.*'

There was nothing amongst these sheets of great interest to Hudson; he put them aside and picked up the notebook. It had a black cover and the initials HS on the fly leaf. Flicking through the pages he saw that there were many baptism and burial entries; it was the rough notebook of Henry Sanders who was the parish clerk until his death in the 1870's. He recognised the carefully executed hand writing:-

'*1st October 1852   Today the railway line passing through Lapworth was used officially for the first time. Eleanor and I walked to Kingswood to observe the special train pass by, but an accident delayed its progress and we returned home having seen nothing.*

October 1854   Kingswood Station was opened today. I did not attend but from reports I believe there were many influential people from the railway company on the platform and there were many speeches.

26th July 1873   Francis Spencer Hildick buried aged 65.
Mr. Hildick, a relation of the Hildick family of Gospel Oak Farm, was shot and killed by his nephew Joseph Parsons who then committed suicide. In the 1850's I remember, Mr. Hildick lived and farmed at Common Farm, Kingswood, Joseph Parsons lived with him. They had no servants and we thought that they were both a little eccentric. When Mr. Gerrard wished to buy the farm, Mr. Hildick retired and went to live in a cottage, I believe they call it Grove Cottage; Parsons went with him. It was there that the tragedy happened, they say in a drunken frenzy. Parsons was buried at night without funeral rites and without an entry in the register.

7th July 1873   Today I am 80 years of age, I have been the parish clerk for 38 years and until the 1840's I was also a cordwainer. My wife Eleanor is three years older than me, we have one daughter, Catherine, but are looked after by a kind niece. My father, William, and my mother, Catherine, were married in 1784 by Rev. Owen Bonnell who also baptised me and three of my seven brothers and sisters.'

Hudson closed the notebook and returned the papers to the box. He would look at them again tomorrow, he was feeling rather tired now. He did not think, however, that other people would be interested in what was little more than parish gossip. Perhaps he should conclude his history with Queen Victoria ascending the throne.

Robert Hudson died in June 1898 before his manuscript was quite finished. His son, Sir Robert Arundell Hudson, brought it to a conclusion and published it in 1904 under the title of 'Memorials of a Warwickshire Parish'.

Appendix 1

THE ANCEINTE MEETS AND BOUNDS OF THE MANOR & LORDSHIP OF LAPWORTH 1784

Beginning at a wooden bridge over Lapworth Brook, called old Lapworth bridge[1] near the eleventh milestone upon the road leading from Birmingham unto or towards Stratford-upon-Avon, and a little below a new brick bridge over the said brook, you go up the middle of the old road now called the Old Holloway until you come into the new Turnpike Road called the Stratford Road. Then keep up the middle of the Turnpike Road until you come opposite the lane called Cross Lane by the old brick kiln, and turn short to the left . . . . . . by the barn called Adkin's barn[2] (which with the farmhouse thereunto belonging is rented by William Broadbury) . . . . . .

. . . . . Then over a style at the top of the third Hawthorne piece into another piece of land held by William Bond of Heneage Legge Esq., called Bakin Hill and crossing the corner of Bakin Hill (where a Cross is made in the ground) you get over the hedge into a lane called Farm Lane[3] (which leads from a Farm called Irelands Farm towards Henley-in-Arden) . . . . . .

. . . . . and going down the ditch of another piece called the second Parson's Piece and by Mander's hedge until you come to a brook called Preston Brook[4] at the bottom thereof. Then you go down the said brook until you come to Lapworth Brook, and then up the brook called Lapworth Brook,[5] on the Bushwood side until you come to a lane called The Ford, otherwise the Ford Lane,[6] leading from Bushwood to Henley-in-Arden, ...

. . . . . then turn to the left by the side of the brook called Lapworth Brook along a lane called Mill Lane, and from the lane keep the old water course until you come to a brick bridge or arch (over the said water course upon Lapworth Millpool Lane) crossing a lane called Mill Lane[7] leading from Lapworth Street towards Henley-in-Arden, ... then keep to the right hand across the meadow called Millpool Meadow (and which heretofore was covered with water and called the Mill Pool) . . . . . .

. . . . . and go up the ditch on the left hand side thereof and into a meadow called Chamberlain's Meadow and go about 20 yards up the ditch to a pear tree where another Cross is made . . . . . . leading to a house[8] in the holding of George Smith and up the ditch of the last mentioned hedge until you come to the house, to a part where a oven lately was (which is now taken down and a small window made where it stood, under which window a Cross is made in the ground). Then go through the said house and a yard into the road called Lapworth Street and turn to the right hand . . . . . .

. . . . . until you come to Bunn Green,[9] then leaving the hedge go across the green, by a small bank where an ash tree formerly stood . . . . . .

. . . . . From there go straight along a slader on the common called Bushwood Common until you come to a road leading across the said common from Bushwood Hall towards Holy Common where a Cross is made in the ground, and then go on down the common[10] . . . . . .

. . . . . and from thence down the water course to a waggon road leading from Lapworth Street to Lowsonford, then turn to the right hand down the middle of the waggon road[11] until you come to a stone which divides the parishes of Rowington and Lapworth (which stone some years ago was placed there by the consent of the inhabitants of both parishes as a mark to mend the road and which road before the stone was set up was mended as follows:- the inhabitants of Lapworth mended one waggon rut and into the middle of the road on the one side and the inhabitants of Rowington one rut and into the middle of the road on the other side thereof). Continue walking down the middle of the said waggon road to a place called Lawson Ford within about 20 yards of a house inhabited by Mary Wilmore, (by the side of a road leading from Lawson Ford to Fynard Green) at the bottom of Moss Meadow (near the brook[12] running along the bottom of Moss Meadow which divides Rowington and Lapworth). Then turn to the left up the brook until you come to a lane called Long Picks Lane[13] leading from Turners Green to the High Chimneys, crossing which you continue to go up the water course until you come to a wooden bridge crossing Sim Lane[14] and so on up the water course which runs across the road leading from Hockley Heath towards Warwick until you cross a lane called Rising Brook Lane.[15] Then turn to the left hand . . . . . .

. . . . . until you come upon the common called Kingswood Common to a Cross made in the ground at the corner of the same, keeping up the ditch by the hedge until you come to a pig stye opposite to a house, the property of Elizabeth Grouby, widow. From there out across the common[16] by an avenue of trees and leaving all poplar trees on the left hand and all the elms on the right, ...

. . . . . go straight across Kingswood Common until you come in a direct line to a large oak tree, called Gospel Oak.[17] Turn to the right along the road leading to Packwood House keeping on until you come to the middle of the top of the lane leading to Spratts Pitts keeping to the middle of the lane, until you come to Spratts Pit[18] or Pond of water through which there was formerly a road. Then follow the water course running from Spratts Pool to Mr. Fetherstone's big pool shooting straight across the same to the Bolt at the Dam and from the Bolt down the water course through the meadow . . . . . .

. . . . . keeping down the water course until you come to a wooden footbridge opposite Packwood Church, then turn on the left hand up a ditch or water course on the side of Stickman's Meadow[19] until you come into the middle of the Turnpike Road leading from Hockley Heath to Warwick near the Turnpike House. Then go through the toll gate[20] and keep the middle of the Turnpike Road . . . . . .

. . . . . then make a straight point across the Stratford Turnpike Road into the road[21] leading from Hockley Heath to Umberslade . . . . . .

. . . . . and go down the middle of the Stratford Road until you come opposite the corner of a hovel belonging to John Greenall. Get over the hedge by a withy tree in to John Greenall's croft and go cornerways over the same to a stile and gate at the corner of a coppice[22] belonging to Isaac Ingram Esq., ...

. . . . . follow the ditch of the field and meadow below the same until you come to the brook called Lapworth Brook.[23] You then follow the stream until you come within about 25 yards of Lapworth new brick bridge upon the Turnpike Road leading from Hockley Heath to Henley-in-Arden and Stratford-upon-Avon. You then follow the old water course, which inclines a little to the left, and continue to the old Lapworth wooden bridge from where you first set out.

Edw. Sadler. Steward of the Manor.

The numbers shown in these extracts of the perambulation correspond with the map on page 19.

Appendix 2

PERAMBULATION OF BOUNDARIES OF KINGSWOOD MANOR 1833

They begin at a cross[1] nearly opposite the house of Joseph Parsons. Then go across the Turnpike Road in a straight line to Richard Kemps meadow. Get over the fence into the meadow, near the gate, and leave a corner of that meadow belonging to Harborough Banks and the greater part of it in Kingswood. Then over the hedge into the next meadow about 18 yards above the old gate place.[2] Then across a meadow of George Ross Esq., in an oblique direction, leaving a corner of it in Kingswood, to a Withy Tree[3] on which a cross is made standing at the Brook course. Then along the Brook course, across the Stratford canal[4] and continue the Brook course to the end of William Bellamy's farm[5] in the tenure of William Bolton. Then turn to the left up the Ditch between Austerton Grounds belonging to William Tibbetts and William Bellamy's farm.[6] Then up an old ditch which was formerly the Boundary of William Bellamy's farm then along the Brook course leaving about two acres of William Bellamy's Meadow in the manor of Rowington and cross the Warwick Canal[7] and still keep the outside fence of William Bellamy's farm till you come to the Turnpike Road called Warwick Lane[8] to Rowington Green. Then across the road and go up Joseph Newbery's Ditch next his meadow. Keep the same Ditch to the Marlpits[9] and continue the Hedgerow to the road from Joseph Newbery's house to Baddesley.[10] Then across the road and through the hedge at the gate, and cross in an oblique direction to the next Close where the Old Ditch was, which may be now seen, and which bears to the left[11] till you come to Rowington Coppice Ditch.[12] Then turn to the left down that Ditch cross the road to Baddelsey[13] and keep the straight fence down Joseph Newbery's Grounds till you come to the Warwick Canal,[14] cross the Canal, and continue the straight fence to Kingswood Brook.[15] Then turn to the right and continue that Brook course[16] till you come to Rising Brook Lane.[17] Keep up the right-hand ditch of Rising Brook Lane adjoining to the lands of the Miss Fetherstones, occupied by John Pearman, to a cross at the beginning of Kingswood new inclosure.[18] Continue on the same ditch leaving a close occupied by Thomas Maids and belonging to Marmion Edward Ferrers in the manor of Kingswood. Follow the same ditch till you come to another part of Kingswood new inclosure where is a cross near a pleck occupied by John Jennings.[19] Keep along the new enclosure next Jenning's Ditch till you come to Jenning's House then straight along the outside fence of Kingswood new Inclosure which Fence belongs part of the way to Marmion Edward Ferrers, and the other part of the way to Benjamin Hildick, in the occupation of Francis Fetherstone. Keep along the fence till you come to the road from Knowle to Kingswood.[20] Cross that road and then turn to the left to the right-hand fence of a close late belonging to Richard Tabberner and now to Benjamin Hildick, afterwards follow the same fence by the side of another close belonging to Benjamin Hildick till you come to the Gospel Oak[21] standing near Benjamin Hildick's Farm House, which oak divides the manors of Kingswood and Packwood. The oak tree belongs half to the Lord of the manor of Kingswood and half to the Lord of the manor of Packwood.

Then turn a little to the right along an old watercourse to a culver made across the watercourse.[22] Then turn down the left-hand fence of a lane called Crab Mill Lane to a cross made in the middle of the lane. Then keep along Crab Mill Lane leaving about two thirds of the lane in Kingswood Manor and Lapworth Parish, and about one third in Packwood. Continue the lane to near Spratts Pits,[23] then through the middle of one of the Pits to the corner of Miss Fetherstone's Brickiln Close. Then turn short to the left[24] along the Miss Fetherstone's Ditch between Thomas Fetherstone's land and Benjamin Hildick's land, rented by Richard Abel, till you come to Timmins Lane.[25] Cross Timmins Lane and go along a ditch between land of Thomas Fetherstone and Benjamin Hildick, late belonging to Joseph Harding in the occupation of Moses Hildick, two closes length along the Ditch. Then into the Pooley Close belonging to Thomas Fetherstone and keep the Straight Ditch leaving the Pooley Close in the manor of Kingswood.[26] Then along the Ditch between Thomas Fetherstone's land, and Mrs Martha Leas' land, in the tenure of Johnathon Billins, called Little Wallers, leaving Little Wallers in Kingswood. Then down the Ditch between land of Martha Lea and John Waller's land, occupied by Richard Heath, leaving Great Wallers in Kingswood. Then across the corner of Martha Lea's Close adjoining to Great Wallers. Then through a Pleck called Carpenter's Pleck,[27] late belonging to John Grafton and now to Martha Lea, and across the Stratford Canal to a mark in the fence on the side of a Pleck belonging to George Ross Esq. Then across the corner of the pleck to a lane leading from Harborough Banks to Chesset Wood[28] and across the lane and down Thomas Smith's garden walk to a Ditch of a high Bank thrown up at Harborough Banks. Then keep along the Ditch next the High Bank leaving the High Bank in Lapworth. Then continue the Ditch till you a second time come to the Stratford Canal.[29] Cross the Canal and continue the ditch of the High Bank till you come to a cross nearly opposite the house of Joseph Parsons where these boundaries began.

Signed:- Joseph Pettifer
Henry Lancaster
Thomas Smith
David Buffery

Charles Smith, Sworn Constable

The numbers shown in this perambulation correspond with the map on page 25.

113

Appendix 3

FARMS AND THE LAND TAX

Tracing the history of Lapworth farms is difficult until the late 18th century and even then would be impossible without the Land Tax Returns and Tithe Apportionment of c1840. The former are extant from 1775 to 1832, they name the tenants throughout the period and the owners between 1798 (1808 at Kingswood) and 1832.

The Land Tax was introduced in the post-Restoration period to supercede various medieval taxes. It was a tax on landed property and became a regular source of revenue in 1692, when a duty of 4s. 0., in the pound was charged on land 'according to the full true yearly value thereof'. Subsequently the rate in the pound varied but in 1798 William Pitt fixed it perpetually at 4s. 0d., in the pound. Those who wished, could redeem it at about 25 years purchase. Despite the changes in the value of land through the decades the Land Tax valuations remained the same as did the charges. The tax was paid by the landowner; charity estates had the tax refunded.

The tenants of a number of Lapworth Farms as traced through the Land Tax are given in the extracts below:-

	Farm Name and Tenant	Date of Ocupation	
1	**LAPWORTH FARM**		A house and about 40 acres of land in Spring Lane.
	John Butwell	there 1768	Also tenant of Brook House Farm.
	William Haycock	c1781-c1798	Financial failure. His twin children were supported by parish.
	John Soden	c1798-c1803	Grazier fattening cattle and sheep prior to butchering. Owner Mr. Ingram.
	James Cheshire	c1803-c1813	
	Benjamin Bissell	c1813-c1830	Owner-occupier. Gave up the tenancy in 1830 but retained ownership.
	Richard Lea	c1830-c1832	
	Charles Aldington	there 1832	Died 1835. At one time the landlord at the Boot Inn.
	Thomas Canning	there c1840	42 acres 3 roods 10 perches.
2	**THE BOOT INN**		A Public House and about 18 acres of land.
	Mary Bott	there c1768-c1785	Widow, died 1787.
	Edward Field	c1785-c1808	Owner-occupier. Also tenant of Spring Cottage Farm. Sold The Boot c1813 to Richard Lea.
	Charles Aldington	c1808-1818	
	John Taylor	c1818-1823	Possibly farmed at Mill House Farm, Kingswood previously.
	Jonathan Billings	c1823-	Owner Martha Lea. His seven children were born at The Boot. The youngest, Henry born 1834, later lived at Catesby House; at his death he left £500 0s. 0d., to Lapworth Charity Estate. The income was to be used to buy blankets and coal
		there c1840	for the 'deserving poor'. 18 acres 0 roods 11 perches.
3	**TUDOR FARM**		A timber framed house and about 25 acres of land at the corner of Catesby Lane and Lapworth Street.
	Hannah Luckman	there 1775-c1785	The widow of Samuel who died in 1775. Their son William, succeeded to the tenancy.
	William Luckman	c1785-c1789	He was already the tenant of Spring Cottage Farm but by 1789 he had left both farms. He was supported by the parish in the 1790's, and was living in Charity Cottage in 1814. He had seven children 1779-91.
	William Cox	c1789-c1832	Owner Mary Lea until 1813, then John Burman.
	William Brown	there 1832	
	William Hawkins	there c1840	25 acres 0 roods 7 perches. Owner Mary Burman.
4 & 5	**LAPWORTH GRANGE**		Also known as Blockbury House. Originally there were two houses and farms totalling about 60 acres together, they became one farm post-1843 when a new house, Lapworth Grange, was built.
	4) William Johns	there-1775-c1781	Owner-occupier, married Mary Culcope. Retained house and some land, but let the rest of the farm to John Cotterill.
	John Cotterill	c1781-c1808	
	Thomas Johns	c1808-c1830	Owner-occupier. Son of William Johns, married Ann the daughter of John Cotterill.
	David Buffery	c1830 there c1840	Property sold to Peter Wooldridge in 1843.
	5) John Cotterill	there 1775-c1813	Onwer-occupier, married Ann Culcope. Retained the house but had let the land to his son-in-law Thomas Johns.
	Thomas Johns	c1813-c1832	Owner of this property by 1827, probably inherited by his wife from her father.
	David Buffery	c1832 there c1840	Property sold to Peter Wooldridge by 1843. 4 and 5 together = 58 acres 2 roods 13 perches.
6a	**TAPSTER FARM AND MILL**		Also known as Windmill Farm. A timber framed house and about 27 acres of land. Later a brick tower mill was built west of the house.
	Thomas Green	there 1768-c1781	Son of Isaac Green, an old Lapworth family.
	Samuel Cookes	c1781-c1798	He was also the tenant of land at Bushwood.
	Samuel Canning	c1798-	Miller. Probably built the windmill c1780's or 1790's. Owner John Brookes.
	John Brookes	there c1840	Owner-occupier.

6b	YARDITCH		No house. About 25 acres of land.
	Isaac Green	there 1775-c1785	Also tenant of Yew Tree Farm, Webb's Land and The Cottage.
	Samuel Cookes	c1785-c1798	Both parts of (No. 6) held together by Cookes.
	Samuel Canning	c1798-c1832	Held both parts of No. 6.
	John Brookes	there 1840	Owner-occupier of both parts of No. 6; together = 52 acres 2 roods 19 perches.
7	MALTHOUSE FARM		A timber framed house and about 54 acres of land.
	John Cooks	there 1775-c1781	
	Thomas Wharr	c1781-c1785	
	William Avery	c1785-c1818	He had eight children all born at this farm. In 1795-6 he was the Overseer of the Poor. Owner Miss Merrix.
	Willaim Dolphin	c1818-c1823	Owner Charles Fetherstone Esq.
	Jo. Fellowes	c1823-c1827	
	William Wheatcroft	c1827-c1830	
	Thomas Canning	there c1830 and c1840	Owner John Fetherstone. Canning had six children (1829-39). He was also the tenant of Lapworth Farm c1840 (see No. 1).
8	THE RECTORY AND GLEBE LAND		House and about 50 acres, property of the rector during his period of office. Part of the land was let for many years to a tenant. From 1813-1839 the whole glebe in the control of the curate, perhaps in lieu of a stipend.
9	BROOMFIELD HOUSE FARM		House and about 27 acres of land. Land owned by the Charles' family since 1755.
	William Bond	there 1775-c1803	Married Mary Culcope, acquired lease of property by inheritance. Also tenant by 1781 of 50 acres more and by 1785 of Lapworth Park Farm. By 1798 had only 75 acres of land.
	William Lea	c1803-1823	He had possibly moved to Dingley Dell by 1827. Died in 1829.
	William King	c1823-c1827	
	Thomas Burman	c1827-1830	Owner-occupier. Married Mary Charles and thus acquired this property.
	James Cheshire	there 1830	At one time the tenant of Lapworth Farm (see No. 1).
	Thomas Cheshire	there 1832 and c1840	Son of above, married 1832. 27 acres 2 roods 08 perches. Owner-occupier.
10	BROOK HOUSE FARM		A small red brick house and about 30 acres of land. Owner 1768 Samuel Mander.
	John Butwell	there 1768-c1785	In 1775 he was also the tenant of Lapworth Farm (see No. 1).
	Joseph Taylor	c1785-	Died 1786, succeeded by his widow, Ann.
	Ann Taylor	-c1798	Moved to the Royal Oak Inn.
	Joseph Payton	c1798-c1813	Owner-occupier. He appears to have come from Nuthurst. He was also the tenant of Lapworth (Moat) Farm and Grove Cottage.
	Robert Cranmer	c1813-c1823	Owner-occupier. Overseer of the Poor.
	Samuel Cranmer	c1823-c1832	Owner-occupier. Overseer of the Poor.
	Thomas Rainbow	c1840	34 acres 1 rood 20 perches. Owner Earl Cornwallis.
11	WOOD AND WATER		No house, about 40 acres of land.
	Mr. Wakefield	c1775-c1781	of Packwood, also tenant of Kershaws.
	William Bond	c1781-1808	also tenant of Broomfield House Farm (see No. 9).
	Thomas Fetherstone	c1808-c1813	Owner-occupier. Lived at Packwood House.
	John Fetherstone	c1813-c1827	Owner-occupier. Lived at Packwood House.
	Charles Fetherstone	c1827-c1832	Owner-occupier. Lived at Packwood House.
	Miss Fetherstone	c1832	also tenant of Webb's land.
	John Fetherstone	c1840	Owner-occupier.
12	WEBB'S LAND LATER CEDAR LAWN		Cottage and about 18 acres of land. Let in two parts 1775-1808, then in one.
12a	About 15 acres		
	William Smith	there 1775	Described as William Smith 'in the lane' as against his father William Smith senior at Bearhouse Farm. Had both a) and b) by 1808. Also held Dingley Dell.
	Benjamin Smith	c1823-c1827	Son of above, born 1785. Owner Thomas Burbury.
	Miss Fetherstone	c1827-c1832	Owner-occupier.
	Joseph Barnbrook	c1840	15 acres 3 roods 9 perches. Owner John Fetherstone.
12b	About 3 acres		
	Isaac Green	there 1775-c1789	Also tenant of Yarditch (see No. 6b), The Cottage and Yew Trees Farm.
	Henry Woodward	c1789-c1808	Also tenant of Mountford Farm.
13	THE COTTAGE		Timber framed cottage in Lapworth Street with about 5 acres of land.
	John Leeson	there 1775-c1781	
	Isaac Green	c1781-c1832	Owner-occupier. Possibly father and son. Nancy Green married Peter Wooldridge in 1790.
	Thomas Baker	there 1840	5 acres 0 roods 29 perches. Owner Peter Wooldridge.

Appendix 4

HOUSES AND BARNS

A great many houses within Lapworth parish have disappeared during this century. The majority of the cottages, particularly along the Old Warwick Road and at Hockley Heath, have been demolished and several other buildings have been completely replaced. Included in these are the *Royal Oak Inn,* the *Bird in Hand Inn,* Hole House Farm, Bear House Farm, Bushwood Grange, Cherry Trees and Terets Cottage. The houses that remain have usually been modernised and added to, and it is often difficult to discern the original core. There are still, however, about 30 houses in the parish which are basically timber framed and have therefore existed since at least the 17th century. The exception is Green Acres which is a comparatively new house built, since 1886, out of old timbers brought from elsewhere, some of which are said to be from the churchyard cottages.

The oldest house in the parish is probably Bushwood Common Farm, a late medieval building, which had originally a single storey hall with a two storey cross wing at each end. Later the hall was ceiled over creating an upper floor and part of the house was bricked round (see V.C.H. Warwickshire vol.5. p.109 for a full description of this and other houses in the parish).

Mountford Farm and High Chimneys Farm are 16th century houses with later added wings. Both have fine brick chimneys, each having one stack with an eight-point star shaped shaft. Both houses have exposed internal timbers and are almost wholly encased in 18th century brick.

Lapworth Park Farm, Tan House Farm and Hole House Farm were probably built in the mid 16th century, all being of the hall and cross wing type. Hole House Farm was a fine house with a group of ornate central chimneys, and a three storey cross wing containing a 17th century staircase. The two other houses have both been considerably enlarged and bricked round, but in places have exposed square framing.

Sands Farm, Arden Hill Farm and Catesby Farm are probably also 16th century buildings. The former, orginally single storey, has an 18th century north east facing wing which formerly contained a crab mill. The house is completely encases in brick and has been much extended. Arden Hill Farm has an 18th century brick facade, but is basically a simple three bay house with an inserted chimney. Catesby Farm, now completely rendered, has matching front gables, a baffle type entrance and much internal exposed timber framing.

Tudor Farm, Kingswood Farm, Windmill Farm and Little Rising all probably date from the 17th century. They are of the hall and cross wing type with a wide fireplace in the central room; they have exposed square framing. Malthouse Farm, also of 17th century build, is of two storey T-plan, with a central chimney and much exposed timbering in the rear room. It has recently been greatly extended by connecting it to an adjacent barn.

Rectory Cottage is also 17th century; it has exposed square framing, inserted dormer windows, and a central chimney. Other houses which are probably of the same century, but may be older, are Drawbridge Farm, Olive Cottage, Vine Cottage and Tapster Brook Cottage. All were probably single storey originally.

Houses which hide their timber framing within a later exterior are The Cottage, the *Boot Inn,* Broomfield House, Yew Tree Cottage, The Round House, and Dowdswell House. Houses wholly built in a later period are Kingswood House, a basically square Queen Ann House, little altered; Lapworth Hill Farm and Hazelwood House. The two latter are apparently late 18th century houses of finely made brick. Lapworth (Moat) Farm was built in 1844, the initials A L, for Alfred Lapworth, and the date, being displayed in large letters, made of blue brick, on the gable end wall.

Many barns and outbuildings in the parish have been demolished or converted into garages, but fine barns and ranges of buildings still remain at Sands Farm (timber framed barn), Bushwood Commom Farm (timber framed and brick barn), Tan House Farm (brick barn), Malthouse Farm (extensive range), and Lapworth Lodge Farm (late 18th century range). The timber framed barn at Arden Hall Farm and the late Victorian outbuildings at Bushwood Grange are in the process of being converted into houses. Those at Tudor Farm and Broomfield House were converted in this way several years ago. An outbuilding at Kingswood House, Victorian in appearance having alternate bands of blue and red bricks, may date from the 1880's when the house was an inn.

Notes & References

INTRODUCTION —

1. Ordnance Survey, *Geological Drift Map* SP 16 NE (1980).
2. Ibid. SP 16 NE (1980) and SP 17 SE (1981).
3. *West Midlands Archaeological News Sheet* No. 12 (1969), p.28 (Department of Extra-Mural Studies, Birmingham University).
4. H. Thorpe, *Birmingham and Its Regional Setting* (British Association of the Advancement of Science 1950), p.88; Victor Skipp, *The Centre of England* (1979), Chapter 4; N. Thomas, 'An Archaeological Gazetteer of Warwickshire', *Transactions of Birmingham and Warwickshire Archaeological Society,* vol.86 (1974).
5. *W. M. Arch, News Sheet* Nos. 9-14 (1966-71).
6. F. W. Shotton, *T.B.A.S.,* vol.68.
7. *W. M. Arch, News Sheet* No. 14 (1971), p.8.
8. N. Thomas, op. cit.
9. *Victoria County History of Warwickshire,* vol.1 — Yarningale Common, p.370; Barnmoor Wood, pp.369 — 70; Liveridge Hill, p.386; Harborough Banks, pp.384 — 6; Beausale, pp.357, 358; N. Thomas, *Guide to Prehistoric England,* p.205 (1960).
10. *Archaeological Journal,* vol.128 (1971), p.195.
11. *V.C.H., Warwickshire,* vol.1, p.384.
12. Victor Skipp, op. cit., pp.72 — 80.
13. Map facing p.1. *T.B.A.S.,* vol.85 (1971-73).
14. *W. M. Arch, News Sheet* No. 12 (1969), p.27. Ibid. No. 14 (1971), pp.14, 17.
15. Victor Skipp, op. cit., p.92. H. Thorpe, op. cit., p.94.
16. See Note 3.
17. *W. M. Arch, News Sheet* No. 20 (1977).
18. *V.C.H., Warwickshire,* vol.5, p.110.
19. Ibid.
20. Ibid. vol.1, p.326a.
21. Ibid.
22. 1 Domesday league = 12 furlongs; 1 square furlong = 10 acres.
23. Gover and Mower, *The Place-Names of Warwickshire,* pp.288, 289.
24. A. H. Smith, *The Place-Name Elements,* vol.2, p.11.
25. Ibid. p.277.
26. Gover and Mower, op. cit., p.288.

CHAPTER 1 —

1. R. Hudson, *Memorials of a Warwickshire Parish* (1904), p.187. I am indebted to Dr. D. A. Rees, Archivist of Jesus College, Oxford, who supplied details of Bonnell's residence in the College.
2. Warwickshire Natural History and Archaeological Society, *Churches of Warwickshire* (1847), vol.1, p.33.
3. William Dugdale, *Antiquities of Warwickshire,* Edn. 1730, p.793.
4. Lapworth Probate Records, Hereford and Worcestershire County Record Office, 008. 7. BA 3585.
5. Analysis of above. All details of farming in this chapter from this source.
6. Lapworth Parish Registers, Warwickshire County Record Office DR (B) 35.
7. I am indebted to Mrs. P. Copson of Warwick County Museum for giving so generously of her time and for her valuable work on the flora of the commons.
8. William Dugdale, op. cit., p.790. Prince's metal said to have been invented by Prince Rupert, is an alloy of copper and zinc. Aurichalcum, erroneous spelling of Latin *orichalcum* = aurichalcite, a yellow copper ore, 'mountain copper'.
9. Birmingham Reference Library, Deed 423866 (1733).
10. H. and W.C.R.O., Will and Inventory of William Overton (1723), 008. 7.BA 3585, 431.
11. Shakespeare Birthplace Record Office, DR 12/56 (1739).
12. S.B.R.O. ER 1/6/8 (1773).
13. William Dugdale, op. cit., p.793.
14. Joy Woodall, *From Hroca to Anne* (1974), pp.49, 51.
15. *Map of Warwickshire,* Yates (1787-9).
16. Culpepper, *Colour Herbal,* Edited by David Potterton (1983).
17. *Map of Warwickshire,* H. Beighton (1725).
18. H. and W.C.R.O., Wills of John and Isaac Green, 008. 7. BA 3585, 490 (1741-2) and 496 (1744).
19. B.R.L., Holte MSS 191, 192.
20. All weather information from J. M. Shotton, *Agricultural Records* (1969) unless otherwise stated.
21. Charles Creighton, *A History of Epidemics in Britain* (1965), vol.2, pp.703-4.
22. Estimated from the Parish Registers by the Cox method, see W. E. Tate, *The Parish Chest,* pp.80-1.
23. W.C.R.O., CR 344/7 and 344/18.
24. H. and W.C.R.O., Will of Edmund Culcope, 008. 7. BA 3585/549 (1771).
25. W.C.R.O., Land Tax Returns, QS/77.
26. W.C.R.O., CR 258/322.
27. James Woodforde, *The Diary of a Country Parson* (1978).
28. C. Creighton, op. cit., pp.362-6.
29. V.C.H. Warwickshire, vol.8, p.280.
30. R. Hudson, op. cit., p.190.
31. W.R.C.O., CR 290.
32. R. Hudson, op. cit., p.193.
33. Woodforde, op. cit., pp.480-1.
34. *Aris's Birmingham Gazette,* (1795), 21 September and 26 October.
35. Victor Skipp, *A History of Greater Birmingham* (1980), p.82.

CHAPTER 2 —

1. B.R.L., 277441.
2. Ibid. the same reference for 1772 and 1775.
3. B.R.L., 413113.
4. Oliver Fairclough, *The Grand Old Mansion* (1984), pp.50-5, for full details of Holte/Bracebridge/Legge affair.
5. V.C.H., Warwickshire, vol.5, p.111.
6. Lapworth Womens Institute Scrapbook (1956).
7. V.C.H., Warwickshire, vol.5, p.110.
8. Ibid. p.111.
9. T.B.A.S., Vol.33, pp.69-70.
10. Ibid. pp.71-2.
11. S.B.R.O., *Archer Collection,* Lapworth 2247.
12. T.B.A.S., vol.33, p.72.
13. *Catalogue of Ancient Deeds,* vol.3, A 13505.
14. H. and W.C.R.O., Will and Inventory Robert Ireland, 1559/60.
15. *Cat. Anct.D.,* vol.5, 12374.
16. Ibid. 12209.
17. Oliver Fairclough, op. cit., pp.22-3; 40., for all details of Holte family and Lapworth estate.

18. B.R.L., Holte MSS 191 (1737); 192 (1746); Jewel Baillie MSS 358B (1753). W.C.R.O., CR 258/321 (1771); -320·1 (1772); -322 (1775); -323 (1779); -324 (1780).
19. W.C.R.O., CR 991 (1892).
20. See note 14.
21. V.C.H., Warwickshire, vol.5, p.194.
22. W.C.R.O., CR 1291/2.
23. B.R.L., 379610.
24. S.B.R.O., DR3/874.
25. W.C.R.O., QS 75/70; CR 955/3 (1807-8).
26. S.B.R.O., DR3/874.
27. V.C.H., Warwickshire, vol.5, p.111-2.
28. *Cat. Anct. D.,* vol.5, 12336.
29. R. Hudson, op. cit., Will of Roger Sly, pp.75-8.
30. John Hannett, *Forest of Arden* (1863) p.164.
31. S.B.R.O., ER 1/6/8.
32. H. and W.C.R.O., 008. 7. BA 3585/435.
33. Deeds of Brome Hall. Generously lent for study by the Smith Family of Brome Hall, to whom I am indebted.
34. W.C.R.O., Land Tax Returns, QS 77.
35. Ibid. Lapworth Parish Registers, DR (B) 35.
36. All the following from Census Returns at W.C.R.O.
37. See note 33.
38. W.C.R.O., QS 75/69.
39. Ibid. Tithe Apportionment, CR 328/30.
40. Gover and Mower, op. cit., p.289.
41. V.C.H. Warwickshire, vol.1, p.384.

CHAPTER 3 —

1. See page 11.
2. Lapworth Probate Records, H. and W.C.R.O., 008.7. BA 3585.
3. Analysis of above.
4. Joy Woodall, op. cit., pp.95-9.
5. Eric Kerridge, *The Farmers of Old England* (1973) p.104.
6. G. E. Mingay, *The Agricultural Revolution* (1977) p.101., Document VIII. For Background to this chapter see also: Chambers and Mingay, *The Agricultural Revolution 1750-1880* (1966); William Marshall, *The Review and Abstract of the County Reports to the Board of Agriculture,* vol.4, Midlands, (1818) Warwickshire, pp.281-329. E. Kerridge, op. cit.
7. H. and W.C.R.O., 008.7. BA 3585, 432 (1723).
8. William Marshall, op. cit., p.300.
9. J. C. Loudon, *An Encyclopedia of Agriculture* (1825) paragraph 6391.
10. See page 12.
11. H. and W.C.R.O., 008.7. BA 3585, 502 (1747); William Baker, 461 (1729); Robert Wilkes, 443 (1726).
12. B.R.L., Holte MSS 191, 192.
13. G. E. Mingay, op. cit., p.7.
14. See Chapter 2, note 18.
15. William Marshall, op. cit., p.293.
16. S.B.R.O., ER 1/6/8 (1773).
17. *Aris's Birmingham Gazette,* 1794-6.
18. I am indebted to Mr. Richard Johns who has generously permitted me to use this valuable family archive so freely.

CHAPTER 4 —

1. V.C.H., Warwickshire, vol.7, p.27.
2. W.R.C.O., Tanworth-in-Arden Perambulation (1767).
3. *Warwick County Records,* vol.2, p.131.
4. W. Dugdale, op. cit., (1765 edition), p.550.
5. *Warwick County Records,* vol.6, p.176.
6. A. Cossons, 'Warwickshire Turnpikes', T.B.A.S., vol.64, p.53, and for much of the detail in this chapter.
7. V.C.H., Warwickshire, vol.7, p.28, and for much of the detail in this chapter.
8. Ibid.
9. A. Cossons, op. cit.
10. *Map of Warwickshire,* Yates (1787-9).
11. V.C.H., Warwickshire, op. cit.
12. Ibid.
13. A. Cossons, op. cit.
14. W. Cooper, *Henley-in-Arden* (1946), p.91.
15. V.C.H., Warwickshire, op. cit.
16. Highways Act, 2 and 3 P. and M. c.8 (1555).
17. W. E. Tate, op. cit., pp.241-2.
18. W.C.R.O., DR (B) 35, Box 5, Highway Accounts.
19. W.C.R.O., DR (B) 35, Lapworth Minute Book 1873.
20. Rowington Parish Archive.

CHAPTER 5 —

1. R. Hudson, op. cit., pp.75-8.
2. W.C.R.O., DR (B) 35.
3. V.C.H., Warwickshire, vol.5, p.116.
4. R. Hudson, op. cit., p.89.
5. Ibid. pp.117-26.
6. Ibid. p.129.
7. Ibid. p.204.
8. W.C.R.O., DR (B) 35, Box 4, Disbursements of the Overseers of the Poor, 1688, 1701.
9. R. Hudson, op. cit., p.232.
10. R. Hudson, op. cit., p.233; W.C.R.O., DR (B) 35, Box 6.
11. W.C.R.O., DR (B) 35.
12. W.C.R.O., DR (B) 35, Box 6, Minute Book.
13. W.C.R.O., DR (B) 35, Overseers of the Poor Accounts.
14. W.C.R.O., DR (B) 35, Box 6, Minute Book.
15. W.C.R.O., CR 1201/4.
16. R. Hudson, op. cit., p.213.
17. Ibid. p.236.
18. *Charity Commissioners Report,* Warwickshire (1836) pp.96-103.
19. V.C.H., Warwickshire, vol.5, p.116.
20. R. Hudson, op. cit., p.237.
21. W.C.R.O., DR (B) 35, Box 6, Minute Book.
22. W.C.R.O., CR 1201/9-14.

CHAPTER 6 —

1. Solihull School, Sutton Coldfield Grammar School and Rugby School all began as 'Free Grammar Schools' in the 16th Century.
2. Patrick Orpen, 'Recruitment Pattern of Schoolmasters in the 17th century', *Warwickshire History,* vol.4. No. 3 (1979), p.76; Patrick Orpen, *Status of Schoolmasters in England 1560-1700,* Thesis at W.C.R.O.
3. Patrick Orpen, Ibid. *Warwickshire History,* vol.4, No. 3 (1979), p.88.
4. Details from this letter and the following one, generously supplied by A. E. Baker, Archivist and Librarian of S.P.C.K.
5. Ibid.
6. W.C.R.O., DR (B) 35, Box 5.
7. See note 24, chap.1.
8. W.C.R.O., CR 244/9.
9. Including those of Rowington people.

10. W.C.R.O., DR (B) 35, Disbursements of the Overseers of the Poor 1783-4.
11. R. Hudson, op. cit., p.213.
12. *Charity Commissioners Report, Warwickshire* (1836), pp.96-103.
13. Ibid. For details of new school and the finance thereof see W.C.R.O., DR (B) 35, Box 6, Feoffees Minute Book.
14. W.C.R.O., Ibid.
15. W.C.R.O., DR (B) 35, Box 5.

CHAPTER 7 —

1. R. Hudson, op. cit., p.204.
2. R. Hudson, op. cit., p.203.
3. W.C.R.O., DR (B) 35, Box 4.
4. W.C.R.O., DR (B) 35, Overseers of the Poor Accounts.
5. J. L. and B. Hammond, *The Village Labourer* (1967), pp.397-400, Appendix B.

CHAPTER 8 —

1. James Woodforde, op. cit., pp.605-6.
2. V.C.H., Warwickshire, vol.2, p.189.
3. R. Hudson, op. cit., p.196.
4. Warwickshire Natural History and Archaeological Society, op. cit., vol.2, p.25.
5. V.C.H., Warwickshire, vol.2, p.189.
6. W.C.R.O., QS 75/92; CR 496.
7. W.C.R.O., DR (B) 35, Overseers of the Poor Accounts, 1816-8.
8. William Cobbett, *Rural Rides* (1909 edition).
9. R. Hudson, op. cit., p.196.
10. V.C.H., Warwickshire, vol.2, p.189.
11. *Charity Commissioners Report, Warwickshire* (1836), pp.96-103.
12. R. Hudson, op. cit., p.196.
13. Clifford Morley, *News From The English Countryside 1750-1850* (1979), pp.242-52.
14. Ibid. p.248.
15. V.C.H., Warwickshire, vol.2, p.189.
16. Charles Creighton, op. cit., vol.2, pp.799-802.
17. Ibid. p.822-5.
18. W.C.R.O., MI 333/5.
19. All weather information from J. M. Shotton, op. cit., unless otherwise stated.
20. Charles Creighton, op. cit., vol.2, p.844.
21. W.C.R.O. Lapworth Microfilm, Reel 1.
22. W.C.R.O. Ibid.

CHAPTER 9 —

1. W.C.R.O. QS 111/8.
2. Charles Hadfield, *The Canal Age* (1968), p.28 and for much of the detail in this chapter.
3. L. T. C. Rolt, *Navigable Waterways* (1973), p.97 and for much of the detail in this chapter.
4. W.C.R.O. QS 111/8/13; -14; -16; -17.
5. L. T. C. Rolt, op. cit., p.98.
6. Lapworth Parish Archive.
7. Charles Hadfield, op. cit., p.30.
8. Lapworth Parish Archive.
9. E. A. Ardayfio, *Development of Warwickshire Canals* vol.2. Thesis at W.C.R.O.
10. L. T. C. Rolt, op. cit., p.99.
11. Charles Hadfield, *British Canals* (1952), p.161.
12. V.C.H., Warwickshire, vol.7, p.35.
13. Charles Hadfield, op. cit., p.161.
14. W.C.R.O. MI 333/5.
15. Charles Hadfield, *The Canal Age* (1968), p.67.
16. Ibid. p.99.
17. W.C.R.O. MI 336/18; MI 370/12.
18. W.C.R.O. MI 267/21.

CHAPTER 10 —

1. V.C.H., Warwickshire, vol.2, p.274.
2. R. A. Pelham, 'The Agricultural Geography of Warwickshire During The Napoleonic Wars As Revealed By The Acreage Returns of 1801' T.B.A.S. vol.68, pp.89-106.
3. A. Murray, *General View of the Agriculture of the County of Warwick* (1815), p.133.
4. W.C.R.O., DR (B) 35, Box 6, Feoffees Minute Book; CR 1201/4.
5. *Charity Commissioners Report Warwickshire* (1836), pp.96-103.
6. W.C.R.O., QS 77.
7. W.C.R.O., CR 328/30/2.
8. W.C.R.O., MI 201/2; MI 267/21; MI 336/18.
9. Lapworth Womens Institute Scrapbook (1956).
10. W.C.R.O., MI 370/12.
11. W.C.R.O., CR 991.

CHAPTER 11 —

1. Rev. E. H. Fenwick, *St. Mary-the-Virgin, Lapworth* (1968).
2. V.C.H., Warwickshire, vol.5, p.112, and for much detail in this chapter.
3. Ibid. p.115.
4. R. Hudson, op. cit., p.182.
5. Johns Family, op. cit.
6. V.C.H., Warwickshire, vol.8, p.524.
7. R. Hudson, op. cit., p.194.
8. Ibid. p.254, and for much detail in this chapter.
9. Charles Lines, *The Book of Warwick* (1985), p.33.
10. R. Hudson, op. cit., p.255.
11. W.R.C.O., CR 328/30/2.
12. W.R.C.O., DR (B) 35, Box 6, Feoffees Minute Book.
13. Warwickshire Natural History and Archaeological Society, op. cit., vol.2, p.25.
14. J. Hannett, op. cit., p.138, note 3.
15. R. Hudson, op. cit., p.256.
16. Ibid. p.257.
17. J. Hannett, op. cit., p.139 and note 5.
18. R. Hudson, op. cit., p.246-9.
19. W.C.R.O., DR (B) 35, Box 4.
20. W.C.R.O. Ibid.

CHAPTER 12 —

1. W.C.R.O., DR (B) 35, Overseers of the Poor Accounts 1816-8.
2. Victor Skipp, op. cit., p.83.
3. Rowington Parish Registers.
4. Peter Laslett, *Family Life and Illicit Love in Earlier Generations* (1977), pp.3, 147, 149.
5. W.C.R.O., DR (B) 35.
6. W.C.R.O., DR (B) 35, Overseers of the Poor Accounts; Charity Feoffees Minute Book; CR 1201/4; MI 333/5; MI 201/2; MI 267/21; MI 336/18.
7. W.C.R.O., CR 328/30/2.
8. W.C.R.O., CR 1201/4.
9. W.C.R.O., DR (B) 35, Box 5.
10. W.C.R.O. Ibid.
11. R. Hudson, op. cit., p.255; W.C.R.O., Lapworth Microfilm Reel 1.
12. Charles Creighton, op. cit., pp.196-208.
13. W.C.R.O., CR 1201/9-14.
14. R. Hudson, op. cit., p.262, note 1.

CHAPTER 13 —

1. Avoncroft Museum Publication, *Bricks and Brickmaking* (1978).

2. H. and W.C.R.O., 008·7. BA 3585, 461 (1729); -503 (1747).
3. Ibid. 008·7. BA 3585, 431 (1723).
4. E. A. Ardayfio, *Development of Warwickshire Canals* vol.2, p.119, Thesis at W.C.R.O.
5. N. Varley, *The Stratford-upon-Avon Canal,* Thesis in own possession.
6. J. C. Loudon, op. cit., paragraph 4661.
7. Robert Malster, 'Malting in Suffolk', Suffolk Industrial Archaeology Society (1978).
8. William Cobbett, *Cottage Economy* (1979), pp.17-8.
9. W.C.R.O., MI 201/2.
10. W.C.R.O., MI 336/18.
11. W.C.R.O., MI 370/12.

CHAPTER 14 —

1. Above from Lapworth School Exhibition material generously lent by Miss K. Smallman, the previous headmistress of the school, to whom I am greatly indebted.
2. R. Hudson, op. cit., p.239.
3. W.C.R.O., MI 370/12.
4. W.C.R.O., MI 336/18.
5. At Lapworth School, most generously lent for study by Mrs. A. Hedley the present headmistress to whom I am greatly indebted.

Weights and Measures

MONETARY CONVERSION

2½d	=	1p
6d	=	2½p
1s. 0d	=	5p
2s. 0d	=	10p
5s. 0d	=	25p
10s. 0d	=	50p
£1 0s. 0d	=	100p
240d	=	£1

SQUARE MEASURE

40 perches	=	1 rood
4 roods	=	1 acre
2½ acres	=	1 hectare

FLOUR WEIGHT

14 lbs	=	1 stone
56 lbs	=	1 bushel
140 lbs	=	1 bag
230 lbs	=	1 sack

100 lbs wheat produces 70 lbs flour
100 lbs flour produces 130 lbs bread
1 quarter wheat = 4½ cwt.

LINEAR MEASURE

1 inch	=	2.54 centimetres		
12 inches	=	1 foot		
3 feet	=	1 yard		
22 yards	=	100 links	=	1 chain
220 yards	=	10 chains	=	1 furlong
1760 yards	=	8 furlongs	=	1 mile
45 inches	=	1 ell		

DRY MEASURE

8 pints	=	1 gallon
2 gallons	=	1 peck
4 pecks	=	1 bushel
1 bushel	=	1 strike
3 bushels	=	1 bag
4 bushels	=	1 coomb
8 bushels	=	1 quarter
36 bushels	=	1 chaldron
40 bushels	=	1 wey

HAY AND STRAW MEASURE

36 lbs straw	=	1 truss
56 lbs old hay	=	1 truss
60 lbs new hay	=	1 truss
36 trusses	=	1 load
1 thrave	=	2 stooks
1 stook	=	12 sheaves

Index of Lapworth Personal and Place Names

Number with asterisk indicates an illustration.

Abel, Richard 113
Adkin's Barn 112
Alcock, Fred 102
Aldington, Charles 114
Allen - Charles 77; Jacob 77
Arden Hill Farm 62*, 81, 116
Arton, G. O. 83
Askew, William 49
Astley, Widow 97
Avern, William 49
Avery, William 63, 115
Aylesbury de - Agnes 22; Philip 22

Baker - Family 99; Thomas 115; William 35
Bakin Hill 112
Baldwin 9
Baldwin, Thomas 55, 81
Ball - Margaret 105, 108; William 81
Barnbrook/Benbroke, Joseph 81, 100, 115
Barnbrook - John 65, 67; Sarah 67; William 94; — 51, 53
Barnet - John 46, 55, 95, 96, 97; Mary 96
Basket, Robert 12, 28
Bate - Thomas 100; William 53, 97
Bayliss - Edward 77, 81; Lydia 16; Matthew 16
Bean, Rev. Charles 11, 15, 85
Bear House Farm 7, 59, 81, 115, 116
Beesley - Mary 93; Sophia 93
Bell Inn 44, 55, 66, 100, 110, 111
Bellamy - John 81; Mrs. 55; William 26, 113
Billings - Henry 83, 114; Jonathan 46, 81, 113, 114
Bird in Hand 27, 42, 77, 81, 102*, 110, 116
Bird, Sarah 64
Bishop, William 46
Bishops of Worcester 9
Bishopsdon de, - Family 110, Sir John 7, 21, 24
Bissell, Benjamin 114
Blockbury House, alias Lapworth Grange 36, 81, 96, 105, 114
Bolton, William 113
Bond - John 15; William 15, 112, 115
Bonnell - Elizabeth 17; Rev. Owen 11, 12, 13, 14, 15, 16, 17, 18, 89, 111
Boot Inn 20, 34, 35, 38, 43*, 44, 55, 62, 65, 77, 81, 83, 93, 94, 96, 100, 102, 106, 114, 116
Bott - Mary 20, 114; William 22, 51
Bradbury/Broadbury - James 31, 81; John 81; Mary 16; Mr. 99; Thomas 81; William 16, 51, 52, 62, 80, 112
Brandeston - Agnes 22; Hugh 22; Rose 22
Bredon House 16, 46, 67, 81, 124*
Brickiln Close 113
Brick Kiln Fields 99
Bridge Close 14
Bridge House, alias The Hollies 77, 101, 109, 110
Brihteah, Bishop of Worcester 9
Briscoe - Jane 98; Robert 100
Brockshires 37
Brome/de Brome - Family 89, 110; Constance 24; Nicholas 24, 28; Robert 28
Brome Hall, alias Bromeham Hall, alias Broom Hall 13, 28*, 29, 30, 31, 48, 63, 81
Brome, Manor of 12, 13, 21
Brommen Priory see High Chimneys
Brookes - John 81, 114, 115; Sarah 53, 92, 95, 96
Brook House Farm 81, 91, 101, 114, 115
Broom Hall see Brome Hall
Broomfield House Farm, alias Broomfield House 15, 58, 81, 109, 115, 116
Brown - John 65; Mary 67; Mrs. 59, 60, 96, 104; William 114
Bryan, Ada 108
Buckle, Thomas 13
Buffery - David 25, 81, 113, 114; Thomas 25, 26
Bumblebees 52, 54, 98*
Bunn - Family 13; Caroline 93; James 51
Bunn Green 13, 14, 51, 112
Burman - John 114; Mary 114; Thomas 115
Bushwood 7, 9, 11, 13, 14, 22, 23, 40, 78, 114
Bushwood Common 13, 14, 20, 70, 87, 112
Bushwood Common Farm 13, 17*, 70, 81, 116
Bushwood Grange 13, 70, 81, 83, 116

Bushwood Hall and Bushwood Hall Farm 13, 14, 18, 22, 23, 35, 52, 81, 96, 111, 112
Bushwood Mill Farm 35
Bushwood Windmill 14
Bushwood Wood 7, 13
Bustin - Child 93; Mr. 93
Buttwell - John 51, 94, 114, 115; Joseph 52; Samuel 66; William 36

Camden - Family 13, 28; Elizabeth 28, 29; John 29
Cameron - Donald 71; Rev. Donald 71, 86, 110; Frances 71; Letitia 71
Canning - Samuel 36, 114, 115; Thomas 81, 114, 115
Carpenter - Elias 53, 95; James 96; Joseph 55, 96, 97, 98; Mrs. 94
Carpenter's Pleck 113
Catesby - Family 84, 89, 110; Edmund 28; Elizabeth 22, 28; George 22; Robert 13; William 22, 84
Catesby Farm 28, 31, 46, 52, 81, 91, 92*, 97, 116
Catesby House 83, 114
Catesby Lane 114
Cattell - Catherine 97, 104; Mary Ann 104; Mr. 52; Sarah Ann 104; William 104
Cedar Lawn, alias Webb's Land 81, 115
Chain House 28, 31, 35, 81, 128*
Chamberlain - George 104; Mrs. 104
Chamberlain's Meadow 112
Charles - Family 115; Mary 115
Chernock, Francis 28
Cherry Trees 27*, 101, 116
Cheshire - James 114, 115; Thomas 81, 115
Chestnut Cottage Farm 81
Childe - Rev. George 70, 86; Georgina 70; Harry 70; Mary Ann 70, 71; Robert 70
Chinn - Isabel 94; William 66
Church Field 9
Church of St. Mary's see General Index
Clark/Clarke - John 22; William 22, 108
Cleese - Mrs. 67, 92; Richard 67; Thomas 66, 67
Cleycrofte 37
Clover, Widow 64
Clues, Charles 20
Cockerill - Sir Charles 21, 24
Collit, Sarah 67
Commander, George 97
Common Farm 26, 81, 111
Constable, John 95, 97
Cook/Cooke/Cookes/Cooks - Henry 14, 23; John 115; Samuel 29, 65, 66, 114, 115
Cooper, W. H. 21, 23, 80
Copt Green 52, 53, 55, 97, 107
Cottage The, 115, 116
Cotterill - Ann 114; John 36, 37, 114; Mr. 38, 51, 52; Richard 101
Couchman - Family 83; Mr. 23
Court - Henry 20; William 49
Courtnell - Family 106; Elizabeth 106; Jacob 108; Mrs. 106
Cox - Lydia 55, 98; Thomas 100; William 54, 98, 114
Craddock, William 95, 97
Cranmer - Robert 91, 115; Samuel 91, 115; Thomas 105
Cricket and Quoits Club 111
Crump, John 95
Culcope - Ann 114; Edmund 12, 13, 14, 15, 57, 58, 59; Elizabeth 15, 59; Mary 15, 37, 114, 115

Danesbury 98
Davey - Alfred Horace 104, 105, 106, 107, 108; Mrs. 109
Day, John 20
Dee, Thomas 53, 95, 97
Deneberht, Bishop of Worcester 9
Denstone, Benjamin 92
Devon House 30, 110
Dingley Dell 27, 103, 115
Divett, Edward 28, 30, 31
Dolphin - Ann 26; Richard 21; William 115
Dowdeswell House 53, 78, 116
Drawbridge Farm, alias Millbourne Farm 49, 52, 55, 81, 98, 116; Plan 56*
Dugard, Miss 109

121

Eades, Mr. 51
Eaton, Rev. J. R. T. 85
Eborall, Edward 52, 54
Edgecox - John 95, 96, 97, 98, 100; Sarah 95, 96
Edkins - Family 35; Benjamin 14, 23; Edward 20
Edwards - John 52; Mr. 51, 62
Egelston Brothers 100
Essenford 40

Fairview 30, 31, 103, 110
Falcon, Mrs. 109
Falks, William 20
Fantham/Fanthom - Mrs. 46, 97; William 53, 95
Farley, Michael 81
Fellowes, Jo. 115
Fenton, Mrs. 102
Ferrers - Family 11, 24; Edward 26;
    Marmion Edward 113
Fetherstone - Family 88, 89; Charles 115;
    Francis 29, 100, 101, 113; John 30, 81, 89, 115;
    Miss 113, 115; Mr. 63, 64; Thomas 26, 52, 113, 115
Field - Edward 38, 114; Mr. 62; Mrs. 65; Richard 26
Finwood Green/Fynard Green 112
Fisher, George 92
Fowler - Mr. 52, 67; Rebecca 52, 80
Frankton, Mr. 52

Garner - Alice 64; Widow 64
Garston, John 25
Gazy, Samuel 94
Gerrard, William 83, 90, 102, 111
Gibbs - George 81, 96, 111; Thomas 81
Gibson the Miller 22
Gilbert - Ann 66; John 46; Michael 66
Gospel Oak The, 12, 112, 113
Gospel Oak Farm 12, 29, 30, 31, 78*, 81, 111
Gowan Bank 90*, 110
Grafton, John 26, 29, 53, 63, 90, 94, 99, 113
Gravelly Hill 14
Greaves, Isaac 81
Green - Family 35; Hester 26; Isaac 14, 20, 52, 114, 115;
    John 14, 37, 52, 100; Mr. 51, 63, 70; Nancy 115;
    Thomas 114; William 14, 20
Green Acres 116
Greenall, John 112
Greenhill - Elizabeth 66; John 20; Joseph 93, 94;
    Mrs. 65, 94; Thomas 66
Greenwood, Charles 21, 24
Grentemaisnil de, Hugh 9
Griffin - Boys 106; Mrs. 106
Grouby, Elizabeth 112
Grove Cottage 27, 111, 115

Hainse, John 25
Hammond - David 100; James 101
Hancox - Daniel 94; Sarah 64
Hands - George 81; Job 81
Hannes, John 78
Harbery Heath, alias *Erdbyr,* alias *Erbury,* alias
    Harborough 12, 28, 30, 41, 48
Harborough Banks 8, 9, 12, 13, 18, 28, 29*, 30, 31, 113
'Harborough Banks' 30
Harborough House 30
Hardin, William 25
Harding - Joseph 113; Mr. 102; Mrs. 102; Thomas 51
Harecourt de, William 84
Hassal, Robert 70
Hawkins - Ann 93; Mrs. 93; Richard 92; William 81, 114
Hawthorne Piece 112
Haycock - Maria 66; William 66, 114
Hazelwood 35, 81, 116
Healstone, William 101
Heath, Richard 81, 91, 94
Hedges, Edward 22
Heritage, William 53, 66, 95
Herlwin, 9
Hicken - Family 83; Ann 81; James 105; Martha 81
Higgens, Thomas 91, 92
High Chimneys Farm, alias Brommen Priory, alias
    Sorrells House 7, 13, 28, 30, 31, 35, 36, 46, 70, 81
    96, 110, 112, 116
Hildick - Benjamin 26, 29, 30, 31, 113; Francis Spencer 111;
    Joseph 29, 30; Martha 29, 30, 81; Moses 29, 113;
    Mr. 37; Robert 29
Hill, Henry 100
Hobday - Joseph 52, 95, 97; Mr. 51, 80
Hockley Heath, alias *Hockelowe,* alias *Huckeloweheth* 7,
    20, 40,
    41, 42, 44, 69, 73, 77, 85, 100, 108, 112, 116
Hodges - Family 83; George 81

Hoese, William 21
Holden, Misses 110
Hole House Farm 20, 68*, 81, 116
Hollies, The see Bridge House
Holte - Family 11; Sir Charles 15, 20, 21, 22, 23, 36;
    Sir Clobery 22; Sir Lister 14, 18, 20, 21, 23, 35;
    Mary 21; Sir Robert 22; Sir Thomas 18, 22
Holy Common 112
Horton - Charles 20, 26; Maria 96; Widow 64;
    William 46, 95, 97
Hoston, William 102
House/Howse - Hannah 81; William 77
Hudson - Misses 109; Mrs. 109; Robert 110, 111;
    Sir Robert Arundell 111
Hullies/Ulelega 48; Big 52
Hulls Garage 101
Hunt - James 100; Thomas 25
Hutton - Ann 93; Thomas 93; William 16

Ingram - Hannah 80, 111; Isaac 112; Mr. 112;
    William 51, 52, 80
Ireland - Elizabeth 22, 24; Robert 22
Irelands Farm, alias Lapworth Hall 14, 22, 23*, 24, 35,
    46, 74, 81, 83, 100, 112

Jeffs, Sarah 98
Jelphs, Mrs. 46
Jennings - Henry 106; John 113; Richard 49
Johns - Ann 114; Richard 39; Thomas 37, 39, 52, 71,
    79, 85, 114; William 37, 38, 39, 44, 69, 79, 114
Johnson, Florence 108
Jones, John 38
Jordan - Lydia 65; Richard 65, 66

Keen, Mr. 93
Kemp, Richard 113
Kendall - Thomas 53, 60, 65; William 52
Kendrick, Widow 64, 92
Kershaw - Family 90; John 77; Misses 89
Kershaws Land 115
Kilner, Rev. Joseph 15, 16, 85
King - Family 83; Joseph 52, 91, 93, 94; Thomas 81, 96;
    William 83, 98, 115
Kingswood 12, 18, 20, 24, 29, 40, 47, 51, 69, 70,
    73, 74, 77, 79, 107, 110, 113
Kingswood Brook 7, 24, 27, 41, 53, 97
Kingswood Brook Cottages 53*
Kingswood Close, alias George Avenue 8
Kingswood Common 12, 20, 26, 27, 30, 31, 53, 79, 112
Kingswood Cottages 25
Kingswood Cross 27
Kingswood Farm 81, 116
Kingswood Gap 7
Kingswood Grange 26, 27, 83, 90, 101, 102, 103, 109*
Kingswood House 103, 116
Kingswood Mission Room 110
Kingswood Station 110, 111
Kingswood Stores 72*

Lancaster - Henry 81, 113; John 101
Lanes and Roads —
    Barrs Lane 20
    Broomhall Lane 9
    Bushwood Lane 14
    Church Lane, alias Ford Lane 7, 40, 52
    Crab Mill Lane 113
    Cross Lane 27, 112
    Dicks Lane, alias Long Picks Lane 7, 9, 77, 78, 112
    Farm Lane 112
    Ford Lane, alias The Ford 112
    Grove Lane 110
    Hole House Lane 52
    Lapworth Street 13, 14, 20, 28, 40, 52, 107, 110, 112, 114
    Mill Lane 27, 31, 77, 112
    Millpool Lane 112
    Old Warwick Road, alias Lapworth Street from Hockley
        Heath to the water tower 15, 27, 28, 30, 40, 41, 44
        45, 47*, 52, 53, 63, 73, 97, 100, 103, 110, 116
    Rising Brook Lane/Rising Lane 27, 112, 113
    Spring Lane, alias Brocshawe Lane, alias Nuthele Lane
        (Nuthill), alias Periwinkle Lane 7, 40, 66, 78, 114
    Station Lane 7, 27, 31, 47, 53, 103, 110
    Stratford Road 7, 15, 20, 45, 52, 63, 100, 104
    Tapster/Tapsford/Topsford Lane 9, 14, 52, 73
    Timmins Lane 113
    Wharf Lane 41, 44, 52, 77, 78, 97, 98
Lapworth/*Hlappawurthin/Lappawurthin* 9
Lapworth, Alfred 89, 116
Lapworth Brook 7, 14, 20, 37, 40, 52, 112; Farm near 37
Lapworth Farm 31, 36, 66, 81, 114, 115

Lapworth Grange - see Blockbury House
Lapworth Hall see also Irelands Farm 18
Lapworth Hill 42
Lapworth Hill Farm 35, 52, 116
Lapworth House and Farm 36, 81, 109
Lapworth Lodge Farm 22, 23, 35, 36*, 51, 62, 81, 83, 87, 96, 99, 116
Lapworth (Moat) Farm 80, 81, 115, 116
Lapworth Park Farm 14, 15, 22, 23, 35, 81, 83, 87, 98, 115, 116
Lea - Martha 113, 114; Mary 114; Richard 114; William 37, 115
Lee, William 102
Leeson - Catherine 65; James 51; John 115; Mrs. 66; William 64, 65
Legge - Lady Anne 21; Heneage 20, 21, 52, 112
Lench, Mr. 51
Linney, Elizabeth 106
Little Rising 116
Liveridge Hill/Liverycheshill/Liveretts 22, 40, 42
Lock - David 66; Elizabeth 66
Long, William 53
Longlands 31
Lowsonford/Lawson Ford 7, 13, 40, 77, 78, 112
Luckman - Elizabeth 65; F. 57; Hannah 114; Samuel 114; Thomas 49; William 53, 65, 114
Lucy - Francis 28; Sir Richard 28

Maids - Alice 93; Hannah 93; Mary 53; Sarah 93; Thomas 51, 53, 64, 65, 95, 113
Malthouse Farm, Kingswood 35, 47, 53, 81, 83, 95, 96, 101
Malthouse Farm, Lapworth 63, 80, 81, 101, 115, 116
Mander - Family 35, 83, 88, 110; Elizabeth 29, 97; John 29, 46, 81; Robert 14, 20, 23, 74, 100; Samuel 23, 66, 115; Sophia 97
Marshall, Family 21, 84, 110
Marston, Charles 104
Martin - John 102; Richard 26
Mason, Thomas 12
Masters, Joseph 92
Meadow Hill Farm 13, 70, 81
Melson, Family 102
Mildmay, Rev. Charles Arundell St. John 72, 85, 86, 89, 97
Mill Farm 23
Mill House Farm 81, 114
Mill Pool 112
Millbourne Farm see Drawbridge Farm
Miller, George 21, 89
Millpool Meadow 112
Mills, Pheobe 93, 94
Montfort de - Sir Richard 22, 48, 84; Rose 22, 48
Moore, Thomas 26
Mortiboys - Family 88; Isaac 37, 51, 52, 64, 80; John 59, 66, 104
Moseley, George 102
Moss Meadow 112
Mount, The 30
Mountford Farm 66, 81, 115, 116

Nash, Thomas 53, 95
Navigation Inn 25, 43*, 44, 100
Neal, Mrs. 98
Needle - Ellen 108; John 30
Newbery - Joseph 113; Thomas 26, 27
Newton, Mary 98
Nicholas, Rector 84

Oak Villa 110
Oilelur, le William 48
Oldfield 14
Old Holloway 112
Old Warwick Road see Lanes and Roads
Olive Cottage 116
Osborne - Family 110; Joseph 31, 46, 81
Overton - Family 12, 99; Thomas 12; William 35, 99

Palmer - Child 93; Shirley 27, 102, 103; His daughter 103; Thomas 46
Pardoe, Mary 93
Pardy, John 94
Park, The 14, 35, 36
Parnell, Benjamin 28, 29
Parsons - Family 83; Henry 51; James 46; Joseph 81, 111, 113; Samuel 26, 53, 94; Thomas 81; William 31
Parson's Piece 112
Partridge, Rev. Charles 106
Paxton, Sir William 21, 24
Payton, Joseph 115

Pearman, John 113
Pettifer, Joseph 113
Phillips, John 94
Phipps, Elizabeth 53
Pinfold 53*
Pinner, Arthur 108
Pinners Bridge 77, 78
Pippard - Cicely 21; Henry 21
Pooley Close 113
Pound Cottages 51, 52, 53, 96, 98
Pountney, John 101
Prat, Thomas 48, 56
Prescot - Rev. Kenrick 85, 105, 110, 111; Mrs. 85, 105, 109
Preston Brook 112
Prior - Ann 65, 66, 67; Lucy 66
Pritchett, John 81
Punch Bowl Inn 27*, 101
Pye - Frances 17; Harriet 17; Rev. Henry Anthony 16, 17, 69, 70, 71, 85, 86, 94

Quinn, Samuel 102
Quinney, Thomas 100

Rainbow, Thomas 81, 97, 101, 115
Rectory Cottage 116
Rectory House 81, 85, 86*, 87*, 115
Reeve - Charles 96; Henry 96; John 46, 53, 95, 96; Sarah 56; Walter 107; William 96, 97
Reynolds - Sarah 95; Thomas 95, 96, 97; William 96
Richmond - Annie 107; Joseph 100; Thomas 100
Rider, Elizabeth 64
Robinson, James 77
Rogers - Richard 77; Thomas 77; - 51
Ross - Family 28; George 113
Round House, The 116
Royal Oak Inn 42, 49, 51, 66, 94, 100, 115, 116

Sadler - Edward 20, 112; William 18, 20, 23
Sanders - Catherine 111; Eleanor 111; George 25; Henry 46, 111; Mr. 67, 105; William 53, 65, 111
Sands Farm 81, 103*, 116
Savage, Harriet 60
Shakespeare - Humphrey 12, 54; John 54
Shaw, William 67
Sheldon, George 31
Sherwood, George 25
Sidaway, Jonathan 93, 94
Sly - Edwin 104, 105, 107; Harriet 104; Nicholas 28; Roger 28, 48, 56; Thomas 34, 49
Smith - Anne 93; Benjamin 115; Charles 113; Child 93; Elizabeth 16, 98; George 16, 67, 112; Isaac 94; John 26, 51, 63; Joseph 23, 35; Maria 98; Mary 108; Richard 30, 31, 46, 77, 81, 100, 102; Thomas 31, 51, 81, 98, 102, 113; William 51, 52, 115
Soden, John 36, 37, 114
Soley, Richard 77
Sorel, Luke 48
Sorrells House see High Chimneys
Sprag - Edward 46, 95, 97; Mrs. 46
Spratts Pits 112, 113; Pool 112
Spring Cottage Farm 65, 80, 81, 114
Spring Rice, Rev. Aubrey 85
Staples - James 98; Mary 60
Stickman's Meadow 112
Stoughton, Timothy 28
Stratford Road see Lanes and Roads
Street Farm 37
Sunnybank 40
Sutton, Samuel 103

Tabberner, Richard 113
Taft, Ephriam 81
Tan House Farm 28, 29, 30, 31, 33*, 35, 63, 81, 94, 99, 116
Tapsford/Topsford 14
Tapster Brook 7, 14, 49
Tapster Brook Farm/Cottage 49, 50*, 51, 81, 116
Tapster Farm, alias Windmill Farm 36, 65*, 81, 114, 116
Tapster Ford 7, 14
Tapster Valley 7
Tapsters 20
Taylor - Ann 113; Jane 30, 31; John 114; Joseph 113; Mrs. 66; Philip 102; William 30, 81
Terets Cottage 116
Terretts, The 27, 102, 103
Thistle Closes 14
Tibbetts/Tibbitts - Thomas 81; William 113
Townsend - Edward 95, 98; Elizabeth 95, 96; Frances 60; John 97; Rev. J. 85; Mary Ann 97; Thomas 53, 96, 97

Tudor Farm 28, 31, 54, 65, 81, 114, 116
Turner, Hannah 94
Turnpike Close 41
Turnpike House 112
Turvey, Thomas 101
Tyndall - Rev. George 54, 71,72, 81, 85, 86; Mrs. 90

Udall, William 23, 83
Ulelega/Hullies 48
Underhill - Sarah 97; Thomas 95, 97, 98; William 96, 97

Vernon, William 83
Village Hall 30
Vine Cottage 116
Viners - Ann 60; Hannah 60; John 97

Wade, Elizabeth 93
Wakefield, Mr. 115
Walker, George 22
Wallers Great 113; Little 113
Wallers, John 113
Walter's Lock 77
Ward - Boy 93; James 95, 97; Thomas 53, 95
Wardell/Wardle - Family 100; William 92
Warden, John 20
Warwick Road see Lanes and Roads under Old Warwick Road
Watton, John 81
Watts, John Edmund 21, 23, 30, 83
Way - Elizabeth 70; James 70; Rev. James 69, 70, 86
Webbs Land 115

Wedge, William 49
Weiss, J. 21, 23, 83
Welshman, Rev. Edward 12, 49, 57, 85
Wharr, Thomas 115
Wheatcroft, William 115
White - John 106; Widow 51
Whitworth, Mr. 109
Wiggett, Edward 108
Wight, John 57
Wilding, Rev. J. 71
Williams - Family 51, 100; Mary 64; Samuel 25
Willpower Garage 51
Wilmore, Mary 112
Wilson - Elizabeth 93; Thomas 93
Windmill Farm see Tapster Farm
Winston House 98
Wood/Woods - Edward 64, 92; John 93; Joseph 70; Thomas 94; Widow 93
Woodcock, Charlotte 60
Woodward - Henry 60, 115; Mr. 66
Wooldridge, Peter 81, 114, 115; - 15

Yarditch 14, 115
Yardley - Edward 66; Mrs. 92
Yeomans - Isaac 104; Sarah 104
Yew Tree Cottage (K) 81, 91
Yew Tree Cottage (L) 116
Yew Tree Farm 53, 81, 83, 115
Yew Tree House 97
Young - Thomas 46; Widow 97

Bredon House, Lapworth Street

General Index

Abergavenny, Earl of 74
Accounts 50, 55, 60, 61, 63, 68, 91, 94
Acreage Returns 1801 79
Acts of Parliament
    Agricultural Childrens Act1873 104;
    Birmingham Canal Act 1768 73;
    Education Act 1870 104;
    Enclosure of Harborough Banks 1863 30, 31;
    Enclosure of Kingswood Common 1807 26, 27;
    Enclosure of Rowington Common Land 1824 70;
    Poor Law Amendment Act 55;
    Public Health Act 1872 46;
    Stratford-upon-Avon Canal Act 16, 73, 74;
    Tithe Commutation Act 1836 85, 87;
    Turnpike Act — Birmingham to Stratford 1726 40;
                  Hatton to Hockley Heath 1766-7 41
Advowson 84
Agriculture 8, 11, 15, 26, 29, 30, 32-8, 52, 53, 79-83, 99, 101
    see Crops, Livestock and Dairying; Convertible
    Husbandy 32, 33, 35; Ley Farming 32, 33; Mixed
    Farming 11, 32, 79; Grazing 12, 13, 26, 79; Arable 79, 81-3; Fallow 33; Grass 12, 13, 34, 64, 81, 82; Mowing
    Grass 29, 83; Rye Grass 29, 34; Ley 32, 33; Meadow 25, 112, 113; Lattermath 37; Pasture 25, 33, 79; Marginal
    Land 79, Department of 83, Effects of
    Refrigeration on, 83; in Arden 32
Agricultural
    Fertilisers 83; Ashes 33; Guano 83; Lime 21, 33, 37, 51, 77, 78; Malt Dust 33; Manure 33; Potash 83;
    Sawdust 33; Soot 33; Implements 32, 33; Pests 33;
    Work — Ploughing 8, 32, 33, 79; Sowing 32;
    Mowing 32; Haymaking 32, 46, 100, 106; Reaping 32;
    Harvest 32, 46, 100, 105, 106; Threshing 32, 35, 71
    Products — Meat 11, 12, 34-6, 38, 64, 80, 97;
    Salted, Smoked 34; Foreign 83; Beef, Pork 83;
    Mutton 66, 83; Fleeces 34; Eggs 85
Alcester 9, 67
Ale and Beer
    Ale 34, 35, 64, 66, 67, 94, 100; Ale houses 63;
    Beer 12, 32, 34, 64, 66, 77, 91, 100, 101;
    Beer houses 27, 77, 101, 102
Allesley 42
Almshouses 97, 98
Alvechurch 85
Animals 11, 26, 32, 34, 35, 99
Apprentices 59, 61, 63, 66, 67, 104; Indentures 67
Archaeological Finds 8, 9
Archdeacon's Visitation 62
Archer, Andrew 85
Arden family 89
Armishaw, Mr. 52
Armorial Bearings 89
Aris's Gazette 17
Ashby St. Leger 22
Aston 22, 26
    Hall 11, 18, 21, 22; Duddeston Hall 18
Atherstone 21
Australia 83

Baddesley Clinton 7, 9, 12, 24, 28, 113; Hall 7
Bagot, Mr. 21
Bailiffs 18, 83, 103
Bakewell, Robert of Dishley 35
Banbury 49, 53
Band of Hope 105
Baptisms 61, 111
Beaudesert 8, 9, 21, 44, 48
Beausale 8
Belbroughton 41
Bells 51, 62; Bell Ringers 51, 71, 94; Bell Ropes 51, 61
Bilston 71, 72
Birmingham 7, 11, 14, 16, 26, 29, 40, 41, 42, 44, 45, 48, 59, 66, 67, 69, 71, 73, 74, 77, 79, 80, 96, 102, 103, 112
    Gun Trade 80; Plateau 6*, 7
Blackburn, Joseph of Nottingham 90
Black Country 69, 73, 77, 79
Books 59, 110
Bordesley 22
Botley 9
Boundaries 8, 9, 10, 20, 21, 22, 112, 113

Bracebridge, Abraham 21, 23
Bradnocks End 20
Bread 11, 15, 17, 32, 37, 54, 64, 66, 80, 94;
    Flour 12, 15, 17, 33, 35-7, 55, 64, 97; Barley 38;
    Wheat 38
Brewing 34, 100, 101; Brewhouses 22, 34, 60; Hops 34, 38
Brick 24, 51, 60, 74, 98, 100, 116;
    Brick Kilns 51, 99, 112; Bricklayers 74, 77, 101, 103;
    Brickmakers 11, 35, 99, 100; Brickmaking 99, 100;
    Brickwork 35, 51, 74, 116; Brickyard 100
Bridges 20, 40, 41, 68, 74, 112
Bristol Channel 7, 9
Bromsgrove 41
Bronze Age 8; Axe Heads 8
Brookhouse Farm, Rowington 13
Brooks and Streams 7, 12, 20, 41, 112, 113
Brown, Isaac 71
Burials 61, 64, 66, 67, 93, 97, 111
Burd, Rev. Charles 85, 110; Marion 110

Canals 16, 70, 71, 73, 74, 77-9, 100-3, 110, 111
    Companies — Birmingham 73; Dudley 73;
    Stratford-upon-Avon 30, 52, 100, 101;
    Canals — Stratford-upon-Avon 7, 16 30, 38, 52, 53, 69, 70, 73-5*, 76*, 77, 79, 101, 113;
    Warwick & Birmingham 7, 73, 74, 79, 113;
    Worcester & Birmingham 73; Shares 73, 74; Navvies 69, 70; Boats 77, 102; Bridges 27, 74, 78, 102;
    Locks 74, 77, 102; Lock Gates 77, 100; Houses 74, 77;
    Towpaths 74, 77;
    Employees — Agent 77; Manager 103, 111;
    Boatmen 77, 100, 102; Lengthmen 77;
    Lock Keepers 77, 100, 103; Canal Side Inns, Shops 77, 102; Cargo 73, 77; Lime Kilns 78
Candles 48, 70, 91
Carmarthenshire 14
Celtic People 8, 9, 10; Names 8
Census 46, 69, 70, 72, 83, 94, 97, 101, 102, 103
Chamberlayne, John, F. R. S. 57
Chadwick End School 106
Chancery, Court of 48, 49, 54
Chantries 48, 49, 84; Chapels 49*, 84, 89, 90, 94;
    Masses 48, 84
Charindon de, William 21
Charities 30, 47, 48, 49, 54, 114
    Charity Estate 37, 46, 48, 49, 52-4, 59, 62, 65, 91, 95, 104; Cottages 53*, 55, 97, 98; Doles 48, 50, 54;
    Feoffees 26, 48-56, 59, 61, 80, 87, 90, 95-97, 110;
    Minute Book 49; Charity Commissioners 54, 71, 80
Chatwin, Mr. 90
Cheltenham 74
Cheshire 21, 102
Chesetts Wood 27; Common 12
Church of St. Mary's 4*, 11, 44, 48, 49, 51, 58*, 61*, 62, 71, 72, 84, 88-90, 97, 110, 111; Building 84, 88-90; Furniture 84, 89, 90: Altar Rails 17, 89*;
    Chancel 54, 84, 89; Chapel 22, 84, 90; Clock 51, 90; Gallery 89, 90; Harmonium 89; Organ 89, 90;
    Pews 88*-90; Pulpit 71, 78; Tower and Spire 84, 90;
    Vestibule 84; Vestry 90, 94; Weather Vane 90;
    Windows 84, 89, 90; Restoration 84, 89, 90, 110;
    Yard 49, 58, 59, 71, 98, 110
Cirencester 16, 69, 85, 86
Claverdon 8, 67
Clayton and Bell 89
Clergy 79, 87
Cloth 64-7;
    Calico 67; Flannel 54, 67; Jersey 34; Linen 29, 51, 54, 67, 93; Making 33, 34
Clothing 54, 55, 59, 61, 64, 66, 67, 91, 94, 97, 100, 108;
    Club 55, 96; Apron 64; Bedgown 66, 92; Breeches 66, 94; Frock 67; Handkerchief 64; Hats 64, 66;
    Petticoats 67, 92; Round Frocks 97; Shifts 92, 93;
    Shirts 66, 94, 97; Shoes 55, 64, 66, 67, 91, 93, 97, 100;
    Stockings 64, 66, 94; Trousers 97
Clowes, Josiah 73, 74
Coaches 29, 41, 42, 44, 45, 73, 100;
    Mail 41*, 42, 44, 69; Stage 29, 41, 42, 44, 71;
    Royal Mail 42; Post Chaise 41, 42, 44; Coachman 41, 103; Coaching Inns 42, 85, 100; Posting House 41;
    Post Boy 41, 44; Post Horn 42

125

Coal 29, 33, 51, 54, 55, 59, 61, 64-6, 68, 73, 74, 77, 78, 92, 97, 100, 104, 105, 114
Cobbett, William 70
Cockerill, Samuel Pepys 24
Coenwlf, King of Mercia 9
Coleshill 71
Common Land 20, 23, 26, 30, 41, 70, 79;
  Encroachments 13, 27, 30; Enclosure 9, 26, 27, 30, 31, 69, 70, 79
Confirmation 110
Corn Laws 72, 83
Cornwallis, Earl 80, 96, 115
Cottages 20, 25, 51-6, 58, 77, 80, 91, 93, 94, 97, 98, 110, 111, 116; Restoration 98
Coventry 7, 42, 69, 72, 74
Coventry Road 41
Cnut 9
Craftsmen 11, 35, 80, 96, 99, 103;
  Blacksmith 11, 13, 51, 90, 96, 99-101, 103; Brickmaker 11, 35, 99, 100; Carpenter 11, 21, 26, 35, 77, 94, 99-101, 103; Cooper 101; Cordwainer 11, 67, 96, 98-101, 103; Hatcheller 35, 99; Maltster 81, 101, 103; Mason 11, 21, 51, 99, 103; Miller 14, 36, 103, 114; Rake Maker 101; Sawyer 103; Stone Mason 94, 101; Tanner 11, 26, 35, 63, 99; Thatcher 53, 65; Wheelwright 11, 99, 100, 101, 103, Wood Turner 28, 100
Crops 11, 15, 32-5, 79;
  Barley 8, 11, 12, 29, 32-4, 36, 38, 79, 83, 87, 101; Beans 33, 38, 79, 83; Clover 34, 83, 87; Corn 15, 35, 36, 61, 79, 80, 85, 94, 97; Flax 33, 35; Fodder 34, 36, 37, 79; Grain 15, 32, 73, 77, 79, 101; Hay 11, 32, 34, 35, 37, 79, 83, 85, 87, 97; Hemp 33, 35; Oats 11, 29, 32-4, 38, 79, 87; Peas 11, 29, 32-4, 38, 79, 83, 97; Potatoes 17, 37, 38, 72, 79, 97; Pulses 33; Rye 33; Seeds 32, 83; Swedes 34, 79; Turnips 34, 79, 83; Vetches 11, 32, 34, 83; Wheat 8, 11, 12, 17, 29, 32, 33, 35-8, 69, 71, 79, 80, 83, 87; Woad 33
Curates 11-7, 69, 71, 85, 106, 110, 115

Dairying 11, 34, 37, 79;
  Dairy 11, 24, 29, 34, 79; Butter 11, 12, 29, 33-5, 38, 66, 80; Buttermilk 11; Cheese 11, 12, 17, 29, 33-7, 64, 66, 79, 80, 83, 94; Foreign 83; Cheese Chamber 11, 29, 34; Making Utensils 29, 34; Milk 11, 12, 29, 34, 35, 37, 64, 80, 83, 85, 87
Dartmouth, Earl of 21
Digby, Mr. 21
Diocese of Lichfield 10; of Worcester 10, 105
Disease and Ill Health 15, 65, 71, 94, 97, 108;
  Cholera 71, 72, 97; Colds 108; Coughs 108; Diphtheria 108; Fever 15, 97; Influenza 97; Measles 15, 72, 97, 108; Rash 15, 97; Ringworm 108; Scabies 93; Scarlet Fever 15, 108; Smallpox 108; Throats 15, 108; Typhus 72, 97, 108; Whooping Cough 97, 104, 108; Vaccination 108; 'Staves Acre Ointment' 108; Lice 97, 108
Doctor 65, 66, 93, 108
Dolton, John 70
Domesday Survey 9
Dorset 103
Drink 15, 52, 64, 66, 67
Dudley 73, 79
Dugdale, Sir William 9, 22
Dunchurch 42

Earlswood Lakes 74
Early Medieval Period 9
Earps of Lambeth 89
Earthworks 8, 9, 12, 13, 30
Eastcote 26
Eden, Sir F. M. 64
Edinburgh 41
Edward I 84
Erdington 22
Eydon, Northants 94

Farmers 11, 22, 23, 26, 32-8, 80-3, 100-2, 114;
  Graziers 36, 114
Ferrers Magazine 98
Fields 11; Communal 32, 37, 52; Strips in - 37, 52
Fishing 21, 103; Fishpond, pool 21, 22, 29;
  Bream, Eel, Perch, Pike, Roach 21
Flowers and Hedges 11, 12, 13, 26, 27
Food 51, 66, 67, 77, 91, 108;
  Bacon 34, 38, 64; Fruit 85; Rice 37, 97; Salt 91; Vegetables 80; see also Bread
Forest of Arden 7, 8
Fountaine, Andrew 22
Fowler, John of Rollright 35

Fuel 29, 64, 66, 67, 91, 95; Fire 64, 95; Cooking Fire 24, 64, 70, 95, 101
Funeral expenses 39, 64, 65, 66, 93
Furniture 29;
  Carpets 17, 29, 59; Chairs 29; Chests 29; Clock 29; Looking Glass 29; Stool 108; Tables 29
Furniture, Soft 29;
  Bedcord, mat, tick 66; Blankets 66, 114: Curtains 29; Feather mattress 29; Sheets 29, 55, 64, 66, 67, 92, 97

Gannow Green 41
Gardens 53, 80, 85, 103;
  Gardener 102, 103; Gardening 106
Geography
  Geographical Position 7; Geology 7; Relief 6*, 7; Drainage 6*, 7; Natural Landscape 8; Woodland 8; Clearings 8; Glacial Drift 7, 8; Watershed 7, 9;
Geological Periods 7
George III 16, 71
George IV 71
Glebe Land 85, 87, 115
Glen de, John 84
Gravel Digging 12, 30
Greaves, Richard 74
Grimshaw, Thomas 48, 49
Gunnild 9
Gunpowder Plot 13

Hair Powder 36
Halesowen 67
Hampton-in-Arden 44
Hampton-on-the-Hill 40
Harborne, Thomas 59, 60
Harvests 15-7, 36, 37, 69-71, 97
Hatton 16, 40, 41, 44
Heath, John 67
Henley-in-Arden 11, 42, 43, 44, 46, 63, 66, 67, 83, 92, 93, 94, 112
Henry VIII 42, 48, 84
Herbs 13, 26; Herbal Cures 13
Highwaymen 15, 42
Hockley Heath
  Club 105; Mop 105
Hockley House 42*, 43, 44, 71, 85
Holyhead 42
Household Utensils
  Chamber Pot 17, Ewer 12; Cooking Equipment 29; Kettle 66
Housekeeping 95, 101
Houses 21, 22, 27, 29, 101, 114, 115, 116;
  Farm 11, 34, 81, 101, 113, 114; Cross Wing 116; Porch 21; Staircase 24, 84, 85, 90, 94, 116; Ceiling 90; Doors 17, 21, 94; Doorway 21, 24; Windows 21; Rooms 21; Bed 24, 29, 60, 108; Dining 17, 24; Drawing 17; Hall 22, 24, 116; Parlour 24, 29, 60, 85; Chamber 21, 24, 85; Sovreign 21, 22; Study 17, 110; Wardrobe 21, 22; Kitchen 22, 24, 29, 60, 85, 86; Pantry 29; Buttery 29, Cellar 29, 85; Chimneys 13, 24, 85, 116; Fireplaces 21, 22, 27, 29; Grate 29; Construction — Timber Framing 12, 14, 24, 30, 85, 114, 115, 116; Ground Sill 24, 84, 49, 85; Walls 21, 74; Gable End 21, 116; Roof 9, 21, 51, 74, 84; Barrel Roof 74; Parapet 21; Floor 51; Glazing 51
Hundreds of Fernecumbe, Fexhole, Hemlingford, Pathlow 9
Hutton, William 16
Hwicce, 10

Income Tax 69
Inland Revenue 103
Inns 34, 42-4, 100, 102, 103, 111, 114, 116;
  Innkeeper 81, 101, 111, 114
Ireland 72
Iron Age 8, 9, 30;
  Forts 8; Tribes — Coritani 8, 10; Cornovvii 8, 10; Dobunni 8, 10

James, William 74
Johnson, Dr. 41; Thomas 17, 86
Jones, John of Islanton 37

Kenilworth 26
Kent 94
Kineton 39
Kings Norton 16, 41, 73, 74
Knowle 7, 12, 41, 66, 113

Lancaster, Earl of 28
Landowners 80, 87, 114
Land Tax 37, 63, 67, 80, 114

Lanes 11, 40, 45, 46, 112, 113;
  Footpaths 27, 31; Bridleways 27
Law and Order 61
  Lawyer 67; Magistrates 92-4; 106; Summons 67, 93;
  Warrants 66, 67, 94; Stocks 63; Petty Sessions 94;
  Quarter Sessions 40
Letters 67, 74
Levies 49, 51, 59, 61, 62, 67, 91
Linear Feature 9
Livestock 15, 29, 32, 33, 34, 83
  Horses 11, 29, 32-5, 41, 42, 45, 73, 77, 79, 93; Breeding
  34; Mares 35; Oxen 45; Cattle 12, 34*-6, 45, 77, 79, 80,
  83, 114; Herds 32; Bulls 11, 29; Cows 11, 12, 20,
  26, 29, 32, 34, 35, 38, 87; Heifers 11; Calves 11, 38,
  85, 87; Breeding 34, 35, 83; Fattening 79; Longhorns 34,
  35, 80; Pigs 11, 12, 29, 32, 34, 35, 45, 83;
  Sheep 11, 12, 17, 20, 26, 29, 32, 34*-6, 45, 79, 80,
  83, 114; Flocks 11, 32; Lambs 32, 85; Old Leicester/
  Warwick 34*; New Leicester 34, 35; Poultry 32;
  Geese 20, 26, 38; Bees 32; Diseases of: Foot Rot 36;
  Foot and Mouth 72
London 16, 21, 40, 41, 42, 44, 73, 74

Macadam, John 42
Malt 32-4, 38, 101; Malthouse 34, 101; Maltkiln 38, 101;
  Maltster 81, 101, 103; Barrels 101
Manorial Courts 18, 20, 24, 28, 61; Court Rolls 18, 20;
  Suit roll 18; Customs 24; Chief Rents 18, 20, 22, 29;
  Heriots 24, 25; Stewards 18, 20, 21, 23
Manors, The Three 19*;
  Brome 18, 22, 28-31; Kingswood 18, 22, 24, 25*, 26, 113;
  Lapworth 18, 22, 112; Boundaries 19*, 20, 21, 25*, 27,
  112, 113; Demesne 21-3, 29, 83; Manor House 21, 22,
  23*, 24, 28*; Lords of 11, 18, 20, 22-4, 28, 29,
  61, 89; Freeholders 18, 63
Markets 33, 37
Marriages 93, 94, 101; Shot-gun 61
Memorandum Book 37, 39
Memorials Of A Warwickshire Parish 110, 111
Meriden 8, 42; Hill 42
Merton College, Oxford 15, 84, 90
Middle Stone Age 8
  Evidence of occupation 8
Militia 63
Mill Pool 14
Mills — Water 12, 14, 22; Wind 14, 36, 103, 114
Moats 14, 29
Monetary Conversion 120
Mont Cenis, Piedmont 84
Mortiboys, William of Nuthurst 70
Murray, Adam 79

Neolithic Age 8
  Farming, settlements 8; Axe at Lapworth 8
Newcastle 41
Nicholas of Worcester 89
Norwich 16
Nuneaton 64, 71
Nuthurst 7, 9, 48, 52, 54, 70, 115;
  Nuthurst Grange 7

Old Stratford 13, 21
Old Swinford 93, 94
Orpen, Patrick 57
Outbuildings 33
  Backhouse 29; Backside 25; Barns 20, 24, 33-5, 51, 85,
  112, 116; Coach House 86; Cow Houses 24, 33,
  35; Crab Mill 116; Dovecote 22; Gate 85, 86, 113;
  Gatehouse 21; Hovel 20, 33; Pigsty 20, 34, 112;
  Stables 20, 22, 24, 33, 35, 44, 85, 86, 96
Oxford 11, 40, 42, 44
Oxfordshire 69

Packwood 12, 30, 52, 102
  Church 112; House 26, 115; Common 12
Paddington 7, 74
Palmer, Joseph 93
Papal Aggression 72
Park 21, 22, 87; Entrance 21; Palings 21; Hunting 14, 21
Parish 11, 40, 45, 61
  Chest 48, 54, 61*; Clerk 54, 55, 59, 60, 111; Officers —
  Churchwardens 30, 31, 51, 61, 62, 110; Constable 51,
  61-3; Overseers of the Poor 20, 30, 31, 46, 49, 55, 59,
  61-8, 91-5, 115; Surveyor of the Highways 46, 51, 61, 62,
  — Highways 46, 54; Highway Rate 45, 46; Registers 11,
  16, 44, 49, 57, 67, 70-2, 85, 93, 94, 100
Parker, Samuel 73
Parr, Dr. Samuel 16
Perambulation 19*, 20, 21, 25*, 27, 112, 113

Pesham de, John 21
Philpot, Dr. Bishop of Worcester 90, 110
Pitt, William 69, 114
Place Names 9, 30
Ponds, Pools 21, 22, 29, 112
Population 9, 11, 15, 16, 35, 36, 69, 70, 71, 91;
  Illegitimacy 93; Mortality 15, 70, 71
Poor 49, 51, 54, 61, 63, 65, 91-8, 111, 114
  By Pay 63, 67; Board & Lodging 94; Firing Money 64-7;
  Nursing 64, 66; Out Door Relief 96; Regular Pay 63-6,
  92; Soup Kitchen 97; Unmarried Mothers 62, 66, 67, 93;
  Widows 51, 64, 92, 94, 95, 97, 98, 114; see also
  Apprentices
Porter, Mr. 38
Post 67, 74, 93; Office 42, 110
Prehistoric Period 7-10
Preston Bagot 9, 21, 73, 94
Prices 17, 37, 38, 69, 87, 91, 97;
  Corn 15, 17, 64, 69, 72, 79
Princes' Metal 12, 30
Princess Victoria 71
Prison 68, 94
Probate Records — Inventories 32-4; Wills 58
Publicans 80, 103; Public House 111

Quakers 16
Quarries 7, 14, 21

Railways 27, 31, 44, 72, 74, 77, 83, 96, 101, 103, 111;
  Birmingham & Oxford Junction 72; Oxford, Worcester
  & Wolverhampton Railway Company 74; Great Western
  72, 111
Railway Station 101, 102, 103, 110, 111;
  Staff — Labourer 102; Platelayer 96, 103; Porter 103;
  Station Master 102, 103; Train 111
Rates 61, 91; Church 61; County 94; Payers 111;
  Rate Book 83
Recipes 39*, 60*
Rectors 12, 15, 16, 49, 54, 69, 81, 84, 85, 87, 90, 94,
  98, 105, 108, 115
Rectory 17, 85, 86*, 87*, 101, 110
Reformation 84
Rent 20, 22, 23, 35, 38, 49, 51, 52, 55, 62, 64, 67, 80,
  91, 93, 97, 98; Charge 87, 97
Richard III 22
Riots 17, 69-71
Rivers —
  Alne 7, 8; Arrow 8; Avon 7, 24, 74; Cole 8; Leam 8
Roads 9, 27, 40-2, 46, 47, 49, 54, 61
  Carriage 27; Waggon 112; Making 40, 41; Repair 45, 62
  95; Stone for 40-2, 46
Robbery 42
Robins, Ebenezer 51
Romano British 9, 10
Romans 7-9, 30;
  Excavation, Kilns, Mortaria, Pottery, Roads 9
Rowington 7, 9, 13, 18, 20, 21, 24, 25, 26, 32, 40, 41,
  47, 54, 59, 70, 72, 78, 93, 94, 96, 104, 112, 113;
  High Cross 40; Pinley Green 40; Pinley Priory 7;
  Poundley End 7; Rowington Green 41, 113
Royal Arms 71
Royal Oak Feast 105
Rubery 41
Rutland 102

Salop 102
School 57-60 —
  House 60; Room 59, 104, 105, 111; Desks 60, 105;
  Slates 105; Staff — Master 12, 46, 51, 54, 55, 57,
  59, 62, 67, 104, 108; Mistress 104; Teacher 105, 110;
  Pupil Teacher 103, 105; Attendance 106-8, 110; Lessons
  59, 95, 104-6; Needlework 85, 105, 109; Examinations
  105, 106; Fees 104, 106; Holidays 105; Log Book 104,
  106, 107, 109; Treats 105; Inspector 105
Schools
  Charity 59; Dame 59, 60, 96, 104; Girls 51, 54, 96;
  Grammar 57; Private 12, 58, 102; Sunday 104, 110;
  Vernacular 57; Village 46, 51, 52, 54, 55, 57, 58*,
  59*, 60, 71, 85, 97, 104, 111
Scotland 103
Settlement, Illegal 67, 94
Shirley 40, 58, 110
Shrewley — Common 9; Heath 41
Shrewsbury 42
Slatter, Decimus 26
Smith, Robert 26
Snape, John 73
Soap 91
Soil 11, 32, 33, 34, 40, 99

127

Solihull 26, 40, 41, 59, 85, 101;
    Rural District Council 47; Rural Sanitary Authority 46, 47, 98, 101, 111
Somerset 102
Stone, Building 7, 21, 85, 89, 90
Stoneleigh 65
Sport 103; Game 36; Shooting 23, 36, 103
Stourbridge 94
Stratford & Henley Coal Company 53
Stratford-upon-Avon 14, 40, 42, 44, 63, 73, 74, 77, 112
Street, G. E. 89
Strike/Bushel 38
Suicide 111
Surveyors 26, 40, 41, 49, 52, 54, 62, 69, 73, 87

Tanning 99; Tanhouse 12; Tanyard 12, 27, 99; Tanners 11, 26, 35, 63, 99; Bark, Skins, Hides 12, 99
Tanworth-in-Arden 7, 9, 22, 26; Ladbrook Park 22
Telford, Thomas 42
Temperance Association 105
Tenants 24, 26, 51, 55, 79, 80, 83, 87, 95, 114, 115
Tiles 7, 9, 51, 60
Tithe 70, 82*, 84, 87;
    Apportionment 23, 80, 94, 114; Commissioner 71, 87; Schedule 80, 87; Modus 87
Tobacco 13
Trades and Occupations 99, 100
    Baker, Banker 103; Box Iron Maker 29; Butcher 101; Carrier 41, 81, 100, 101, 103; Clerk 77, 100, 102; Coach Builder 103; Coal Dealer 37, 38, 78, 81, 100; Corn Dealer 101; Dress Makers 96, 101, 103; Draper 103; Flour Dealer 101; Hat Maker 103; Jeweller 102, 103; Metal Worker 102; Milliner 103; Ostler 44; Shop Keeper 103; Spectacle Maker 103; Steel Toy Maker 29; Tailor 91, 95, 100, 101; Wharfinger 80; Domestic Servants 29, 88, 89, 95, 97, 101-4, 111; Gamekeeper 23, 36, 102, 103; Nurse 102; Laundry Woman 66, 101; Agricultural Labourers 30, 46, 71, 80, 81, 91, 95, 97, 100, 101; Carter's Boy 96; Cowman 96; Day Labourer 26; Wage Labourer 32; see also Craftsmen
Transport — Carts 33, 41, 45, 46, 93; Tumbrels 33; Wagons 33, 41, 45, 46
Travellers 15, 70, 100, 111; Soldiers, Sailors 70; with Passes 70
Trees 13, 14, 22, 26, 27, 36, 112
    Alder 36; Ash 8, 36, 57; Elm 36, 112; Oak 8, 22, 36, 99, 112, 113

Turnpike 15, 40, 41, 63, 94, 112, 113
    Act 41; Gate 41, 42, 112; Trust 40, 42, 44, 63; Tolls 45, 68 — Collectors 41; House 41, 112; Office 77: Fares 44

Umberslade 112

Vagrants 63, 70

Wages 46, 91, 97
War 37, 63, 69, 70
    America 16; France 16, 37, 63, 69, 70; Invasion 63, 69; Napoleonic 52, 69, 91; Waterloo 70
Warmington 44
Warwick 7, 8, 11, 40, 44, 45, 63, 64, 66, 67, 85, 86, 93, 94, 104: St. Mary's Church 11, 85
Warwick, Earl of 48, 85
Weather 14-7, 32, 36, 38, 39, 69-72, 79, 97, 107
Webster, Mr. of Canley 35
Wedgenock Park 28
Weights & Measures 120
Wellesbourne 24, 67
West, James of Alscott Park 74
West Bromwich 96
Wharves 25, 53, 73, 77
White, Gilbert of Selbourne 16
Whitelands Training College, London 105
Wilcox, Mr. 20
William IV 71
Wood, Woodland 8, 9, 13, 26, 36, 61, 82, 83, 100, 101
    Coppices 36, 113; Plantations 36; Products 36; Timber 23, 36, 37, 51, 89, 100
Wool 11, 12, 29, 34, 35, 83
    Spinning 35, 64; Wheel 29, 34, 35; Carding 35, 64
Wolverhampton 42, 72
Woodforde, Parson James 17, 69
Wootton Wawen 7, 42, 70, 74
Worcester, Bishops of 9, 13, 57, 90, 110
Worcestershire 102
Workhouse 55, 96, 98

Yard 24, 33; Court 22, 86; Fold 25, 35
Yarn 34, 35
Yorkshire 110

The Chain House, Lapworth Street